EMPIRE OF LOVE ✑

MATT K. MATSUDA

Empire of Love

Histories

of France

and

the Pacific

OXFORD
UNIVERSITY PRESS

2005

OXFORD
UNIVERSITY PRESS

Oxford   New York
Auckland   Bangkok   Buenos Aires   Cape Town   Chennai
Dar es Salaam   Delhi   Hong Kong   Istanbul   Karachi   Kolkata
Kuala Lumpur   Madrid   Melbourne   Mexico City   Mumbai   Nairobi
São Paulo   Shanghai   Taipei   Tokyo   Toronto

Published by Oxford University Press, Inc.
198 Madison Avenue, New York, New York 10016

www.oup.com

Oxford is a registered trademark of Oxford University Press

Library of Congress Cataloging-in-Publication Data
Matsuda, Matt K.
Empire of love : histories of France and the Pacific / Matt K. Matsuda.
   p. cm.
Includes bibliographical references and index.
ISBN 978-0-19-516295-0
1. France—Colonies. 2. Imperialism. 3. Acculturation. 4. France—
Civilization. I. Title.
JV1827.M335 2005
325'.344'0995—dc22   2004043437

Printed in the United States of America
on acid-free paper

ACKNOWLEDGMENTS ✐

Like the stories they tell, the notes and fragments of this work have been pieced together during peregrinations around the world with the aid and support of friends, scholars, and loved ones in Europe, Asia, and the Pacific. The dedication is to my family in California.

In the South Pacific, a particular thanks for the insights and encouragement of Robert Aldrich at the University of Sydney, whose support and pioneering work have made much of this possible. At the Australia National University, Canberra, thanks to Dipesh Chakrabarty and the Centre for Cross-Cultural Research, and the fabled Research School of Pacific and Asian Studies, particularly the generosity of Bronwen Douglas, with regards to Donald Denoon and Brij Lal. In Melbourne, gracious recognition to the estimable Greg Dening, and to Charles Sowerwine. My friends Alastair Davidson and Kathleen Weekley, between Wollongong and Ouroux-en-Morvan, are with me wherever I go.

In Auckland, Aotearoa–New Zealand, I am indebted to the good works and hospitality of Hugh Laracy and his family. My way to Noumea, New Caledonia, was opened by the generosity of Paul DeDeckker, Université Française du Pacifique, and the archival energies of Ismet Kurtovich. Frédéric Angleviel has provided me with more challenges than I can ever hope to meet. Thanks to the Centre Culturel Jean Marie Tjibaou for research assistance and recommendations, and, in Hienghène, to Jean Philippe Tjibaou for his patient introduction to things Kanak. In Tahiti, debts are owed to Jean Marc Regnault, Université de Polynésie Française, Veronique Mu

Liepmann of the Musée de Tahiti et des îles, Robert Koenig, Société des Etudes Océaniennes, and the *équipe* at the Service des Archives Territoriales, Tipaerui. For helping me imagine larger and comparative questions thanks to Stewart Firth and Sandra Tarte at the University of the South Pacific, Laucala, Fiji. Thanks also to the helpful staff at the National Archives, Suva, the insights of Vincent Lobendahn, and the inspiration of Epeli Hauʻofa.

My gracious thanks to my students and colleagues at Rutgers University, and the special support of John Gillis, Jackson Lears, Bonnie Smith, and Don Roden. Thanks also to Alice Bullard, Eric Jennings, Herman Lebovics, and Christine Skwiot, and to those who have allowed me to research and present my work across the United States. In France, *remerciements* to Marie-Colette Depierre and Sébastien Leboucher, John-Simon Loche, Jean-Pierre Melot, Gaby Marcon, and Mme. Fradin and M. Prisot of La Maison Pierre Loti at Rochefort. Regards to Isabelle Merle, Christian Genet, Francis Macouin of the Musée Guimet in Paris, and the directors and staffs of the Service des Archives de la Marine, the collections of the Musée de l'Homme, the Musée des Arts Océaniens et Africains, Le Centre des Archives du Monde du Travail in Roubaix, the Centre des Archives d'Outre-Mer at Aix-en-Provence, and the Bibliothèque Nationale de France in Paris.

In Rome, thanks to Pères Carlo Maria Schianchi and Hubert Bonnet-Eymard for access to the collections of the Padri Maristi. In Japan I have profited much from contacts with the Maison Franco-Japonaise in Tokyo and the Institut Franco-Japonais in Kyoto. Thanks to my friends Yutaka Sasaki and Kiyofumi Tsubaki for their kindness. In Hanoi, my thanks to Phan Huy Le. At the University of Hawaiʻi, Manoa, thanks also to Geoffrey White, Tisha Hickson, David Hanlon, and David Chappell for inspiring and allowing me to participate in rethinking Pacific histories.

This book was written and completed under the watchful eye of my editor, Susan Ferber; thanks to her, Robert Milks, my readers, and Oxford University Press for seeing it through. For so many years, Matt Symonds and Maria Spada have kept me coming and going across another ocean—the Atlantic. Priceless thanks to Jaap Talsma and Marjan Schwegman in the Netherlands and around the world for their many insights on love and history.

Parts of this book have appeared in earlier versions in scholarly journals. I am grateful to the editors of these publications for permission to reprint this material here: "The Tears of Madame Chrysanthème: Love and History in France's Japan," *French Cultural Studies*, vol. ii, no. i (2000), Sage Publications; "Pierre Loti and the Empire of Love," *Raritan*, vol. 22, no. 2 (2002); "Geopolitics of Desire," *Proceedings of the Western Society for French History*, vol. 27.

CONTENTS ∽

EMPIRE OF LOVE

Idylls and imperialists: Entangled lives in the Pacific.
Two native girls and European man by a palm tree (1847),
Charles-Claude Antiq. Source: National Library of Australia

INTRODUCTION ✑

EMPIRE OF LOVE
Histories of France and the Pacific

The territorial archives of French Polynesia are kept up a winding
roadway in the hills of Tipaerui, a green valley whose summits over-
look Papeete, Tahiti. Among the scores of registers, requisitions,
and cartons filled with stamped, scripted orders and reports to bureaus and
ministries remain references to a striking project that made its way into both
French literature and administrative practice in the nineteenth century: the
forging of an Empire of Love in the Pacific.

The following stories focus on the historical constitution—and con-
testation—of that project. The navigator Louis-Antoine de Bougainville
famously set one of the narrative myths for Europe and the world in the
1760s by reporting of his reception in Matavai Bay, about ten kilometers
from Tipaerui, "The canoes were filled with women, who in the charm of
their features conceded nothing to most European females . . . most of these
nymphs were naked, for the men and old women who were with them had
taken off the loin-cloths which they usually wore." His enthusiastic tales
purposefully underscored notions of sensuality and erotic attraction as constituents of a French presence in the Pacific. These launched an exotic genre
that never separated itself from reports of unpredictable, yet generous, local
hosts and "island women" of ripe sensuality and easy sexual encounter.[1]

Within two generations, Pacific encounters would be overwhelmingly
colonial, coded in languages and practices of dominance and possession—
yet no less amorously defined. The Tipaerui archives conserve instructions
from nineteenth-century colonial commanders to their station heads that

illustrate this at the most local level. Notes to a gendarme on the island of Rapa begin with exhortations of responsibility: "You will take, from this date, command of the post on Rapa," a charge that includes organizing a school, mail service, weather station, supply house, and administrative office. These primary colonial institutions are enclosed within a familiar logic: "You will make all efforts to extend throughout this small population your beneficial and civilizing action." This evocation of the famous French imperial "civilizing mission" is in turn contained within the largest priority: "Your role will consist above all in making the natives love France, their new patrie."[2]

Bougainville's tales and the imperatives informing the gendarme's posting and charge raise arresting questions. What historical configurations placed "France" and "natives" in relations of "love" for and against "empire" and "patrie"? What roles do these configurations play in writing of "the Pacific" as a place of Oceanic, Asian, and European engagements? I address these questions by interrogating empire as a shifting arrangement of Pacific places, bounded by and invested in demonstrations of love as vital constituents of French imperial projects. Whether a yearning for exotic sensuality or political affinity, love was historically implicated in practices of rule, resistance, and alliance from Polynesia to Southeast Asia.

The following chapters detail the operations of love and empire within different constituencies, outlining and examining the specific presumptions, challenges, and legacies of men and women who were Tahitian monarchs, Kanak warriors from New Caledonia, French bourgeois politicos, poor white Oceanic emigrants, deported prisoners, Futunan chiefs, Central American Indians and laborers, East and Southeast Asian denizens of treaty ports and colonial compounds. These stories—about power and art, work and slavery, faith and tradition, class and race, family and ideology— lend local distinction to multiple perspectives that constituted the greater narration of an "Empire of Love" in a French Pacific. There was no singular experience, yet the apparently dissimilar expressions of "love" here emanate from a consistent historical configuration: all are bound up in negotiating tensions provoked by multiple appropriations of and struggles over *amour* for and against empire.

The stories emerge in multiple locations and contexts, and so I begin with space and places, trying to reimagine European Pacific histories restructured as Oceanic moments and crossings. From Europe, the Pacific was a world apart, lacking the immediate and contiguous significances of the Mediterranean or the Atlantic. What to make of this great space, one third of the surface of the planet, which touches no part of Europe at all?

French maritime writers called it the *Grand Ocean*, a vast expanse whose shores touched both East and West, an emptiness of routes and exchanges in the manner of the desert sands and caravans of the European "Orient."[3] In such narrations the Pacific was remote, written and drawn into being through distance in time and space. A familiar narration imposed "isolation" upon Pacific peoples: "slow development" in 1900 Tahiti was blamed on "her isolation from the rest of the world, her great distance from the mother country"; the "inferior degree of humanity" in New Caledonia, attributed to the "extreme isolation" of the islands.[4] Such attributions, always in reference to Europe, ignored centuries of Pacific migration and navigation, in many ways interrupted by colonial boundaries themselves.

In contrast to the clichés of a vast and void Pacific, scholars such as Epeli Hau'ofa have reimagined empty ocean as a "Sea of Islands," replacing distance with connection, rethinking presumably isolated Islanders as mobile, *Oceanic* peoples. Pacific space also can be seen in traditional Micronesian navigational charts of the Marshall Islands, constructed frameworks of rigid sticks, joined and bound to map seafaring routes and deep ocean swell patterns. Such models present island groups as points of crossing supported by the framework of their multiple interconnections where currents and tides refract, the negative of a paper map in which landfalls register as positive space, and water as emptiness, a forbidding barrier.[5]

To take such navigational representation—in all its nautical, astronomical, and mythical richness—as metaphor is reckless, yet also revelatory: rather than isolated, the Pacific is full of entangled histories. For all the narratives imposed upon the Pacific, here "the Pacific" shapes European history in return. Stories of an interloping Europe are reconfigured by a "chart" for which the framework of sticks itself takes on the particular shape of time, space, and destination, as opposed to an Occidental map in which all points are enclosed by the formal border of the illustration.[6]

These redefinitions are absorbing. Such an approach draws together the Oceanic and the European by pursuing Bronwen Douglas's "strategic appropriation of others' concepts."[7] Thinking through navigational crossings illuminates certain aspects of French maritime policy—particularly the imagination for defining the Pacific by a mapping of points and intersections of staging, supply, and transfer. In 1843, one French writer asserted that Pacific islands would "probably never be more than *points de relâche*"; in 1900 another pointed to "those famous *points d'appui* which ought to be [our] bases of operation or ports of refuge." In their literal definitions evoking points of rest and force, these markers declare control not of larger regions, but a mastery of critical maritime passages and places of crossing and provision.[8]

History drawn through such particular locations should give little pause; even European scholars with no consciousness of the Grand Ocean have long profited from the sort of locale-specific thinking in which Pacific studies have been so heavily invested. Such approaches have made possible ethnographic-historical studies of small villages, regionally specific commemorations and festivals, obscure revolts and rebellions, ephemeral *mentalités*, discursive practices, and *lieux de mémoire*. In Pacific history, scholars such as Greg Dening and Nicholas Thomas have repeatedly demonstrated through studies of encounter, exchange, and mutual representation how instances—or a series of connected instances—can incorporate stirring generalities about a population, culture, or a given age.[9]

Points de relâche and *points d'appui* engage histories of the Pacific through such sets of unique locations, each rich with specific moments and outward resonances constituting tidal and wave patterns of meanings. These indicate shifting routes and navigations shaped by contacts, encounters, and cultural transferences between other Oceanic locations. Imagined as this series of locations and instances, a "French Pacific" would be defined less by a political or institutional narrative of conquest and adventure than as an underscoring of moments and places where European, Oceanic, American, and Asian temporalities and geographies came together. Such an approach might be profitably defined by Hauʻofaʻs "Sea" framing Marshall Sahlinsʻs memorable turn of phrase, "Islands of History," evocative wordings that strongly capture mythic distinction and apartness, yet also the deep implication of Pacific places in contested schemes of time and chronology.[10]

This emphasis on particularities is in fact perfectly consistent with academic histories of the region, which concur that French empire in Oceania was a haphazard creation, an unpredictable set of ministerial decisions, faits accomplis by naval commanders, responses to settler agitation, islander concerns, nationalist pressure, and the presence of other European powers. The geography of a French Pacific over the nineteenth century was never that of a positively defined and defended area but the tracing of a constantly shifting series of points that gained and lost significance in accordance with political, commercial, and ideological fortunes.

How did this tenuous array of points and sites constitute an Empire of Love? The very instability of its own presumed territory supplies many responses. What made the "French Pacific" a unique area was the way in which multiple and often contingent claims intersected in the region. The daily colonial authority of Britain's India or of expanding frontier narratives in Australia and the Americas was widely dispersed among numerous

conflicting parties, both local and imperial, often with only tentative authority over extraordinary varieties of peoples and circumstances. This underscored the Pacific as less a site of colonial history or expansionist territorial
mastery than of highly unstable and charged encounters, especially for the
French who never had commanding settlements such as Australia and New
Zealand and only consolidated their control of "Indochina" very late in the
nineteenth century.[11]

For the "French" Pacific, extended over Polynesia and the penal colony
of New Caledonia in the south, Oceania was much more a realm of shifting struggles and accommodations than settler colonies. Writing from Papeete in 1843, Armand Bruat, governor of the French Possessions in Oceania,
reported, "Many people are in error because they suppose that the government has the goal of creating a colony for products of exportation, whereas
the small size of the islands, the lack of manpower and working populations
. . . throw disfavor upon their occupation." At the same moment, the Tahitian Queen Pomare would note, "The only Frenchmen who resided upon
my islands before the year 1842 were nine and nine only."[12]

With such fitful debuts, compelling narratives played a critical role in
attracting, shaping, defining—and maintaining—a French presence in the
Pacific. Through monarchies, empires, and republics, missionaries, traders,
and admirals began marking stations, territories, and protectorates, but the
"Empire" existed heavily in the realm of words, emotions, and Enlightenment visions: the exile tales of Chateaubriand, sensuous New Cythera
of Bougainville, generous mockery of Diderot. Royal South Seas missions
created a topography of loss, of memory, ruin, and secrets: the disappearance of La Pérouse as opposed to the heroic, if ultimately fatal, successes
of Cook.[13]

The French romance of nineteenth-century imperialism is inexpli-
cable without these literary and philosophical templates; as such, what
was "French" about the "Empire" developed as a curious concatenation of
story and unrealized ambition of possession. Havelock Ellis once suggested
a "French mode" for parts of the Pacific drawn from eighteenth-century
sentimentalism. "These French voyagers and missionaries—although there
were some notable but more sober-minded English and other sailors among
them—were delighted and intoxicated as these strange manners and customs, often so gracious and fantastic, opened out before their astonished
vision."[14]

Patricia Seed has suggested how, from the sixteenth century, property-
centered English colonialism focused on settlements and plantations,
whereas French empire, shaped by a politics of ceremony and royal favor,
was characterized by "seeking an alliance and watching the faces and ges-

tures of indigenous peoples for signs of assent."[15] In the nineteenth century, sentimentalism and politics of affinity were reconfigured into varieties of attachment to peoples, nations, and new territories. In his classic *De l'amour* (1822), Stendhal proposed varieties of European sentimental character, from the jealousy of Italians to the mysticism of Germans. The postrevolutionary French, he thought, were unique in combining politics and emotions, having "sacrificed love to the needs of the 'passion nationale.'" What becomes clear is that French imperialists and ideologues often regarded their "assimilation" of colonial subjects as a genuinely heartfelt meeting of sensibilities, quite distinct from mere Anglo-Saxon "exploitation."[16]

Popular sensationalist tomes such as *L'art d'aimer aux colonies* (1927) also theorized uniquely French characteristics, pointedly comparing Cook's and Bougainville's tales of Tahitian women by asserting, "one will notice how differently the matter is recounted by the two celebrated navigators." The English Cook mentions "the offerings of Venus," but it is Bougainville, "more frank" and without "false modesty," who sets the tone by admitting that some of his sailors gave themselves up to erotic pleasures.[17] In these Pacific tales we clearly see what was presumed particular about French empire—a curious yet historic assertion of erotic imagination, common attraction, nation, and Latin fraternity.

Such narration made colonies and territories attractive and desirable. Writing in 1881, Admiral Brossard de Corbigny described a Central Oceania where "today the population, isolated from the rest of the world, lives there miserably and without industry." Although evoking "isolation," the admiral also believed he saw how empire could bring advantages to both islanders and colonialists by establishing *point de relâche* coaling stations and "cargo ships from Panama to Sydney."[18] Such promotion of imperial interests as mutual advantage was part of the *mission civilisatrice* that gave ideological shape to amorous imaginings by rendering empire an enlightened force bringing benefit to the world. Where French empire extended under royal then republican rule in the nineteenth century, perhaps the most compelling of civilizing narratives was that which reconfigured possession into passion, and drew the legacies of sentimentalism into the age of the nation: imperialism registered in languages of *love*.

In her *Europe in Love, Love in Europe*, Luisa Passerini has proposed: "When they think of Europe most people have in their minds images of something other than love: things economic, military, or commercial. This research . . . tries to reconnect the study of intellectual history and the study of international encounters and relations with historical writing on emotions, literature, and cultural production."[19]

Passerini's insight is doubly applicable to empire and colonialism. Classic studies of the commercial and economic logic of imperialism go back to Hobson and Lenin, and military histories have been the stock in trade of conquest, pacification, and administration narratives. "Love" might appear inappropriate to such narrations. Yet the historian Vince Rafael has excavated the "White Love" of Filipino elites for supposed American progressivism and Japanese pan-Asian modernity. Scholars as different as John Hirst and Jane Samson have woven narratives of Australia as a "Sentimental Nation" and followed the colonial logic of British "Imperial Benevolence."[20] Studies by Alice Conklin, Julia Clancy-Smith, Frances Gouda, and Antoinette Burton have expanded the intersections between ideologies of humanitarianism, male-female roles, and material and sentimental domesticity in imperial projects. One of the doyennes of such research, Ann Stoler, has repeatedly shown how deployments of affect and intimacy can be as much parts of empire as articulations of more familiar "civilizing mission" components such as economic development, primary education, or hygiene and health projects.[21]

Far from an intimate emotion resistant to power and opaque to imperial authority, love can be, and was, part of authority—a potent organizing force and site of contest. In an 1886 piece for a Saigon newspaper, the town mayor Jules Blancsubé extolled "the vitality of this Cochinchine which I love with passion, which we all want great and prosperous, which we all aspire to see become a useful auxiliary to France." Blancsubé saw his personal fulfillment in making the first colony of French Indochina into "a new and considerable force for our beloved patrie." As Blancsubé understood, his love for Cochinchine was but an example of a tremendous source of political power dedicated to the service of the patrie—the true beloved. He had complete faith in his project—and also his imperial subjects: "The love of these people for France, the trust they have put in us, certainly form our greatest force in this affair."[22]

Projects such as Blancsubé's were abetted, advanced, and challenged by villagers, mandarins, and armed rebels with overlapping notions of affinity and alliance. Such contests mark the shifting borders of a forcefully articulated yet always uncertain Empire of Love. Not a bounded space but a waxing and waning set of locations, the empire emanated from particular confluences of authority and event, sites and moments where Oceanic worlds and Asian territories interconnected with European and American transits from France to the Grand Ocean.

The historiographical boundaries of this empire depend upon differing claims of possession. As such, I attend to subjects and sites that necessarily fall within French colonial jurisdiction (like the Etablissments Français de l'Océanie) but also some—notably in the Americas and Asia—that seemingly do not. Stories unfolding in Japan are tied to struggles in Polynesia, Central American heroism and tragedy appropriated to the logic of Western France and Australian waters. The French Pacific of Oceania, Asia, the Americas—and Europe—provides sentimental and exotic idylls articulated within a military, commercial, religious, and emotional cartography. My choices are selectively defined by a history of a "French Pacific" that is only fitfully about colonies and how they were administered. Generally, I seek rather *imperialism* at what I describe as exemplary *points de relâche* and *points d'appui*, the connected moments of a political, economic, administrative, and aesthetic system.[23]

The first chapter visits a small drydock town on the Atlantic coast of France where a fetishistic writer and his patron created an Oceania of delirious fantasy. Focusing on the naval officer and *littérateur* Pierre Loti and his powerful patron Juliette Adam, we see how the "romance" of this unlikely couple allowed them to create a popular overseas empire, which for both reflected back upon their highly emotional ideas of the nation. In chapter 2, we journey to Panama, where romantic Jesuit ruins, isthmian peoples, and a French canal project illuminate Saint Simonian communities of love plotting to conquer the Pacific transit with a passionate Gallic nationalism. In the Pacific islands of Wallis and Futuna, church fathers confront the house of Lavelua, the king Niuliki, and the sacred and profane alliances of a martyr's love that will create the first saint in the South Seas. Tahiti situates us where violent warfare is written into and out of naval ledgers and Oceanic histories, as erotic loves for Tahitian "natives" are implicated in battles and alliances between Queen Pomare and French naval officers struggling for control of the Society Islands. In New Caledonia, European settlers, administrators, and penal colony deportees face local Kanak resistance to an imperial project dedicated to creating love matches and households in the service of colonial settlement.

The peregrination through Indochina is perhaps the most obvious expression of love as politics, as we examine how love of country, possession of the "native," and colonial marriage are consistent figures in France's articulation of its Southeast Asian colonies, and how these same figures are reiterated by Vietnamese both in colonial collaboration and armed resistance. At the end of our voyage, we sweep north to Japan to see France's own history in crisis through the tears of Madame Chrysanthème weeping in a tea house above Nagasaki harbor—and at the Paris Opera. Here we engage

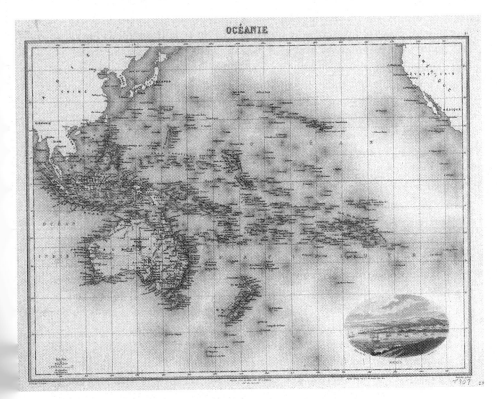

The grand ocean: An empire of love?
French mapping of *Océanie*; inset of Noumea harbor,
New Caledonia. Source: National Library of Australia

Japanese and French debates on the nature of political, economic, civic, and sentimental life east and west, and the possibilities of love in modern states as they mutually struggle to define what is common to all of the above studies: conflicting engagements with *amour* for and against empire.

The uneven frameworks of such an Empire of Love in the Pacific were shaped politically and assayed for European audiences by literary tales and imperialist bravado by the middle of the nineteenth century. Hardly any figure incorporated and exploited that moment better than the writer and naval officer Pierre Loti, *né* Julien Viaud. His life (1850–1923) neatly encompassed the decades and peregrinations of the chapters just mentioned, and as a novelist he created the indelible Princess Rarahu, Madame Chrysanthème, and Breton sailors Yann and Sylvestre (and himself, "Loti," after a Tahitian flower) in stories whose popularity carried his name far beyond his literary readership. His talent coupled with his military status regularly inscribed his prose in the reports and papers of warship commanders, colonial propagandists, mass-circulation journalists, and ministers of the navy.

As a fleet officer, Loti's missions guaranteed French naval and maritime authority in the treaty ports of Asia and in the island colonies. As a cultural figure his exotic love stories occasioned fashion trends for things Polynesian or Asian (as well as Turkish and Arab) and were staged as popular operas by producers in Paris, London, and New York. An admiring Henry James noted of the Frenchman's characters, "We live with their simplicity, and we generally love their ways. Above all we love their loves, and there is no one like Loti for making us fond of his lovers."[24]

Loti's exotic lovers were drawn from empire; that empire was in turn shaped in reference to the changing France of his lifetime, and for him, no figure better incarnated that France than his sometime muse and always patron, Juliette Adam. As a liberal thinker under the Second Empire and later Republican grandee, the politically powerful and long-lived Adam (1836–1936) was Loti's protector and one of few women he both loved and pointedly respected. Proclaimed "The Great Frenchwoman" by Léon Gambetta, Adam's long editorship of her own *Nouvelle Revue*, her partisan engagements, her political salon, and her numerous writings on international affairs, moral philosophy, feminism, and religion ably captured the collusion of love and nationalist politics at the heart of French empire.

Loti and Adam wander in and out of the chapters as accomplices, not as "colonial" figures themselves but as *points de relâche* and *points d'appui*—providing shifting engagements of imperialism behind the literary and political production of Asia and the South Seas. From strategic positions across the

Pacific, Loti filled notebooks with mordant observations and bitter nostalgia for Western imports and habits which to him signified the collapse and extinction of Pacific "tradition." From Paris, Adam published essays on Asian and Oceanic empire, interfered in New Caledonian policy, and articulated the meanings of a truly Gallic, Latin, French world presence. The two corresponded about a timeless Oceania and Orient of childhood imagination, and fashioned love stories in which passionate longing, loss, and nostalgia would become necessary elements of imperial mastery.[25]

Sailing away from Tahiti in his 1878 *The Marriage of Loti* (published first by Adam), Loti reflected on his Polynesian paramour Rarahu, "He was beginning to love her, really love her. Far away he wonders what has become of his dusky love, whether she pines for him." The formulaic iteration of such South Seas clichés betrays the way in which the possibility of a French Pacific was deeply encoded in the contiguous expression of love and politics. Loti's friend the novelist Paul Bourget established his own 1889 axioms for "l'amour moderne" by suggesting, "Total love supposes possession, as courage supposes danger. One who loves is to a lover as a soldier in times of peace is to a soldier in times of war." As lovers are soldiers, so imperialism is possession; thus are Loti's sentiments constituted of island pleasures made possible by duty to France.[26]

As Loti sails away, he is left wondering, like a proper lover and determined colonialist, about the fulfillment of his own presence. Loti's own imperial authority is here configured through the analysis and embrace of "pleasures of the text," the very attractions, enjoyments, seductions, and strategies of empire and narration that made each other possible. Saidya Hartman has deftly sketched out the ways in which terms such as "enjoy" can be juridically grounded, as in "to have, possess, and use with satisfaction; to occupy or have the benefit of." The pleasures of imperialism then, are readily evoked where such "enjoyment" in story or practice is a satisfied exercise of possession and occupation.[27]

Love of empire would prove deeply ambivalent—a craving for and "enjoyment" of the master's status and attentions of colonial subjects, yet marked by strong anxieties: boundaries of race, social order, and civilizational status were complicated by the baptized souls of Island monarchs, the mixed métis liaisons of Asians and Europeans, outright military resistance, and the successful "mimicry" of native officials or economic modernization.[28] "Love" was thus never merely a generic island sensuality but—like the shifting *points d'appui*—an unstable and potentially violent series of contested crossings underscored by multiple, highly political appropriations of devotion and alliance. Max Radiguet concluded his *The Last Savages* about the Marquesas Islands (1842–1859) with the line, "The presence of an armed force at Nukahiva will only result in fear and respect for the name of France. That is already something, but it remains now to make it loved and blessed."[29]

By the mid-twentieth century, the Cambodian prince Sisowath You-tévong would provide an ideal expression of this politically amorous vision: "France has gathered around her many civilizations which have marked the artistic, philosophical, and spiritual history of humanity; these civiliza-tions . . . consent to enrich themselves, to love and to serve, but not to give themselves up. What is created in the habits of the common life, voluntarily accepted or not, is not a relation of servitude, but one of love."[30] It is exactly the tensions between such love and servitude that I examine as they manifest themselves in the shaping of empire.

Such imperial passion and authority well framed the enormous and con-tradictory ambitions of European nations in the Pacific from the mid-nineteenth to the early twentieth centuries. The result of the double-bind-ing of romantic desire with the project of drawing all of the Earth's peoples into a grand narrative of Western civilization would be a fin-de-siècle crisis of *finitude*. In geopoetic terms, an 1889 travel guide *Guide de France en Océ-anie* captured a voyage across the Pacific not as an infinite expanse but as an oppressive blue enclosure: "As Baudelaire said, we feel the idea of the infinite evaporate, replaced by a vague sentiment of the finite, of narrowness, of imprisonment itself."[31]

Politically and ideologically, the imperialism of the later nineteenth century was not privileged to the sense of expansion into the marvelous described by Stephen Greenblatt that characterized the imperial visions of the Spanish, Portuguese, Dutch, and English of the late European Renais-sance—or the French of the Enlightenment. Those suddenly larger uni-verses of unimagined new peoples, new species of plants and animals, newly discovered regions, such as the Pacific itself, stood in marked contrast to the appropriated globe of fin-de-siècle imperial powers. Britain already had an empire upon which the sun never set; Germany clamored for a place in the sun; from the west coast of North America, the United States had reached the limits of a continent and now looked to the Pacific as a closing act for the "Manifest Destiny" of its expansion. Within these imperial limits, Loti lamented, "Colonies represented for me the gateway into the unknown; but where would it lead me now, to what oceans that I have not explored?"[32]

The expression of colonial empire by the turn of the century would turn from "discovery," adventure, and territorial claims to administration, most visible in the colonial expositions of London and Paris where island peoples, earlier displayed as living artifacts, were now putatively "protected" by and brought into subordinate identification with metropolitan masters as parts of nation-states. At the International Colonial Congress of 1900, French delegates declared, "The period of conquest has ended; the period of development needs to begin." The president of the Republic, René Waldeck-Rousseau, shifted colonial policy from "assimilation" to "association," a new French community of territories and protectorates whose ideological space promised "economic strength and human development" for the overseas territories themselves.[33]

For colonial governors such as Jean Louis de Lanessan and Albert Sarrault, or the diplomat and geographer Auguste Pavie, this was supposedly the new age of formal enlightened rule. For Loti, the acknowledgment of such projects was lamentable, for it gave authority and visibility to what he disliked about imperialism: the reality of colonies, interests, and administrators. Yet he might have appreciated how much this later administrative practice was itself discursively shaped by languages of love, such that Laotian villagers might respond to Pavie's presence in their territories, "You are father of our family and of our people. We salute you like ignorant children . . . for a long time already, before seeing you at Luang-Prabang, we knew you and we have loved you."[34]

The men and women of Loti's era, from the mid-nineteenth century to the first decades of the twentieth century, had created a new global domination by wedding a "civilizing mission" to the romantic legacies of discovery voyages, premised upon figurative erasure of the political and economic networks that organized colonialism as a system, what the *universitaire* and critic Félicien Challayé would soon call "a reign of political oppression having for its goal the economic exploitation of subject peoples." Loti's own life, abetted by Adam's political and literary influence, aggressively occluded these; his empire could only be beautiful and sad, fashioned to justify idylls of fatal exoticism. The colonialism that succeeded him nonetheless was founded upon the Empire of Love.[35] As Challayé, in the 1930s, would admit, "When I left on my first great voyages thirty-five years ago I naively believed what had been taught me. . . . I believed France the most benevolent of all colonial powers, and that the loyalty of her subjects attested to their gratitude."[36]

In a 1931 report on Pacific naval strategy, and Tahiti in particular, Rear Admiral Raoul Castex summarized the shifting imperialist world and the legacies from Loti's era: "What the Americans do not absorb, the Chinese take. Several bureaucrats are the only ones who still remind France today of the island which has never played any role in our history and our expansion other than awakening in us picturesque and literary impressions of Queen Pomare, Rarahu, and other fantasies à la Pierre Loti."[37] As we shall see Castex was not correct; Tahiti, as Polynesia and the Pacific, have had significant histories—the admiral took for absence what was in fact a construction: the lovely void of the French Pacific. In this, he inadvertently complimented Loti, master of nostalgia, who in remaining unreconciled to the twentieth century shaped and incarnated the imperial legacy of the nineteenth.

Such were the ebb and flow of empire and its fictions, the managing and exploiting of bodies and territories set within a desire for boundless rule and literary romance. Figures such as Loti and Adam, with their talent and narrative authority, were one part of the story. Peoples in Polynesia, Melanesia, and Asia were another, where they accommodated and appropriated French outlanders, or where, like the Pomares in Tahiti, or Ataï and Niuliki in New Caledonia and Futuna, they wrote and fought back. As I have noted, the "reality" of French imperialism in the Pacific was more fragmentary than comprehensive, often the result of initiatives taken by actors in the islands rather than by ministerial committees in Paris. Local conflicts over property or religion, exchange opportunities between foreign traders and island peoples, the sudden death of an important leader or the arrival of a naval frigate might have a greater impact on island life than any "colonial policy," however imagined. What I seek are those navigational points where narration and event joined, located in instances channeled by the "tides" of ideology and imagination that are so much parts of empire.

These scattered moments are the *points de relâche*, the joints and contacts articulating the stick-chart of Pacific empire. I have attempted to underscore some of these moments as they mark a territory reconfigured from place of encounter and imagination to one of possession and administration. In the locations and instances I examine, the dream of totality, the assertion of power, and the desire for desire itself can all be understood as histories written by and for the Pacific, by peoples of islands and oceans, and for those drawn to the Pacific as a region of promises and passions within which to shape the boundaries of an Empire of Love.

ONE

ROCHEFORT

The Family Romance of the French Pacific

Rochefort, with its tile roofs and shutters, is a charming provincial town on the Atlantic coast of France. Once the unique site of the royal rope-works established by Colbert to outfit the navy of Louis XIV, Rochefort's maritime glory was carried into the nineteenth century by a large complement of riggers and fitters who plied their trades on cutters and torpedo boats in the town's armory. It might not be too much to say that Rochefort shaped French empire, particularly at the moment European interests turned toward the vast expanse of the distant Pacific. Part of this can be traced to the town's strong naval and maritime histories. Yet from the later nineteenth century, many Rochefort residents could also simply point out the importance of the Oceanic world to one of the town's most renowned native sons: heading off the main tree-lined square toward whitewashed blocks of residences and market streets was the family home of the novelist and naval officer Pierre Loti, the former Julien Viaud. Known for his tales of South America and Easter Island, of Tahiti and the Pacific in the 1870s, Loti had cruised around Indochina and landed in Japan in the 1880s, adding East Asia to his repertoire of narrated lands of what the French called the Grand Ocean.[1]

What Loti created was a French Pacific as an Empire of Love. As Louis Antoine de Bougainville and Denis Diderot shaped a paradisical noble savagery for Tahiti in the legacy of the eighteenth-century Enlightenment, so Loti wrote, collected, and dramatized into being a romance of the Pacific for the late-nineteenth-century age of European empire and fin-de-siècle culture. With his patron and muse, Juliette Adam, Loti created a romantic French Pacific by rewriting the sensual idealism of Bougainville for the political sensibilities of post-1870s European bourgeois nationalism, telling

Empire as collection: The view from home.
Pierre Loti in his pagoda chambers.
Source: Collection Christian Genet

tales of naval missions and amorous liaisons that erased the distinctions between love story and imperial ideology. From Tahiti to Indochina to Japan and around the wider Pacific, Loti penned seductive stories and traveled on warships making claims of possession, outlining idylls of exoticism, mapping out a strategic and sentimental geography through which successive French regimes radiated naval and maritime power.

As an exoticist writer and sailor (later captain), Loti was an ideal figure to express nineteenth-century empire as a love story. He succeeded by narrating imperialism as a kind of family romance—a performance of loving sons become brothers-in-arms in service to the mother country. Tahitian tales such as *The Marriage of Loti* (1880) featured Occidental officers moved by personal passions, yet bound by duty, a delicate balance of sensibility and patriotism. Affection for fellow sailors and liaisons with local women in Asia and Oceania were parts of attractive episodes shaping an understated but encompassing love story: *l'amour de la patrie*. In "marrying" the Polynesian princess Rarahu, Loti not only affirms his desire for his bride, but gains the favor of Tahitian ruler Queen Pomare.

As the title of *The Marriage* indicates, Loti's pursuit of *l'amour* was built less upon masculine heroics than a conscious attention to roles, alliances, and institutions. The protagonist of many of his own stories, Loti posed himself not so much as rakish adventurer but eternal suitor. Sensitive to his presentation of empire, he shaped his most popular fictions with gestures to European marriage and attempts at domestic affection. This suited bourgeois sensibilities; as the mordant essayist Emile Bergerat put it in his study of French attachments, "the code . . . only recognizes marriage, that is, the case of love publicly declared and guaranteed . . . outside of marriage, one does not love."[2] Through the fated couples of his Breton novels, the royally doomed Princess Rarahu, and the prostituted Japanese Madame Chrysanthème, Loti used the formalities of matrimony to temper and charm legacies of colonial warfare, unequal treaties, exploited mistresses, and deadly epidemic disease. In marrying the empire, he courted his audience with tales of ostensibly amorous, duty-bound men and alluring women, placing respectability and sentiment at the heart of colonial relationships—as did European settlers, missionary priests, and administrators across the Pacific extolling the virtues of colonial households and love of France to subject peoples.

It was from Rochefort—where he was born in 1850 and grew up as a small boy and later returned to establish a residence filled with eccentric collections and rooms styled on pagodas, temples, mosques, and medieval chambers—that Loti transformed Asia and the Pacific into writing. That the author's imperialism and exotic tales were so strongly associated with his home in Rochefort is highly significant. Never comfortable in Paris and an indifferent supporter of the French government (which he called "this pitiful grocer's daughter of a Republic"), Loti carried out colonial missions around the globe yet remained something of a provincial all his life. His Empire of Love across the seas was firmly rooted in local concerns, particularly his displeasure with empire at home: the "internal colonization" of local towns and villages in France by institutions and policies dictated by the republic, the encroachment of Paris upon regions such as the Atlantic coast.

While Ministers Jules Ferry and Charles de Saulce de Freycinet extolled national rail networks, industrial development, and compulsory elementary education in the 1880s, Loti wrote to Juliette Adam of his "horror for all that is progress, ideas and modern things." Loti's own voyaging, his empire of the faraway, was an attempt to maintain his own past; never geopolitical in ambition, it was ultimately located in a domestic space: the familiarity of Rochefort where he had collected feathers and shells and dreamed of the world as a child. He preferred to be among "men raised in the country-side, among sailors, among sons of fishermen." This beloved, now changing, France was the place whose naïve grandeur he tried to preserve by using his naval missions to find what he imagined were innocent or primitive worlds abroad, and to fill his home with art and artifacts reminiscent of his child-hood. These, along with his Pacific paramour stories, were less mementos of distant lands, than expressions of his own displacement. He ceaselessly wrote of seeking love while surrounding himself with objects at Rochefort, intoning, "It is undoubtedly because the persistence of certain things always known ends up deluding us about our own stability, our own existence."[3]

In Loti's case, this losing battle—a melancholy ambition to preserve his own corner of France—rested upon his imperial status abroad. Affections lost to a colonizing Paris at home might yet be recovered by seeking them in empire across the sea. In one letter to his friend the renowned actress Sarah Bernhardt, Loti described with exemplary satisfaction receiving orders for a naval mission, the moment to "begin again to live and to love," to find again "another life, another friendship, *un autre amour*." Whether as the site of objects and icons amassed for collections or as the originary locale for child-hood dreams become exotic romances, Loti's Rochefort was the heart of the Empire of Love.

He began in the 1870s with journalistic pieces of his naval voyages to journals and newspapers, using his time aboard ship throughout the 1880s and 1890s to draft stories and novels. His first tale of a Turkish lover,

Aziyadé (1879), sold indifferently until it was reissued in the wake of his succeeding smash success—the Tahitian love story *The Marriage of Loti*. The Polynesian idyll of a young naval officer's "marriage" (a temporary arrangement) to a local princess quickly sold out its first editions, occasioned a fad for the style of ribbons worn by its heroine Rarahu, and was made into an opera with choruses of sweet island maidens. Julien Viaud had come from a Huguenot family with a history of financial setbacks and a fear of the auction order barring the entrance to the family home. Now he was out of debt and on his way to becoming Pierre Loti—a pen name he adopted from his own sailor-hero. Loti's story is a tale of sharp talent and better luck, but even more of exoticism and empire as a production of business and politics.[4]

The star of this promising but unknown author rose when his publisher Calmann-Lévy allied with the formidable Juliette Adam to create the *Nouvelle Revue*, an arts, science, politics, and literature rival to the *Revue des deux mondes*. Through the keen patronage of Adam, her literary salon, and the *Nouvelle*, Loti's novels and travel writings were serialized and proliferated to a popular reading public. He immediately felt the cultural pull of Paris. His *Rarahu* was given its familiar title *The Marriage of Loti* by Adam, and her connections with many writers including Maupassant, Goncourt, Bourget, and Daudet helped keep Loti in good company and make him famous.

A self-declared promoter of new talent, Adam cast a wide shadow across the fin de siècle and belle époque. A strong, charming, and well-connected woman, Adam was an ardent bourgeois republican, intellectual, and patriot who would be declared "La Grande Française" in 1879 and the "Grandmother of la Patrie" in 1918. Married to Edmond Adam, a banker and senator, Juliette Adam wrote early polemics against the philosophy of Pierre-Joseph Proudohn (she supported his socialism but not his antifeminism), kept company with George Sand and Victor Hugo, and maintained a glittering republican salon at the joint request of erstwhile political foes such as Adolphe Thiers and Léon Gambetta. Nationalists and imperialists seeking a "noble, warlike, and sheltering" icon for France needed not resort solely to myths and symbols of Marianne to express their attachment to the patrie. Adam's presence ably filled that role.[5]

A central figure in the revanchist (revenge) strain in politics from the Franco-Prussian War to the Great War, Adam once mused, "Not one day in forty-four years have I forgotten to wind the old clock of my heart which will sound the hour of *La Revanche*." She promoted France's moral and intellectual regeneration and championed writers consistent with such sensibilities. Asked at a dinner of dignitaries including Gambetta and Gladstone to explain the purpose of her *Nouvelle Revue*, she replied, "to oppose Bismarck, to demand the restoration of the Alsace-Lorraine, and to lift from the minds of our young writers the shadow of depression cast by national defeat."[6]

The nineteenth century was the great era of the French novelist and essayist—Hugo, Stendhal, Sand, Flaubert, Dumas, Balzac—and also of a certain territory of the audience, the community of the literate, which through books, story-installments, articles, the popular press, and salons and writing prizes would shape a celebrated "national" literature. Adam was comfortable in all circles, dining with academicians, journalists, and publishers, often at the invitation of family friends such as press lord Emile de Girardin, whose *Petit Journal* circulated close to a million copies. The business of literature was the mapping out and writing of the nation-state, the accumulated narrations of a civilization's history and genius.

Adam was not merely a patron; at the *Nouvelle* she reserved for herself a regular feature, "Letters on Foreign Policy," in which she set forth her influential views on Germany, Austria, England, Russia, Greece, Hungary, China, and Japan (she often is credited with having helped secure the Franco-Russian alliance treaty of 1894), and she later published a detailed study of British policy in Egypt. At the turn of the century, political actors and cultural taste-makers such as Adam focused on the urgencies of post-1870 Europe and continued the business of shaping republican power and selecting the writers of France as nation and, in Loti's case, of empire.

What might have attracted Adam in selecting for the *Nouvelle Revue* the Tahitian tale that launched Loti's literary career? Pacific connections can be suggested by the writings of Charles-Victor Crosnier de Varigny—finance minister to Kamehameha V in Hawai'i—whose own *Fourteen Years in the Sandwich Islands, 1855–1868*, was published just after the Franco-Prussian War. His stories and recollections apologetically begin, "I do not know whether the history of a small kingdom of Oceania will attract the interest of a public so much concerned at this moment with so many difficult questions. I sometimes begin to doubt it." Yet de Varigny presses ahead, suggesting, "The more we feel depressed by the world around us the more we resort to the charms of fiction." Beautiful stories can restore a wounded civilization; to this lifting of "the shadow of depression" equally contained in Adam's nationalist literary project, de Varigny adds his own Oceanic inspiration: "All the problems that preoccupy Europe have been encountered in this small society and have there found a solution." In this, de Varigny reiterates the classic vision of the apartness and simplicity of islands as microcosmic sites of experiment, ideal, and longing.[7]

The Marriage of Loti proffers no overtly political solutions to a shaken France, yet its intensely poetic distractions are an ideological project in themselves. In retrospect, Loti might seem an odd figure to have had such

Power and persuasion: Juliette Adam and her famous salon.
Pierre Loti to the far right in naval uniform.
Source: Collection Christian Genet

an impact on colonial writing and policy with his ambivalence toward Paris, weak republicanism, and glorious, gauzy romances and melancholy wanderings. Yet from the 1870s to the turn of the century, it was exactly his attention to sentimental love stories that made him ideal for Adam. In her own *Jean et Pascal* (1905), Adam would write of a French girl trying to win the affection of an Alsatian officer, a tale that Gambetta reviewed as indicative of her philosophy: "The analysis of the two most noble passions which can capture the heart of man: love and patriotism." In this tale Pascal is in love with the sister of Jean, his friend and fellow soldier ("my brother-in-arms"), but insists, "I do not wish to love, I will not love. . . . I keep myself for she to whom I am pledged body and soul, who demands too little of my blood. . . . I swear, my passion for France makes me sectarian, fanatic. My heart is struck by her name, even on just speaking it, it beats almost to burst from my chest, because I adore her!"

Jean tries to show his friend that patriotism and "personal sentiment" are not incompatible, but can be readily integrated: "Would it be wrong to love France in a young French girl?" In her earlier *La Chanson des nouveaux époux* (1882), Adam's hero—again a military officer—tells his new wife, "My cult for la patrie is the shape of my existence; she is my existence itself. I do not act except under her impulsion, I do not love except through her love. Your image appears to me as the visible image of la patrie, your beauty her true expression. I confuse you with her, and it is in her that I am yours."[8]

In many of Adam's works such personal, political, military, and matrimonial evocations of love form the main lines of her nationalist narratives. Loti, with a more refined talent, seduced his readers for empire along equal lines, although with more charm and less didacticism. He wrote sensuous tales of naval officers visiting colonies, lingering on details of language and physiognomy, local landscapes, and his own precious feelings, yet generally shunned the reality of colonial institutions. Adam promoted the ideal of an impassioned French nation, and of empire as sentimental and civilizing. Loti's empire was bounded by tales of France in search of love and the disappointments and tragedies of unrealized desire. The stories the two produced masked the violence of their projects: Adam's belligerent anti-German patriotism, Loti's colonialism rendered as picturesque loss and melancholy.

Bounded by common literary visions and linked by well-orchestrated social connections, Adam worked with Julien Viaud to make Pierre Loti the impresario of empire as a terrain of imagination and romantic disenchantment. Loti used his talent to render empire sensual and melancholy, Adam provided the critical forum for presenting politics to the public in crafted narratives. At the launching of the *Nouvelle Revue,* Adam announced, "As republican politics seem to have resolved themselves into nothing more or less than a distribution of rewards, my political salon has ceased to interest me." This hardly meant she was giving up her political engagements. Rather, she understood how better to pursue them by other and more compelling means. Dramatic literature would be a powerful tool to advance her interests. For one so well situated in social and cultural networks, editing the *Revue* was a base of power greater than meetings with senators and deputies.

Literature, love, and politics were all very much as one for Adam. With the support of her eminent contributors and allies she would refashion her own France by impressing her passions into a program of great writing and popular distribution, the end of which was unapologetically a revitalized, republican love of the country. "With all my heart and soul, I am determined to make my review a credit to French letters, a reflection of republican disinterestedness, patriotism, and dignity."[9]

Although Calmann-Lévy remained Loti's key publisher, it was with Adam that Loti forged his powerful alliance of love, empire, and history. Adam—La Grande Française, incarnation of the republic—called herself Loti's "moral and intellectual mother" (she was thirteen years his senior) and chided him affectionately, "My dear Loti, I think that I know much of friendly love, you love me with filial love, *n'est-ce pas?*" Skeptical of the republic, Loti nonetheless responded in kind to Adam's vocabulary of love, closing his letters "I love you with all my heart and take your hands with the tenderness of a son."[10] The Great Frenchwoman created her man, and he executed her desires, helping her shape a space for French empire by sending her the letters and dedicating to her the manuscripts that made him famous.

Loti is a writer whose reputation is now much less than when he lived. Respected and extraordinarily popular as an artist in his own time, forgotten soon after, revived by his fans as a magician in a technocratic era and derided as a shallow imperialist, Loti's works and life hover at the margins of French literature and historical consciousness. Although elected to the Académie Française in 1891, he has proven a rather mortal Immortal; one easy to like, easy to despise and ignore.

His career and highly visible life as author and imperialist are exemplary for the ways they shaped and followed the social and cultural changes taking place within France at the turn of the twentieth century, particularly regarding literary culture and the articulation of overseas empire. Loti's work somewhat follows British literary studies suggesting that adventure romance developed as an assertive masculine genre, self-consciously opposed to the feverish decadence of Naturalism. In an 1887 essay, the widely popular Rider Haggard called Emile Zola's mordant fiction "unmanly," and Loti notably gained his place at the Académie Française by beating out Zola for a seat left open by the death of Octave Feuillet. After a widely publicized contest, Loti unsettled his audience with an inaugural oration rather bluntly attacking Zola's writing: "The condemnation of Naturalism is, furthermore, in this: that it takes uniquely as its subjects the dregs of people of the big cities where the authors indulge themselves." Zola, present in the back of the room, reportedly wore a thin smile as Loti denounced "these peasants, these laborers, the same as all those one would pick up in the dance halls of Belleville." Loti also assaulted Naturalism's "morbid phenomena, particular to the boundaries of Paris."

Here, Loti's politics are in fully array. Most obvious was his dislike of Paris but as well his contempt for the working class. Paris was not only republic but city of the proletariat and the Commune, the new society that violated his search for nobility. Although he articulated no self-conscious theory of popular empire as a "safety-valve" for worker agitations at home, Loti clearly believed it his duty to move literature away from what he called the "coarseness and cynicism" of urban class struggle to the "ideal and eternal" sensibilities of imperial romance.[11] During the Franco-Prussian War, he had been assigned to naval duty and had passed the struggle in his favored way: at sea, preserving his vision of privileged adventure, defending a real France that would one day be found only abroad.

In his Académie address, Loti predicted that the world described by Zola and his "school" would pass away once abandoned by "the unhealthy curiosity which sustains it." For his part, Loti focused on rewriting domestic and adventure themes of the nineteenth century novel to become the imperialist of an Empire of Love. Initially he seemed to revive some of the cult of sentiment popular in the eighteenth century, binding passions and exquisite descriptions to exotic locales in the manner of a Chateaubriand. Adam regularly published the essays and serialized the stories in the *Nouvelle*.

Lauded (and derided) as a "sensitive" writer, Loti's approach characterized a generation, then faded. In the first decade of the twentieth century a younger generation of writer–naval officers, like the doctor Victor Ségalen, would denounce Loti as an "impressionist tourist" and develop a highly theoretical exoticism based upon an ethnographic *littérature coloniale* of subject peoples and places. Writers such as André Gide, with a dramatic life and anticolonialism drawn around a morally ambiguous psychology and sexuality, made Loti's decorative work seem hopelessly precious in comparison. In the 1920s, colonial peoples in Africa and Asia began to write back, in local languages and in French and English. Dashing yet disrespected, Loti would be both fabulously admired and pointedly anachronistic in his own lifetime.[12]

He shared characteristics with yet remained distinct from other imperial romantics. British contemporaries such as Rudyard Kipling, Haggard, Arthur Conan Doyle, and Robert Louis Stevenson became best known for sending manly heroes on distant quests, presumably in flight from the emasculating "domestic realism" of George Eliot and the prosaic mannered tales of Victorian drawing rooms. Although equally seeking adventures, Loti always remained far from his contemporaries' sense of epic voyages and rugged self-reliance. Rather, his superiors wrote him up as a commendable if rather "dreamy" sailor, and in later age he chauffeured women's groups to the gravesite of his heroine Aziyadé. Both critics and admirers noted the large female audience for his novels. Romain Rolland rather acidly offered, "Women are crazy about this little nephew of Chateaubriand for whom . . . five or six white, yellow, and red women have died for love."[13]

If Haggard's tales, for example, *King Solomon's Mines,* underscored late-nineteenth-century romance as a domain of manly, supernatural adventure and regenerative violence, Loti's work continued to configure romance as sentimental attachment.[14] His naval commissions and appeal to not only male but also female readers suited Juliette Adam, whose salon propagated such fashionings of refinement, excitement, and patriotic devotion. In her anti-Proudhonian writings, Adam had herself denounced that philosopher's violent pomposity ("what I love most in the world is that warlike mood") and established instead that, "love, and not force, can become the revelation of the ideal. . . . It is due to the growing influence of sentiment that war is tending to disappear."[15]

Adam's own *revanchisme* after 1870 was hardly pacifist, and she managed to refashion her love of humanity into patriotic identity partly by engaging Loti as the man of imperialism and romance. The long *affaire* of the imposing Adam and "sensitive" Loti was a love story very much of its time. She was the strong "masculine" woman, he the dreamy and "feminine" man. She could be demonstrably political and intellectual because her status and talent were allied with love of country. He could be sentimental because his passion was primarily for men and the military.[16]

These projects were well located in international affairs. Through the end of the century, the French Third Republic reckoned with the new European order that threatened the homeland of the *mission civilisatrice.* After the Franco-Prussian War, writers and critics such as Jules Davray felt obliged to declare *la ville lumière* "still the most virtuous city in France, and in Europe," because of French amorous creativity. Davray insisted that in his hometown "what is always *new and unexpected* are the lovers." Using "love,"

Davray followed a rhetorical line that, in the analysis of Claude Digeon, created the post-1870s German as "an amorphous being, indistinct, without desires, without will."[17]

This view, propagated in innumerable writings and in French elementary education would have powerful resonance—even in the colonies—for decades. The Francophile Vietnamese novelist Nguyên Phan-Long created a military veteran character, a M. Minh, to express his views in 1921. Minh, having fought for the French in Europe, warns against a "dead world" to come, intoning, "Germany, disciplined and organized by Kultur has already given us a foretaste." The French, Minh suggests, also flirted with the dangers of an "arid, analytical" society, but at the time of their revolution "felt the need to live again by the heart, to refresh the soul with springs of love and enthusiasm. The word 'sensibility' came back into conversations."[18]

Loti ably recaptured much of that emotional sensibility for empire and adapted it to his own version of love of France. Adam also insisted upon the finesse of sensibilities in defining her own Gallic moral philosophy, giving her ideas political weight through a phenomenology of love. There are, she proposed, "three states in the universe: matter, mind, and soul. Brute matter [read: Prussia] is composed of elements in disintegration, corruption, and suspension." Mind [French ésprit], by contrast, is a "reconstructive force, the impulsion of organic life, the search for forms." The soul is the expression of actions and "movements in harmony with their milieux." Notably, action imposed by the soul is that which "directs devotion and heroism to their ends," heroism being "the most undeniable affirmation of the Divine in Man." Lest this appear overly abstract, Adam herself makes manifestly clear, "the more ideas are abstract, the more power they have on the soul of psychic man. So it is with the idea of la patrie, the most abstract of human ideas, that which will make [a man] most lovingly [plus amoureusement] sacrifice his life."[19]

These evocations of love as heroism, sacrifice, and devotion also were the common elements of the Empire of Love Adam created with Loti. Against the strident heroics of British adventurism, or the heavy hand of the Teutons, Loti posed himself a truly manly writer and soldier of a different sort. As he and Adam understood, men of the post-1870s French empire would no longer be (if they ever had been) mere warriors or adventurers, but men with hearts who manifested or provoked great passions, like the "so well loved" Admiral Amédée Courbet, upon whose death in the Pescadores Islands, Loti reported to Le Figaro, "all of the sailors wept." The military was a particularly rich source of such sentiment. A companion of Loti's also wrote of Courbet's passing, "Farewell my Admiral! . . . your name will be brilliant in the history of your country; it will remain loved and honored in our hearts."

In praising the career and many missions to Asia of Vice Admiral Bergasse Dupetit Thouars, a fellow officer spoke of his colleague's ability to manifest "that trust which doubles the forces of an army or a fleet, which makes everything possible . . . strength, spirit, and daring even in action." For this, "one must unite in oneself an ensemble of qualities rarely concentrated in one officer," the first and foremost being "one must love the men."[20]

Colonial reports of the time, such as that of Captain Francis Garnier's death in Tonkin, were similarly structured around such emotionally resonant narratives, what Dupetit Thouars's fellow officers called "the perfect accord between duty . . . dignity of life, and constant abnegation." For Garnier, "there remained to him only a few piastres, a few effects, and his saber. The old officer in charge of the inventory wept hot tears upon closing the trunk of his commander. How to think of a leader who could inspire such affection!" When prosaically entreating Adam for recommendations on the behalf of impoverished friends, Loti equally employed this brothers-in-arms vocabulary: "This matter concerns a poor sailor . . . whom I love with a fraternal affection."[21] In his fiction and artworks Loti gave this affection corporeal form with his proud, sensual descriptions of sailors and his classically robust sketches of their handsome faces and muscular torsos. His work materialized the masculine devotion and erotic attraction embraced by brothers and lovers of nation and empire.

In prose and art, and in the costume balls that filled the rooms of Rochefort, empire was this family romance, a sensual binding of loving sons and brothers to each other under the mère patrie and the history of her glory. For Adam, as the great mother of the republicans, the Empire of Love was a means to extol the transcendent development of the nation; for Loti, it was an opportunity to maintain the beloved maternal and fraternal experience of his regional France. These were remarkably common projects. As one scholar has explained the dialectic, concepts of nation based upon territorial acquisition and historical change are generated from "the notion of the folk as an organic entity with a natural relation to the nurturing place, the motherland."[22] Loti's affection for local Rochefort perfectly complemented Adam's maternal role as the republic.

As a political and cultural figure, Adam was an insistent presence, particularly on questions of patrie and divided affections. She was perfectly aware of the devotion she imposed upon her charges. In *Nouvelle Revue* editorials, she bluntly asserted her patriotism and scorned weak governments in Paris: "All those who are suffering from disillusionment, who are indignant to see our politicians prefer their personal interests to the national cause, come to me." In her *Chanson des nouveaux epoux,* she adopted the voice of a young wife, demanding of her military officer husband, "Are we compelled to forgive the patrie everything, to accept everything from her, even pain and injury? . . . the greater my love, the more profound my terror when I fear that you will not hesitate for one moment to prefer the patrie to me." But her husband has already chosen his beloved: "Do you believe that it is for a uniform, for a rank that I have chosen what you ironically call 'the noble military estate?' No, it is a cult of an ideal being, it is for love."[23]

In his memoirs, Loti reflected on such associations from his own childhood, insisting, "The love one has for a mother is the only which is truly pure, truly unchangeable, the only which carries no selfishness of any kind, which bears no disappointments or bitterness." Such reflections were the core of his imperialism, a sentimental configuration of empire as domestic familiarity and affection. "Take these sailors, these spahis, all these abandoned young men exhausting their lives far away on the sea or in lands of exile . . . in the deepest and most sacred corners of their hearts, often in a sanctuary, you will find an old sitting mother."[24] Expressions of love—especially masculine, brotherly love under the sign of maternal devotion—were not only consistent with French imperial pursuits but also incarnated those pursuits.

As an imperialist, Loti was one who mixed French provincial, conservative values of distinction with overseas expansionist opportunities. Self-absorbed and ill at ease with both Paris and the harsh realities of colonies, he is best seen as a working professional sailor and writer, with a strong yearning for local nobility. He regarded with suspicion "those at Paris who send out to be killed . . . the brave children of Bretagne," yet his critics and some friends also called him a narcissist par excellence, an identification that marked him an embodiment of French empire: if he lacked the blue-blooded superiority of an aristocrat, or the regal Parisian bearing of a Juliette Adam, he could at least command servants and mistresses in other parts of the world. And this he did, both on his naval missions and in his writings.[25]

A continentalist like Adam, Loti nonetheless took full advantage of his positions abroad. In a famous exchange, Prime Minister Jules Ferry had debated Deputy Paul Déroulède on whether to follow a policy of empire, or one of strict attention to Germany. Ferry declaimed, "You will end by making me think you prefer Alsace-Lorraine to France. Must we hypnotize ourselves with lost provinces, and should we not take compensation elsewhere?" Déroulède retorted, "That is just the point. . . . I have lost two children and you offer me twenty domestics!"[26] Loti captured both sides of this argument.

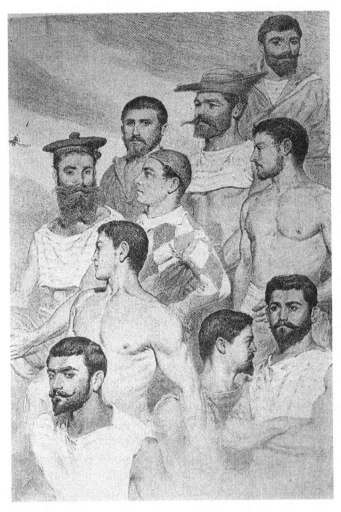

"One must love the men."
A passion for duties and bodies: Pierre Loti's illustration of the
sailors of the *Triomphante*. Source: Collection Christian Genet

His France was also a riven family: he despised the "banality" of the republic, while supporting the colonial expansion through which he gained the lovers, brokers, guides, and servants who populated his stories. He found the noble status denied him at home abroad.

Landing in Nagasaki, Loti's conflation of status, marriage, and imperial authority is clear. His *Madame Chrysanthème* (1887) is based upon his own experience contracting a temporary "wife" in the treaty port: "I wished in the first place to speak to M. Kangarou, who is interpreter, laundryman, and matrimonial agent. Nothing could be easier; they knew him and were willing to go in search of him. . . . Next I demanded a well-served repast, composed of the greatest delicacies in Japan. Better and better! They rushed to the kitchen to order it." His colonial engagement was indeed built upon marriage as the empire of twenty domestics.[27]

In *The Marriage of Loti*, the main character spends the last chapters of the book searching for children rumored to belong to his brother who preceded him to Tahiti as a sailor. He never finds them; these "marriages" produced not children but servants. Loti's contribution to empire was to translate those lives from colonial servitude into exotic characters, evidence of his true mastery—the literary Empire of Love.

With a growing prestige as a *romancier* and his promotion to commandant, Loti's authority over narratives became indivisible from his naval rank; his renown illustrates how little distinction was often made between "official" documents and "fiction" in the writing of nineteenth-century empire. Many were the writers, historians, and political journalists who cited his tales to capture their own adventures and impressions of the South Pacific, or East and Southeast Asia, including the future president Paul Deschanel, who pressed for French naval connections in Tahiti by remarking, "one must read *The Marriage of Loti*." The negotiation of colonial marriage recurred in Indochina, where the scholar Albert de Pouvourville paused to observe, "Getting stuck with the natives! This is not about the little wives of Loti, which white women call congaïs." In her *Un Barrage contre le Pacifique*, Marguerite Duras described a young woman "dying of impatience" to go to the colonies; as for her husband, "like her, he too had fallen prey to the mysterious writings of Pierre Loti." In memoirs of the beloved Admiral Courbet in New Caledonia, colonial Hélène Lainé noted, "here am I fifty-seven years after Courbet's death drawing on the pages of Pierre Loti."[28]

Such admissions are so regular in the French Pacific documentation and literature of Loti's lifetime that his tales are not merely "representations" of Asia and the Pacific but, rather, themselves producers of possible territories of French empire. Journalists, colonial bureaucrats, colonists, politicians, and naval commanders created their own official, archival "documents" and historical records out of the narratives established by his "fictions." In many cases, reality for them was already one of his stories.

By the end of the nineteenth century, Loti as writer was an authoritative narrator of the Orient from the Bosporous to the Indian Ocean to the Sea of Japan, across the Pacific and around the American continents. His notebooks and sketchbooks became the literary analogues for his formal diaries and naval reports, his ships' logs and registers. With his high profile and military status, Loti's writings were given front-page treatment. In a notable 1885 incident, French forces shelled the Red River delta in pursuit of Chinese and Tonkinese "Black Banner pirates," accused of ambushing a French expeditionary party. Loti's accounts for *Le Figaro* (he was a friend of the publisher Gaston Calmette) emphasized the bloody French massacre of the Tonkinese to such a degree that a displeased Ministry of the Navy had him recalled from Southeast Asia.

He entreated Juliette Adam to "use a little of your sovereign influence to save me," and was rescued from deskbound oblivion with the help of her ministerial connections. Vaguely accused of having harmed the name of France, Loti defended himself using the language of love that he refined and employed so effectively in his fiction: "I asked Alphonse Daudet to tell the public, the journalists, of my indignation . . . how I love them, those rough sailors, how I am with them, how I am theirs. . . . I love this calling and the men of the sea above anything else."[29]

Here we see Loti's and Adam's empire in full relief. Some forms of imperialism, such as Tahitian marriages and fraternal affection for sailors were safe to narrate; others, as the Tonkin massacre, were not. Of this, Loti was extremely self-conscious. During his reprimand he bitterly wrote of his critics, "the people cry horror because it is the first time that the realities of war—and an exotic war—are put before their eyes. That's the whole problem; it is true, I should have soothed and calmed their nerves."

Proud of his reports, Loti nonetheless sarcastically recognized the limits of his colonial writing. Empire was to be made attractive. He enthusiastically penned the foreword for a former shipmate's account of the Tonkin campaign that was much to his sensibilities. Reflecting on his friend's return from a dangerous sortie he fairly gushed, "And your return on board the *Bayard*, that unforgettable return where the admiral, weeping, embraced you, while tears ran down the faces of so many good sailors. . . . I read that as through a veil that clouded my eyes, for never had a drama moved me so much as this simple tale." As if to reinforce the critical role of the writer and of stories in shaping empire, Loti concluded, "There where I wept other readers of whatever sort will also weep; believe me that there, where I was captivated, the others will be captivated as well, and that your work will leave in all a noble emotion after the book is closed."[30]

In the same era, purportedly humanitarian imperialists such as Auguste Pavie in Laos and Pierre Savorgnan de Brazza in Africa—the latter a Loti friend also supported by Juliette Adam—became wildly popular by developing such generous, emotionally resonant reputations. Colonial officials such as Governor Lacascade in Rapa (1887) entreated local inhabitants, "Always love France who wants nothing but your happiness and that of your children. In a word, make yourself worthy of the title she has given you, and of the protection you will always find under her flag." Empire and acceptability were exploited, at times tested, and constantly renegotiated as divergent reports, writings, and story-lines were gradually and deliberately shaped into an accommodating and attractive imperialism for the Empire of Love.[31]

Adam made sure this empire had an audience, supporting Loti and working tirelessly to expand the bourgeois audience of the *Nouvelle Revue*. Her own writings also specifically shaped this empire. In her *Jean et Pascal*, Jean's father is serving the navy out of Saigon. In her early *Le Mandarin* (1860), she invokes Pé-Kang, "descendent of Confucius," who comes to Second Empire Paris from China in search of ways to enlighten himself and his country. Introduced to the works of Jules Michelet and Victor Durand (notably Durand's *L'Amour*), Pé-Kang rejoices "without object and without form, a powerful, eternal love took possession of my heart." To Durand he writes ecstatically, "Dear Sir . . . I affirm that this book captures the Chinese ideal." To Michelet, "Master, I have understood your teachings and you have unveiled the thoughts of my heart; would that my gratitude equaled the good you have given."[32] Such consistent narratives (love, ideology, and devotion to France) are primary sources for understanding Adam's elaboration of nation and empire.

For Loti, an additional and extraordinary source bears extended commentary. In Loti's Rochefort, the old Viaud family home was a profound expression of the Empire of Love. The residence was more than a home base for a writer retreating from a "long season of *ennui*" in Paris; it was a fantasy of French provincial bourgeois comfort enclosed by a seductive and domesticated universe of the exotic. At Rochefort, Loti ceaselessly reshaped his rooms, and the residence is in many ways a topography of his France and its empire in the later nineteenth century. The rooms are articulated around the plan of a bourgeois localism infused by nostalgias of aristocracy and peasantry, interlocked with phantasmagoric impressions of empire and exotica from the Near East, Africa, Asia, and Oceania. Loti's intimate private quarters are whitewashed, austere and adorned by a crucifix. The family rooms are heavy in drapery and decoration, the grand halls European Gothic and Renaissance.

The carnival of objects assembled at Rochefort by Loti was in the tradition of the *cabinet de curiosités* of privileged and impassioned individuals, and serves as a resplendent figure for the question of why Loti should be an impresario of a work on love, empire, and history. His collections were his personal domain, his repository of memories and promises. As Krzystof Pomain has argued, such personal collections are crossed by two dominant themes, "that of totality, and that of desire." Such imperatives of desire "express themselves also in the words that one gives, at least in French, to the one who applies himself to amass objects and to form a cabinet: '*Amateur,* singular, masculine, [he] who loves something.'"[33]

Loti's collection was the work of such an amateur—nonsystematic, deeply and romantically obsessive. He bartered in Oceania, looted from Southeast Asia, and bought and photographed courtesans in Japan. In his youth, he offered a striking and perhaps unintentional definition of the Empire of Love as collection: "When I am at last a mariner, I will be able to possess all those things that I have dreamt of for so long." Empire was military strategy and civilizing mission, yet it was also imagination and fantasy; it accumulated in the halls and chambers of Rochefort under the sign of *possession.*[34]

What Loti wanted to possess was a certain idea of France. Rochefort's empire rooms, where he stored his foreign treasures, his bronzes, carpets, idols, and carvings, are exotic facsimiles of mosques, pagodas, and temples. Most deliberately evoked an immemorial past, such as the *salle chinoise,* about which Juliette Adam remarked: "The grandeur of such an old empire speaks of a civilization left by time, searching to distract and still astonish in its old age." Yet such temporal exoticism only enclosed the true place of timelessness, according to Adam: "I speak of the room of she to whom I was the other [l'autre], the room of his mother where nothing had been touched." The mother of la patrie recognized the doubled maternal space of the revered "old sitting mother" at the heart of Loti's empire: Adam was the France of the republic he served as a dutiful son, but Madame Viaud kept the inner chambers of Loti's Rochefort-based France, the ultimate object of his love.[35]

Loti's local world was arranged to stand sentinel over obsessive memories of a storybook past, including a "petit musée," a child's collection of seashells and natural objects. In his maturity, Loti was not really even a collector but a *fetishist.* He worshipped his home as the template for the family romance that became his Empire of Love: the memory place of his mother, and his beloved older brother Gustave who had gone to Tahiti as a sailor, kept a local mistress, collected shells, masks, and carvings, and written young Pierre, "Do not doubt all the pretty things I will bring back for your museum." In 1865 this first brother-in-arms died of cholera on a naval mission to Southeast Asia, his body released into the Bay of Bengal. Pierre was left with the goldfish pond his brother had made him behind the family home. "It was during my reveries of mourning . . . that I began to devote to him my cult, a bit fetishistic."[36]

Gustave's romance and fatal end were Loti's autobiographical means for writing himself into a storied French Pacific tradition. Through longing and melancholy Loti identified the Great Ocean of Bougainville, who claimed for Enlightenment France to have found the sensual paradise he sought, and La Pérouse, whose disappearance in the South Seas raised oceanic death to the status of myth. Loti, through his literary and naval project, consolidated this tradition at the turn of the nineteenth century in the most obvious way: he made plain in his writings, his home, and collections how the longing for the Great Ocean was the melancholy of a changing, increasingly unfamiliar France. As Loti wrote to Gustave in 1876, "My brother, where are our future plans, where is Oceania, where are our dreams, where is the past, where is France?"[37]

At the end of the century, Loti's *cabinet* imperialism fascinates less as exemplary of French colonial plans or missions, more as part of a European culture in transition; the dying "traditions" of other lands he so lamented were taking place not far away but close to home. Of his Rochefort past, he wrote, "It was still the time of modest local trades which 'progress' has everywhere replaced." A supposed "fatal impact" in the Pacific, or the decline of the East were the distant tableaux of Loti's dissatisfaction with a changing Europe, and the republic's "modernization" of regional France. In letters to Juliette Adam in the 1880s, he lamented, "There will come a time when the earth will be very troubling and tedious (ennuyeuse) to inhabit, when it will be rendered the same from one end to the other, and one will not even be able to try to travel to be distracted a little."[38] When the local childhood world Loti loved and tried to recover overseas were not equal to his reveries, he sought to preserve his dreams by restoring their imagined surroundings in beloved miniature at Rochefort. For the world beyond the continent, his amateur Empire was the attempt to seize the fantastic and faraway and preserve them in the form of the collection.

The heart of empire was literally at home for Loti. In a well-known essay, *A Pilgrimmage to Angkor* (1912), the writer's Indochinese adventure is so completely framed by domestic evocations of Rochefort that it is difficult to say which is the subject of the piece. The work epitomizes the connections between his literary Empire of Love, and that of his collecting. He reflected, "The ruins of Angkor, how well I remember a certain April evening, a bit veiled, how they appeared to me in a vision. This took place in my childhood 'museum'—a small room at the top of my family home where I had brought together many shells, island birds, Oceanic weapons and jewels, everything that could make me speak of faraway lands."[39] Collecting objects throughout his life preserved these childhood dreams. Like his evocation of the "old sitting mother" and his beloved sailors carrying on for Gustave as the figures of his only indisputable loves, Loti's collecting was a primary source of empire as domestic comfort and affection.

It was from his collections that Loti developed the exoticism that made him such an attractive imperialist. As the colonial author Clotilde Chivas-Baron explained the exoticist project in a 1927 essay, such genre writers produced tales of "great voyagers" appealing to "the milieu of the average sedentary Frenchman." These tales and figures incarnated "the prestige of those who will traverse the endless seas and oceans, those who will live in the lands of pineapples, bananas, mangos, and orchids . . . those who have seen blacks and Chinese with their own eyes." It was thus, she suggested, that the colonial ideal was planted and took root "in the enthusiastic brains" of her fellow Frenchmen. Loti himself used the same vocabulary: empire was not colonies; rather colonies were childhood desires: "the totality of faraway hot countries with their palm trees, their giant flowers, their black peoples, their beasts, their adventures."[40]

Loti had none of the scientific collector spirit that motivated scholars such as Emile Guimet, who would found the Museum of Asiatic Arts in Lyon and later Paris. Not for Loti were the thoughtful historical classification and anthropological interpretations of his pieces in terms of cultural tradition, ritual practices, or religious beliefs. The house at Rochefort, with its idiosyncratic objects, was distinctly out of step with the great age of state collections, the erudite ambitions of a true scholarly Orientalist such as Guimet, or Paul Rivet's later Musée de l'homme and its scientific anthropology. In 1850 the Louvre divided its naval and ethnographic museum into two departments—one still housing general collections for the navy, the other now consecrated to the formal study of art objects. In 1859 Paul Broca and associates founded the Paris Anthropological Society, dominating French thought with scientific applications of racial differentiation and European superiority. In 1867 Napoleon III decreed a Museum of National Antiquities to house the burgeoning study of comparative anthropology.[41]

Yet Loti was not alone in the pursuit of empire as exotic collection. Although monarchy and republic moved to appropriate the world in nationally organized, scientifically premised exhibits and expositions throughout the later nineteenth century, French imperial culture also had a uniquely Loti-like face in the same period, one that domesticated and enclosed appealing storybook histories. Consider a set of Suchard chocolate trading cards (1880–1910) targeted at children, particularly those printed for Tahiti. "This is the type of woman celebrated by Pierre Loti" suggests the legend on card 277, a fitting companion to Loti's cabinet imperialism. The evocation of the Tahitian "wife" and lover Rarahu presumed knowledge of Loti's tale and connected his *Marriage* to other colonial projects. Here was empire very much à la Loti: colonialism as a pastime for children, a set of wondrous images and descriptions; faraway lands and peoples in the form of a collection. Featuring images of colonial "natives" and landscapes printed with pithy observations designed to inculcate a sense of French empire, the over three hundred cards were part of a promotion that allowed collectors to create formal albums of empire that, when complete, could be redeemed for promotional prizes including bicycles, chimes, cameras, phonographs, and—in greatest supply—atlases of the colonies. It was empire commodified, circulated, like Loti's stories, ultimately to seduce the reader with colorful pictures, colonial instruction and—in this case—perhaps even desirable goods.

The cards themselves are steeped in the colonial logic of Loti's *Marriage*: union with and appropriation of the local. Card 248 teaches the ways Asia and Europe can flavor each other's urban planning: "Saigon is a delicious Western town, but even in the European quarters it still has a cachet of exoticism which increases the attraction." Card 252, a local river scene, labors with surreal determination to maintain some slight French hegemony in the landscape: "Except for the presence of a few sampans, a few natives, and except also for the climate, the river, the banks, and bridge are not very Far Eastern." Notable stereotypes about dark Melanesians and light Polynesians are promoted. The Tahitian woman who earned the Loti appellation is praised for her "European traits in a coloring of café au lait," and for being "gladly covered with flowers."[42] She is indeed the celebrated Loti "wife," the attractive and desirable face of empire.

The colonial Suchard cards belonged to a larger promotional collection dedicated to a young person's "Picturesque France," a set of regional images rendering both nation and empire assemblages of local color, custom, and costume. Likewise, Loti created at Rochefort an invitation to perform both France and other civilizations in a phantasmagoria of stone, wood, bronze, gold and silver. For him, the past and the faraway were not always overseas. Along with his Japanese pagoda, Chinese throne, and Turkish and Arab chambers, Loti designed the main hall as a medieval replica of soaring vaults, stained glass, and heraldry. A simple dining area is contrived to be a peasant family's place of refuge, from its low timber beams and stone floor to its rude wooden benches and iron pots and cooking rings. Rooms at Rochefort had the stylings of a Europe no less exotic than the Orient.

Indeed, Loti's most popular book, dedicated with filial affection to the grand Juliette, was *Pecheur de l'islande* (1886), an exoticist tale with very "local" flavor: it follows the lives of Breton fishermen, their hard existence on the rugged coast, betrothals to local beauties, and dangerous months-long fishing voyages to Icelandic waters. These challenges and travails, reprinted in multiple and illustrated editions for young readers, are intertwined with portraits of wise, long-suffering aunts and hopeful, waiting young women, a world of simple values, earnest love, and traditional costumes. Loti's empire remained grounded in dual exoticisms: faraway lands and detailed evocations of regional France.

The binding of near and far is often pointed. The author's brave souls, Yann and Sylvestre, will lose their lives as men of the sea, the latter through an effective colonial plot twist, in Asia: "One day he was called to the office where it was announced to him that he was ordered to China to serve in the fleet in Formosa." Sylvestre's picturesque posting through the Indian Ocean will be overtaken when he is shot down in a colonial war while "smiling disdainfully" at a Chinese soldier whom he dares to fire at him during a skirmish. In Sylvestre's death Loti narrates the dream of exotica and its harsh disappearance, both at home and abroad, the lost sailors and the lost France he loved. As a coda, Loti offers the tragic drowning of Yann as a macabre inversion of matrimonial metaphors. Overtaken in a storm, the last local hero is pulled, struggling, into the depths. "Deep mystery enveloped this monstrous marriage. Dark fluttering veils and storm-tossed curtains had been drawn to conceal this festival, the bride had filled the air with her loud voice, drowning out his cries." If Loti saw the world abroad of French colonialism despoiled, so also did he read back a bitter anguish for the images and comforts of a disappearing France in a time of national consolidation.[43]

Hoping to console and conserve the past he imagined, Loti collected objects that comforted him as evidence of a stable and ordered world. Loti's home *was* empire, neither as rude white conqueror or enlightened progressive administrator but in timeless guises: as monk and aesthete, or in an imagined despotic model of the Chinese Middle Kingdom, the cannibal native island chief, the childhood he loved. He was supreme; resident and sovereign in a home furnished with the sensuous objects, images, textures, and totems that defined his true France from the republic.

Loti's supreme terror was reserved for the passing of his own aristocracy; its end meant "I would no longer be loved." It was through empire that Loti hoped to exercise and preserve the most singular quality of an aristocrat: *privilege*, the special status he craved. In Rochefort and abroad he delighted in describing such authority, as in the formalities leading up to his own treaty-port "marriage" to Madame Chrysanthème: "By way of a chair they gave me a square cushion of black velvet. . . . The two little women who are servants of the house, and my humble servants too, awaited my orders in attitudes expressive of the profoundest humility." His own household at Rochefort obeyed these principles. Respectably settled with Blanche Franc de Ferrière, Loti maintained a second ménage for a young Basque woman, Crucita Gainza. Although he never formally recognized her, she bore him sons he wanted; that was her role. It is no wonder that upon retreating to Rochefort, Loti brought his incarnate empire and "marriages" with him; they were the material signature of places and peoples, the status with which he could command love and order affections to satisfy his desires.[44]

What do we know of Loti's universe of objects? Scholars of the house can choose their theme by following the chronology of construction and addition: Turkish salon, 1877–1894; Arab chamber, 1884; Japanese pagoda, 1886; Gothic chamber, 1887; peasant, Renaissance, mosque, mummy, monastic, and Chinese rooms, 1895–1903. Loti has been a popular biographer's subject and a general life would properly emphasize the author's attachment to things Turkish and Arab, his one "true" love the Circassian Aziyadé, his poetic adherence to Islam, and his problematic defense of the Ottomans down to and including the denial of the Armenian genocide. Loti fans and scholars have detailed his Orientalist preferences for the spiritual and picturesque.

For our purposes, we can note the preeminence of the Oceanic and Asian articulations that uniquely marked Loti and his Empire of Love. The collections, some still preserved at the Rochefort residence, have been transformed by the state—Loti might appreciate the irony—into a national museum. Most—including all substantial traces of the Japanese pagoda collections—were dispersed after the writer's death, but the auction catalogues with their rigorous descriptions and enumerations describe furniture, paintings, ceramics, sculpted and encrusted woods, textiles, and potteries. One notices special lots devoted to "Arts de l'Océanie." Item 181, a flat boomerang, comes complete with a handwritten note by Loti, noting that the "indisputably Australian" object was found by him on Easter Island, where he made a port of call as a young sailor on the *Flore* in 1871. Loti adored speculation: "The presence of this boomerang on Easter Island ... seems to constitute a curious document concerning the migration of the peoples of the Great Southern Ocean in distant epochs."[45]

This fascination with time immemorial marks the collection: carved stone faces, fetish statuettes, ceremonial masks. Yet as always, timelessness is distinctly historical for Loti, sharply marked by home and his family romance of empire. In memories of brother Gustave, Loti recalled, "He made me a present of a large book which was called *Travels in Polynesia*, and this was the only book I loved as a little child." Following his brother, Loti's first literary affections and naval assignments were in the South Pacific. The islands of Oceania were always part of his love for home.[46]

He developed his talent for bringing the Pacific to France in imperial service. It was on Easter Island that Loti drafted his first reports of the Grand Ocean: notes and sketches (he was charged by the captain with keeping an artistic record) that would become semi-ethnographic adventures when presented to and published by *L'Illustration*. His narratives were shaped by his twin role as artist and imperialist: topographies and ethnologies—sketches of lakes and valleys, writings on local customs, reports filed with his superiors for dispatch to the naval ministry.

These writings are indistinguishable from many nineteenth-century European Pacific impressions: details of savages, wild, barbaric behaviors, curiosity and exchange. Some of the reports are lamentable to a later age. It was on this stopover that the crew fulfilled part of its mission by toppling and laboriously decapitating one of the island's famous moai, leaving a desecrated trunk and carting away the two-ton head to Paris, where it sits today in the Jardin des Plantes.

The odd melancholy that suffused Loti's writings returned to reporters watching the auction of these collections, those admirers of the writer "attracted by a pious curiosity, to contemplate these relics of a grand voyager and of a great, pained writer, imaginative, at once childlike, ancient, and a bit savage, who laid bare his sensibility perhaps even more than Baudelaire."[47] The remote and exotic ultimately returned to the realm of domestic familiarity, as the pieces gathered from around the world came back to Loti's family. The collection to which the Oceanic lot belonged brought in over one hundred thousand francs to the sellers—the writer's children.

Loti would certainly have appreciated the windfall less than one journalist's report that the auction had brought about "sensations of the infinite, in the triple sense of humanity, time, and space. We obsessively turned yesterday . . . toward chance, uncertainty, toward the dispersal of all things, of the "Loti objects" come from the far reaches of the earth."[48] Another article captured in fewer words the uneasy sensibility that haunted the former Julien Viaud with its simple headline: "The *Souvenirs* of Pierre Loti have been sold."

TWO

PANAMA

Geopolitics of Desire

The town of Rochefort on the river Loire and her most famous native
son, Pierre Loti, were well known in the late nineteenth century.
Loti's residence and reputation attracted Parisian luminaries, and
his writings on Tahiti, Japan, Indochina, and other Pacific ports of call
made this maritime town an outpost for the ideological romance of empire.
In 1886, a little-known writer and publicist named Augustin Garçon also
staked a claim to Rochefort's role in the Pacific. His argument proposed
directly linking the distant Grand Ocean with the maritime communities
of the French mainland, a transit of communication, commercial advantage,
and national pride extending from the far reaches of the Pacific to Europe's
Atlantic coast. "We note," he said, "that the center of the Gulf of Gascogne
will become an intermediate point which will attract the vessels coming
from the isthmus. We find there a port which will be perfectly situated, that
being Rochefort, on a good river with easy docking facilities at the heart of
very rich departments."

Once again, Rochefort integrally shaped French thinking about the
Pacific. Garçon envisioned a direct rail line to connect the warehouses of
Rochefort with the rest of France and Europe. From here, he suggested,
could be distributed "the products of Oceania in all directions," making
Rochefort the "stockhouse of this corner of the globe."[1] Garçon recognized
the town's historic maritime importance by detailing its history and strategic
potential as a center for global trade. His argument lay in the evocation of a
singular idea—the linking of Rochefort to Oceania through "the isthmus";
not a geographical detail of the French coastline but of the Grand Ocean.
As he argued his case, he knew full well a French *Compagnie universelle* was

"Glory for la patrie . . . and a touch of romance."
Workers, families, and machines on the isthmus. *Percement du canal de Panama* (1888–1903). Source: National Library of Australia

making his plan possible with a project that would render the Pacific an extension of the Atlantic through the greatest capitalist enterprise of the era—the Panama Canal.

"Panama" is an engrossing story; a great feat of capital, engineering, and medical science, a ruthless tale of disease, labor exploitation, unbelievable political skullduggery, and the ultimate success of American imperialism and gunboat diplomacy under Theodore Roosevelt. But first it was a French dream and disaster, one that ultimately brought down a government, ruined politicians and financial houses, took the savings of thousands of small investors, and shattered a generation of imaginings about the glory of a French Pacific. Those imaginings had been an *histoire d'amour* gone wrong. As the Americans took over the isthmus, the canal-publicist Willis John Abbott assessed his French predecessors: "Their emotionalism leads them to support any great national enterprise that promises glory for la patrie [and] . . . has in it a touch of romance."[2]

This was not merely the view of a wily American. In his 1889 "sociological" study of varieties of French love, *L'Amour en République*, writer Emile Bergerat had argued, "Our people is essentially imaginative, idealistic, and chimerical; we believe everything our poets tell us, and if told that there were tramways on the moon not only would we believe it, we would buy shares." The 1880s and 1890s were the decades of such a project, the French Panama romance and failure. Here was a grand scheme that offered the conquest of the Pacific and the unity of the globe through the joint-stock company, the nation-state translated into capital. Through the investment of thousands of stockholders, the proud *mission civilisatrice* would know its finest moments. As Garçon put it, "Our nation will show that to its venerable distinguishing qualities has been added perseverance, and that she will never abandon her role as initiator of all that concerns progress and civilization." With a grand sweep of history he declared, "Civilization, the arts as well as industry of Europe will bring to life these immense territories bathed by the Pacific. The stockholders and capitalists who, with their financial aid, permit the realization of this immense interoceanic canal project have claim to all of our thanks for the intelligent and patriotic employment of their capital."[3]

While Garçon pondered the future of the Pacific from Rochefort, the salon of Juliette Adam had a visitor recently returned from a triumphant business and lecture tour of the United States. The Great Frenchwoman welcomed the man acclaimed as her counterpart, the Great Frenchman. A strong supporter and patron of Adam's *La Nouvelle Revue*, Ferdinand de Lesseps had come to talk about Panama. The aristocratic Lesseps, confidant of monarchs, presidents, and financiers, was a heroic figure.[4] In the 1860s, his backers created the company that had excavated the Suez Canal, making them rich and him a worldwide celebrity. Now, Lesseps, some eighty thousand French investors, and several republican governments were poised to dominate the Pacific, to gain the fabled coast of East Asia, and to spread the benefits of progress and civilization throughout Oceania with what the future president Paul Deschanel called a "veritable economic, political, and military revolution."[5]

As with most great undertakings of late-nineteenth-century France, Adam was there to provide a forum. The lead article in the very first issue of her *Nouvelle Revue* (1879) is a detailed and enthusiastic assessment of the Panama Canal project—penned by none other than Lesseps himself. In her opening letter from the editor, Adam creates a passionate, patriotic context for the discussion with her blunt critique of other European powers: "England and Germany, in our old world, have given us a show of certain progress on the order of movement or by accumulation of force. But their governmental systems create obstacles to forward movement of the overall social body." The imperatives of unity and egalitarian social progress she explored throughout her philosophy and in her republicanism are here programmatically set against a favorite trope: the mere "accumulation of force" of her rivals. As always, however, Adam does not eschew force, so long as it can be joined with love in a distinctly French passion. This she called the "violent love we have for Gaul," springing from "our sentiment of Latin fraternity, our passion for liberty."[6] This violent love and fraternity, of the "Latin" sort that linked France to Central America, would be reiterated by numerous French thinkers and planners and ultimately expressed in the promotion of grand common causes—like the audacious challenge of the Canal.

The revolutionary potential of the Canal lay in realizing the ancient dream of an interoceanic sea passage to India and East Asia—a transit interrupted centuries before by European encounters with the Americas. Lesseps himself was not shy about drawing on and completing this legend. In Adam's salon, as in the United States and across Europe, he referred to himself as a sort of "Christopher Columbus voyaging on to the discovery of a new hemisphere." His engineers spoke of "tearing down" the barrier "which turned back Colombus and Cortès from their ardent search for the lands of the Pacific." French newspapers enthusiastically repeated Lesseps's imperial vision. *La Liberté* lauded this "push to human progress," and argued "it is the route . . . of Europe to Oceania, to Japan, to China, to the rich and magnificent countries which we still call "the Far East." *Le Gaulois* waxed,

"The piercing of the isthmus of Panama is a grandiose work, of first-rate utility, civilizing."[7]

The *Compagnie du Canal Interocéanique* itself issued regular bulletins to underscore the popular sentiment. Henry Bionne, the general secretary of the company, declared "Panama commands an immense space, almost an entire hemisphere" and called the future canal "the great highway of the world," which from Europe would run "to America, to Oceania, to Japan, to China, and back." In this vast domain, the merchant marine would "show its colors and link together the lands of the Pacific where French interests are calling." The canal would make a "French Pacific" through a masterstroke not of conquest or territorial expansion but by integrating, relaying, and connecting a set of disparate points into a tenuous web of empire. The great routes meeting at Panama would be "linked with well-placed French stepping-stones: Martinique, Guadeloupe, the Marquesas, Tahiti, New Caledonia, Cochinchine," and Bionne promised riches of trade as French wines, silks, and manufactures found "new and vast markets among the consumer countries of the Pacific basin and the China Sea."[8]

As a child, Pierre Loti had played with carvings and picture books and fantasized about the joining of France and the Grand Ocean. Waking one morning, he found in his room "necklaces of shells threaded in human hair, feather headdresses, ornaments of gloomy and primitive and savage simplicity hung about in every direction as if distant Polynesia had come to me during the night." The explanation for this miracle? "My brother, who had returned to Europe by a mail packet-boat from Panama."[9]

The child Loti dreamed the isthmus as the bearer of both his brother and of the Pacific world. Gustave had only landed and embarked; there was no canal to transit in his time. A generation later, all aspects of French policy in the Pacific were ultimately tied to the project at Panama, whereby the Great Ocean became an extension of France. Far-flung territories previously thought of as outposts such as New Caledonia were strategically reimagined as linchpins of empire. "The capital Noumea grows in importance every day from the channeling of the Panamanian isthmus," wrote Garçon, making the Melanesian colony "an excellent base for stationing and refitting our navy." Even the mythic paradise of Tahiti was annexed in 1880 with the canal in mind. At King Pomare's formal signing of union with the French state, the governor proclaimed the islands would soon know "a new era of progress and prosperity, worthy of the epoch which will see the barrier of Panama fall, making Tahiti the natural connection of all transpacific steam navigation, the most beautiful and fortunate land of them all. Vive la France! Vive Tahiti!" Four years later, Paul Deschanel was arguing for more French public education on Tahiti, Bora-Bora, and Huahiné, to "familiarize our fellow citizens about the geography, history, morals, administration, and resources of a colony which can become one of the most frequented points on the globe."[10]

The rest of the world watched "French" Panama with keen interest. Japanese scholar Inagaki Manjiro noted, "If M. de Lesseps' scheme of the Panama canal should happen to be completed . . . undoubtedly the Pacific Ocean would be revolutionized in every way." He plainly observed, "The French occupation of Tahiti and Rapa—both containing good harbors—in 1880 was with the distinct object of controlling the sea route from Panama to Sydney, Brisbane, and Auckland." Back in France, Auguste Garçon demonstrated that Pierre Loti was not the only Frenchman to be able to imagine the Pacific both from Rochefort and Japan. "Upon the opening of the canal, it is possible that Europe could counter-balance the influence of the United States, and that we could take back the place we held in Japan." The constitution of the French Pacific, from the Japanese islands in the far north to the Society Islands and New Caledonia in the far south, rested with the success of the canal. Lacking the immediate proximity and significance of the Mediterranean or Atlantic, the far Pacific could yet be made part of France by linking it bodily to the Atlantic world already known. That would be accomplished by piercing the isthmus and having the waters of the two great oceans meet under a French-controlled strategic *point d'appui*—the canal.[11]

Before Panama became a dream of global commerce and mastery, much less a terrain of survey, hydrography, and capital calculation, it was a space for French imaginings to shape humanitarian, spiritual, and political principles. For Félix Belly, a journalist and historian, the European encounter with Central America fulfilled Columbus's notion of "having seriously found the earthly paradise of the scripture." Subsequent colonial settlement, occupation, and revolution reinforced the isthmus's destiny as a place of primary affinity for France, the national liberation wars of the 1810s and 1820s that separated Latin America from Spain touted as direct evocations of French revolutionary principles. "It is in these new countries, without precedents, without education, without roots in the past, that our principles of [17]89 are the best understood and the most strictly applied."[12]

For Belly, new revolutionary states in Central America were not only youthful and unspoiled, they were as such natural children of the great Latin France, whose maternal love would affectionately guide their development. Whereas Phillip II "inspired them all to the most violent repulsion, France attracts them by being nothing more than . . . the interpreter of eternal verities of humanity, and by encouraging their own emancipation." Ranged against such generosity, the Spanish are a cruel empire in decline. "The Castillian genius is hard, proud, and empty," marked by "aridity of heart."

If Belly's rhetoric was self-serving, it was a prescription with which many isthmian Indians of the Panamanian coast could at least partly agree. As one Kuna chief, Néle de Kantule, put it, "When my old ancestors knew the Spaniards were coming they had to flee away to the forest where they slept. Some Spaniards got hold of the Indians and tied them up and they threw them away and they died." Evoking a Spanish madness for gold, Kantule ponders, "Those people who come from another country, they believe we are living in a stolen country. No, we have not stolen the country we are living in. Now the Spaniards are after us and they are going to rob us of our country."[13]

In his own attacks, Belly joins such testimonies and complaints by transferring Latin history away from a pitiful and desiccated Spanish empire of blood aristocracy to the promise and tenacity of the Indians and Hispanic Americans: "It is from their villages that shines love of family, goodness without reserve, and hospitality beyond measure." At the heart of this all-encompassing love is a remarkably Gallic prescription; succeeding Spain, France is the new Latin beacon. "It was not from their blood that the Hispanic-Americans have drawn their true qualities, it is from the sudden light of 89, which has enlightened the entire world."[14]

Latin America would thus be enfolded within the revolutionary French Empire of Love. The eminent anarchist geographer Elisée Réclus, traveling through Central America in the 1850s, also invoked French revolutionary traditions from both 1789 and 1848: "The moral influence of France is such that in these countries her new revolution strongly supports their spirits." Full of excitement for the possibilities of a new man in a new world, Réclus was for a short time a banana planter on the isthmus. As his biographers relate, "he saw in this type of colonization . . . the possibility of seeing born a new man capable of the organization of a new society—a utopia shared by a good number of anarchists."[15]

Important French voices took the idea of aiding and guiding Latin American affairs a bit too seriously. Notable among them was Louis Napoleon Bonaparte who, along with the Austrian Archduke Maximillian, made a disastrous intervention in Mexico in the 1860s. Bonaparte's craving for an empire in the New World was longstanding, for it was he, then still a future emperor, who in 1846 insisted, "The joining of the Atlantic and Pacific Oceans by means of a canal crossing the center of the New World is a matter whose importance cannot be doubted." By championing a canal project, Bonaparte declared himself for trade and communication with China, Japan, New Zealand, New Holland, the western United States, and "the hastening . . . by several centuries of the progress of Christianity and the civilization of the globe."[16]

The future emperor was not alone in his imaginings. Canal projects had been proposed since the first Europeans came upon the isthmus and correctly reckoned the lay of its geography, and French speculators were always in the forefront, with grand schemes defined through civilization and humanitarian principle. In 1860, Athanase Airiau of the Paris "Society for a *Canal Interocéanique*" said, "It is to France that belongs the initiative to establish a canal," a case he made by appeal to national character: "This exploration, attentive, disinterested, will conform to the aptitudes and penchants of our nation, to the allure of our generous policies, our humanitarian tendencies around which one can rally, yet which are no less eminently honorable." In a separate letter to the French government, Airiau would strongly emphasize the particularly Latin qualities of French colonialism by cautioning, "It is important, in effect, that the Panamanian isthmus always have a sufficient colonial force at its disposition . . . to preserve South America from the invasion of the Monroe Doctrine which dreams despotically of Latin submission to its profit, to the detriment of our Old Europe."

Airiau's compatriot Léon Faucher also pressed the matter by distinguishing French and British imperial ideologies. In fact, "Frenchness" was understandable only by pursuing and assessing imperial ambitions. Compared to the cold egoism of British indirect rule, French "assimilation" was a politics of embrace and sympathy. "The English race never associates itself with any other in interest or in ideas, it is absolutely incapable and antipathetic to the work of assimilation. . . . England's conquests take the road of substitution and not fusion; the other races flee or are extinguished before her." It was thus that "it is France which will henceforth march at the head of civilization and progress."[17] Empire itself revealed that Panama and the Pacific should rightly belong to Gaul, the Enlightenment, and the Revolution.

Airiau's canal project perfectly illustrates this sort of self-reading of generous and brotherly empire; his plans detail not only an engineering scheme, but an extraordinary spiritual and ideological topography. In elegant renderings and elevations he lays out, in addition to a canal route, plans for a perfectly octagonal city to be built around the waterway, with quais dedicated to England, Holland, America, France, and other nations of the globe, complemented by boulevards named for Panama and other South American territories. The city would be divided into mathematically exact sections within northern and southern basins and detailed with symbolic districts, places named for Asian and African animals, for Central American and European peoples, and for famous figures drawn from myth and history such as Athena or Simon Bolivar. The world's states would each have legations in the center of the octagon around an artificial inland sea dotted with small communities named for French towns such as Rouen and Bordeaux.[18] In these extraordinary plans, the Panama Canal in particular and canals in general were much more than feats of engineering, the triumph of nineteenth-century man and science over nature; they were human quests and utopian, spiritual locales for creating a world united under a brotherhood of commerce, progress, and faith. In an 1848 interoceanic proposal, Claude Drigon of the Maritime Company of Saint Pius claimed to work for "the world as a fatherland whose citizens are all brothers, because they are all children of the same God," and he called his fellow canal-planners "missionaries of European civilization," and "benefactors of the human species."[19]

Nowhere were such grand sentiments more clearly realized than at the site of the Orient waterway that would make Panama seem possible—Suez. In 1904, the German scholar Wolf von Schiebrand drew together Napoleonic histories and the Egyptian project by noting, "Napoleon saw the future importance of an interoceanic canal through the isthmus [of Panama], and because of his clear perception of it, the American negotiation for the Louisiana Purchase almost failed." Nevertheless, the emperor's plans remained without practical application "until after the Suez canal had been built, thus showing that the immense engineering difficulties of such an undertaking could be overcome."[20] In 1846, the same year the Bonapartist nephew Louis Napoleon had first proposed a Panama crossing, an advisory company was formed by French Saint-Simonians to move ahead with a Suez canal project.

Claude Henri de Rouvroy, the Comte de Saint-Simon (who died in 1825), had been a visionary aristocrat who, appalled by the effects of industrialization in Europe, had advocated a new society based on control of work by scientists, engineers, and artists. After his death, some of his followers, under the charismatic Prosper Barthélemy "*Père*" Enfantin, created a semi-mystical cult, advocated communal living and free love, and established sections in the United States and Egypt. Juliette Adam was one of many who traced this history, chronicling how "The Father" and his sons left for Egypt, "and there studied a system to dam the Nile and to pierce the isthmus of Suez. Enfantin and his disciples were marvelously endowed with the capacity for undertaking great enterprises."[21]

Juliette Adam was intrigued by Saint-Simonian ideas for personal as well as philosophical reasons. As the bold author of the feminist *Idées Anti-*

Proudhoniennes, which defended George Sand and Daniel Stern, Juliette (then Lamessine)'s rigorous arguments on female equality attracted the attention of Enfantin, who had his delegates invite her to a Saint-Simonian banquet. In fact, noted Adam in her memoirs, the banquet was an affair that "the heads of the Saint-Simonian school proposed to give in my honor," so impressed were they by her equalitarian principles and, as she discovered, beauty. One of the delegates, Lambert-Bey, "invited me especially in the Père Enfantin's name, who saw in me, as Saint-Simon had seen in Madame de Staël—fancy, how flattering it was!—the woman hoped for since the school's foundation, the legislative woman, the feminine Messiah."[22]

Lamessine declined ("I did not feel myself sufficiently matured") but later engaged Enfantin at a salon. In general she found the Saint-Simonians compelling but odd, particularly on the question of free love, about which she remarked "they wished to reform manners not by virtue, but by license . . . there are certain obligations necessary to preserve a woman's dignity which she cannot find outside of social duties, nor in unbridled love." She was an astute observer of the tensions within the remarkable configuration of Saint-Simonianism. For all of its technocratic trappings, it was driven by constant renegotiations of the idea of love: passionate and affectionate, profoundly humanitarian, spiritually redemptive. Despite its grandiose "gospel of great public works, railroads, maritime canals, [and] free trade," Adam would note in her memoirs, "Its keynote was love, love and pity for the oppressed, for the poor, for the fallen woman, for the sinner, for Satan himself."[23]

This idea of love, allied to industrial progress, was the foundation of Saint-Simonian engineering. Indeed, within his detailed plans for the corporate restructuring of nineteenth-century society, Saint-Simon had lectured, "Humanity, you do not yet know your religion, law, and life, for religion is love, your law is association, your life is happiness." Enfantin himself warned against men's attachment to glory, which only "could give birth to pride"; better to cultivate the "womanly type of love," for "love alone can call back humanity." The settlement and canal projects of the Saint-Simonians were, in a sense, a working form of "utopian socialism"—a productive challenge with commercial benefits but also a commitment to creating alternative communities.

The Saint-Simonians seriously pursued such communities. In letters from Egypt in the 1830s, Enfantin wrote of the new world underway: "Engineers, farmers, doctors, teachers, artists, I have already brought here a small colony which I enlarge little by little according to the needs of *service,* and which I increase even more as the first arrivals have given proof of their talent and utility."[24] He reported with satisfaction the schools, hospitals, and dams built, and very much linked his group's achievements to greater projects of colonization. He wrote directly on this subject in works such as *Colonisation d'Algérie*, in which he hoped to consolidate French military, administrative, and commercial interests in North Africa by direct settlement and exploitation of the land. Consistent with his philosophy of love and humanity, this was to be done in an enlightened fashion, "not . . . ransacking or exterminating the people, nor putting them in chains, but raising them to the sentiment of civilization and association of which we have always been the most generous representatives." By the latter, he meant "the French," a point he made with a derisory analogy to the British unloading of prisoners in Australia and the Pacific: "Some people have dreamed of making Algeria the Botany Bay of France; that would be . . . to awkwardly copy England . . . it would be more monstrous than bringing back buccaneers and pirates, looters of the Americas, butchers of the Oceanic islands and of India."[25]

What Enfantin sought were projects "worthy of the nineteenth century and of France." To this end, Suez had long interested the eccentric but technically formidable Saint-Simonians. Enfantin, a graduate of the École Polytechnique, would himself ultimately become director of a company that would help build France's railway network; for decades he and his followers saw in the ancient land of the Pharaohs and their own social, humanitarian, and philanthropic ideas the perfect meeting of circumstances for undertaking the work of the human race. The writer and journalist Maxime du Camp narrated the messianic Enfantin's voyage to Egypt in search of (as Lamessine would appreciate) the mystical great mother, taking his "family" of followers on a quest to fulfill Old Pacuvius's promise that "the homeland where you will find yourselves is there." Obtaining permission from Mehemet-Ali, the pasha of Egypt, the Saint-Simonians began to engineer the Suez transit, hoping to unite humanity by linking the Occident of the European Mediterranean with the Orient beyond the Red Sea as far as India and possibly East Asia. It was a project that ultimately overtaxed their resources, faith, and bodies. Enfantin's letters were filled with grievances over Mehemet-Ali's greater interest in irrigation projects than interoceanic canals, and fearful evocations of "many quarantines," and "a sad state of events." Enfantin wept over the many lives lost to disease and inhospitable conditions, and ultimately the project was abandoned.[26]

⤜

Though the Saint-Simonians failed, the canal project ultimately did succeed under French direction. On December 8, 1834, Enfantin wrote a letter to the French consul in Alexandria, "especially recommending the good friendship of Monsieur Ferdinand de Lesseps, as one of the best hearts that I know."[27] He flattered Lesseps, but also himself, for the Lesseps name was legendary in diplomatic circles; Lesseps's own grandfather, uncles, and father, Mathieu, had served Catherine the Great, Napoleon, and Talleyrand; the father also had been long distinguished in French and Egyptian relations, a post that Ferdinand himself would take on in the 1830s, when he met and aided Enfantin and his projects.

Lesseps was the man whose name became synonymous with the Suez undertaking. For many French, particularly investors, Central America and Panama would simply be continuations of Lesseps's success in Egypt, where he obtained concessions from the Sultans and Khedive and negotiated a complex package of industrial and financial interests to realize the Suez Canal. In the 1880s, Lesseps's own canal company presented Panama as simply the Western counterpart to Suez, the last gate to unlock before the world was open to the unlimited circulation of prosperity from Asia to America to Europe and round again. An 1888 special commission of the French railways anticipated increased traffic, reporting, "Suez has greatly profited France by the increase of maritime traffic and greatly facilitated the relationship of the metropole with its colonies. From this it could only be expected that the Panama Canal will extend the glory of France and be profitable to its interests."[28] East and West would become one; for Europeans, Columbus's Orient at last would be fully gained.

Lesseps's vision was not only that of an extraordinary engineering project but also one of reshaping the nation and historical time itself. The joint-stock company, the mutual investment of France, would be the expression of the unity of the people engaged in an enterprise for global progress. Where the original Saint-Simonians had failed with their cultish philosophy, Lesseps would succeed with the engagement of his general public. Where the Saint-Simonians under Enfantin had been the select, Lesseps would be the nation. His canal project was not special communities, but a geography of "patriotism, 80 million interests, 100 million machines, 30 million employees," figures of capital transformed into work and will. At the height of his popularity in the mid-1880s, Lesseps sought to distance himself from the cultish aspects of the "Saint-Simonian aberration, so justly forgotten," while happily drawing from their ranks "perfect engineers, distinguished economists, and financiers of the first order." French elites had been long partisan on this distinction. At a dinner with Paris notables in the 1860s including Charles Reybaud and Louis Jourdan, Juliette Adam noted in her memoirs, "Except for [Emile] de Girardin and myself, all were Saint-Simonians . . . and M. Girardin lauded himself for being the closest friend of M. de Lesseps." Not surprisingly, prominent Saint-Simonians such as Lambert-Bey complained of Lesseps's disregard for their contributions, fulminating "Lesseps is abominable . . . to have taken for his unique profit the works of the Saint-Simonians."[29]

Like his *Grand* counterpart Juliette Adam, Lesseps admired yet was skeptical of Saint-Simonian attachment to the passions. Nonetheless, Lesseps himself maintained an inherent logic of love in his own canal projects; as Adam, he did so by reimagining his own idea of love as a passion for France. Lesseps would create through the common cause of his investment company a moment of simultaneous action that would unite an "ardent" France. "I love the present, I think to abandon absolutely hopes of the future and regrets of the past; it matters that all the French unite as in a *phalange* to defend the tricolor."[30]

In Lesseps's hands, the Saint-Simonian religion of love became the phalange of patriotic grandeur. As with Juliette Adam's maternal nationalism, Lesseps located his technical assessment of Panama Canal proposals as much in European geopolitics as in Central American hydrography. After the Franco-Prussian War, military strategists, empire builders, and nationalists—the latter, like Adam, particularly appalled by the seizure of the Alsace-Lorraine—blamed what they saw as a general French ignorance of geography for the debacle. Imperial competition and now-reduced national boundaries made clear the dangers of failing to understand, protect, preserve, and adequately exploit and expand territories at home and abroad. The geographer Eliseé Réclus, a familiar of Saint-Simon, Fourier, and Proudhon, had long extolled the natural endowments of "our beautiful France, so remarkable among all for the variety of her lands and the harmony of her contrasts." As a patriotic project he wrote approvingly of consolidating regional France by railroads: "The inhabitants have been torn away from a savage life and participate in the general movement of society." He also lauded public schooling and other institutions that a generation hence would so displease the nostalgic temper of a Pierre Loti. Such internal colonization was particular to Réclus for "not having cost blood; this conquest of lands will be no less useful and will be much longer lasting than that of so many faraway colonies purchased at the price of thousands of precious lives."[31]

After 1870, Reclus's idealist, organic vision was amplified from nationalist pride into colonial expansionism. Local geographical societies across France were suddenly popular, becoming defenders of provincial heritages and powerful lobbies for imperial projects in Africa, Asia, and Oceania. Lesseps drew his *Nouvelle Revue* piece from the discussions of an important Congrès Géographique of 1879. Tracing recent history, he proclaimed, "Geographical studies, formerly neglected in France, have been restored to honor following a painful testing which has demonstrated their utility." His plan to "unite the Atlantic to the Pacific Ocean" was a project of grand purpose, part of a movement that had "ceased to be the domain of a small number of the privileged," becoming rather something "to impassion the public."[32]

Lesseps's genius was to transform a history of capital investment, economic development, and business lobbies into a grandiose histoire d'amour. His presentation of capitalism as devotion to France was strongly returned in extraordinary expressions of affection. Chasing his carriages on the boulevards, small investors adored him from the street, while major intellectual figures such as Ernest Renan covered him with gratuitous praise at the Académie Française, not—so it seemed—for the money he was going to make for his shareholders but for his genius in reimagining the Saint-Simonian project of love and universal brotherhood. "The true reason of your ascendancy is that people detect in you a heart full of sympathy for all that is human, a genuine passion for ameliorating the lot of your fellow creatures. You have in you that *misereror super turbas* (O have pity upon the masses) which is the sentiment of all great organizers." To this he added a personal, enthusiastic coda, "People love you and like to see you and before you have opened your mouth you are cheered."[33] The senator Léon Renault grandly conflated Lesseps's financial, political, and sentimental genius by announcing, "there is very much a clientele of ordinary people gathered around the illustrious founder of the Panama Company. Isn't there something there which moves our patriotism, which carries along not only our accepting solidarity with the enterprise . . . but at the very least [also] the mark of our sympathies?"[34]

The canal company promoted Lesseps as both man and principle of public works as benefactor to the country, and by extension, humanity. He made Adam's violent love of French passion and fraternity the sources of his authority. In his address to the Académie, Lesseps lauded the historian Henri Martin for the scholar's commitment to historical "justice," declaiming, "and this love of justice in his mind comes from that *amour de la patrie* in his heart."[35] Whether engaging the rightness of history or making plans for a transoceanic future, Lesseps's projects were based on the mastery of a particular language and narrative: the national love story.

Although he incarnated the canal through the rapt attention of the Immortals in the Académie and the sublime affection of the masses, Lesseps's grand vision fell far short of the dreams of an international octagonal city of brotherhood and commerce, or even a Saint-Simonian community of love and work at the crossroads of the world. The French company proved woefully inadequate at handling either its administrative or engineering duties. The capital for the project was quickly expended, and new issues of shares and last-ditch efforts to save the shares with bonds could not overcome the reality that hundreds of millions in francs disappeared with less than a third of the work done. Reports of Panamanian warehouses filled with snow shovels (inaccurate but damaging), abandoned private rail lines, fabulous mansions for the company agents, and scandalous salaries for family members of the directors became the common currency of Panama reporting.

Although the dream would ultimately be realized, it would be at the cost of scores of lives, and not by the French. The company went into receivership in 1893 in the largest financial scandal of the age, directly taking the savings of tens of thousands of small investors, many of whom had borrowed or mortgaged properties for shares. The Americans would buy out a bankrupt enterprise, engineer a crude secession of Panama from Colombia, and complete the canal under Theodore Roosevelt. Lesseps's egregious financial and manpower miscalculations, and his delusions about the terrain and hydrography of Panama—which made him insist on a sea-level canal, as in Suez—led to the shattering collapse of the company, many financial institutions, and members of the political class corrupted by bribery and greed.

In the Chamber of Deputies, Jules Delahaye excoriated his fellows, "Panama, it is evil itself which has overtaken the limbs of the social body. . . . Panama is shameless waste, a mad scramble under the sun with the fortune of our citizens, the poor and the needy, by those men having the mission to protect and defend them."[36] As the value of shares plummeted and the company was taken over amid illegal payoffs and falsified documents, the republican government fell in crisis.

For the French, Panama, the fabled door to the riches and wonders of the Pacific, became a sign of all that was wrong with the republic. In the wake of the collapse rose the antisemitic journalism of Edmond Drumont who claimed a financial conspiracy of Jewish bankers and radicals, a hysteria that crystallized in the Dreyfus affair, which would divide the nation for years. In an attack on Joseph Reinach, relative of one of the lead Panama financiers, Baron de Reinach, Drumont demanded, "What do you think of your esteemed father-in-law, thief, German agent, and corrupter of politicians? . . . In any case this masonic and Jewish world will have received a blow from which it will never recover." Even the Church did not evade suspicion. Journalists for *La Libre Parole* suggested of the republic's pro-colonial bishop, "I've almost forgotten Monseigneur Freppel, who wanted to interest M. de Lesseps in his diocesean works."[37] Amid murder, suicide, scandal, and indictment, politicians, cabinet ministers, and members of the press were hauled into court and off to prison for enriching themselves at the public expense. Lesseps's "nation" of ordinary Frenchmen was wiped out.

Hoping to rescue the canal concession one last time, the ingenious engineer, adventurer, and speculator Philippe Bunau-Varilla argued (self-interestedly, but correctly) that losing the project would be "not only a financial disaster; it would also determinately be a political and social danger." Picking up on anti-German sentiment, he rewrote the narrative of the French republic, seeing the "sinister diplomacy" of Bismarck behind disasters beginning with Napoleon III in Mexico and ending with Panama.

According to Bunau-Varilla, these failures were deliberately orchestrated plots to crush France's most singular strength: her Gallic sentiment and spirit. He excoriated Louis Napoleon for being duped into using "the bayonets of France" to put an Austrian on a Latin throne, a foolish plan whose reversal and humiliation "formed the antechamber of the disastrous war of 1870–1." Subsequently, suggested Bunau-Varilla, "I . . . clearly and definitely saw that the fate of France was linked with that of Panama, because that enterprise was a part of her honor and of her heart." Bismarck's purported manipulation of the financial press to cause the Company's collapse was a deliberate attempt to weaken French resolve at the very core of the nation's ideology, by having the republic "prostrated like a mother who has lost faith in the honor of her sons."[38] The Empire of Love was struck a mortal blow.

Across the Atlantic, Americans would pick up on the "Frenchness" of the Panama failure. As the Compagnie Universelle was unraveling, American journalists thought they knew what had happened in Paris and Panama, adopting the notion of shattered spirits, though with an attention not to prostrate mothers but frivolous mistresses. "In this atmosphere of lavish extravagance caused by the financial corruption . . . the morals of the French force were broken; there was no determined spirit of conquest; interest centered in champagne and women; the canal was neglected."

What had begun as a triumph of savoir-faire collapsed, apparently, not in ignorance of hydrography, malaria, or capital markets, but in moral exhaustion and excesses of "champagne and women." Lesseps himself might have expected such *cherchez la femme* attacks. His insistence on a sea-level canal without locks was impracticable in the mountainous and elevated terrain of Panama, yet from the beginning he had tied together the feminine and natural by arguing, "I have declared myself for a sea-level canal, without locks, because locks are against nature, and I am for nature, because nature is like a woman, she is always right." As a *gallant*, Lesseps had argued, "one must always help nature," but in this case his chivalry and cupidity would not serve him well.[39]

Through registers of fraternity and patriotism, Panama provided a generation of politicians, communitarians, technocrats, and capitalists with dreams of humanitarian love bound to the enrichment of global civilization. When the canal company collapsed in 1893, blame was fixed upon the cultivation or corruption of French morals. But not everyone defined Panama through the canal, necessary reference though it was. In 1887, Paul Gauguin, seeking to "live like a savage" would flee Paris and Brittany. He gave up his life as a *remiser*, or stock adviser, for a company that had traded small shares for the Panama canal company. Perhaps it is unsurprising to learn that in seeking to live the native life his first thoughts turned not to Tahiti and the Marquesas, where he would become immortalized as a painter, nor Martinique (his other choice), but to Panama.

After leaving France in 1887 with companion artist Charles Laval, Gauguin's brief sojourn in Panama probably gave him good reason to head for Tahiti, although his desire for an elysian place was amazingly undiminished. He had read and envied *The Marriage of Loti* and his hope was to obtain land somewhere and to live "on fish and fruit for nothing . . . without anxiety for the day or for the morrow."[40] Gauguin sought only somewhere with a French colonial presence and had little interest in the canal project or championing or profiting from it in any way. For him Panama was distance, isolation, and—like the Saint-Simonians—a semi-religious and spiritual quest. But he was still a colonial; his search for anything but Europe was contradicted by his choice of French imperial jurisdictions. In Panama he wound up on the isthmus with no resources and he had to slog through his days as a common laborer with a pickaxe to earn his keep. He refused to paint portraits of the despicable company agents, complained bitterly and justifiably about the conditions, the weather, the work, and the authorities, and got arrested for urinating in public. In all, it was a trying sojourn that sent him anonymous, unhappy, and soon packing for Martinique, and finally Tahiti and the Marquesas.[41]

Despite the difficult circumstances, Panama was—as Gauguin demonstrated at first—clearly not without its apparent attractions in the 1880s. Yet as in Gauguin's imagination, Panama for canal-era explorers existed largely within a temporality of finitude, one of things too late. Literature dating from mid-century is grandiose and charged with humanitarian idealism; in later decades these paeans to brotherhood are marked by litanies of technical accomplishment blunted by transformed histories and created nostalgias. The canal project drew on the former and invented the latter; the jungle was only the antipode to the rending of nature at the canal site.

When Lesseps visited the isthmus in 1886, accompanying journalists filed stories which spoke of mystery and odd isolation: "We found the indian village of Gatun on the left bank of the Charges [River]. It sits now on a veritable island, the canal having cut the loop at the summit of which sits the village. Nothing is more curious than this assemblage of square little houses with roofs of palm leaf."[42] These strange islands, stranded now in time and space, were creations of the Compagnie's own engineers and excavation projects. The island imagery even continued under the "Big Job" of the Americans, Willis Abbot noting, "Despite its isthmian character, the Canal Zone, Uncle Sam's most southernly outpost, may be called an island," as it was "walled in by the tangled jungle."[43]

Within the temporal boundaries of this island, "French" Panama of the nineteenth century meant an odd romanticism, a vision of nature both bestial and extraordinary, a sublime land of giant animals, riotous vegetation, primitive peoples, and a landscape of earlier centuries in European exploration and conquest of the New World. It was a land to capture, classify, and savor before it disappeared. Writing for *Le Figaro* in 1880, journalist Adrien Marx described the isthmus both through "the sweet murmurings of its limpid flowers," and—ironically—"the angelic kiss of the mosquitoes and the caress of the vampire bat." Traveling down the isthmus in the 1880s and 1890s, the adventurers Charles Autigeon and Albert Larthe, and the surveyors Lucien Napoléon Bonaparte Wyse and Armand Reclus, working together but writing in separate accounts, noted a world part savage, part melancholic splendor. Wyse, the illegitimate son of Princess Laetitia Bonaparte, and originally Lesseps's lieutenant, begins his account with the Linnean cataloguing ambition to subsume all of natural history into a "planetary consciousness" of types and species, some forty-odd pages describing and ennumerating in Latin the geologic formations and flora of the isthmus, the river gorges and lithic striations, the palms, bamboos, and tropical flowers.[44] Larthe makes an important point about what "Panama" meant to Europe, by beginning his chronicle: "Lately much has been written about the isthmus of Panama, but all of it concerns the Canal; we thought it would be interesting to bring different scenes of Indian life to the attention of our readers."[45]

Far from a site of interest solely as an ambitious engineering project, the isthmus was a world onto itself, a thin, twisted branch of land extended out "between two immense seas," home to some of the most "isolated" peoples on Earth. Calling the isthmus an "immense obstacle to communications," Larthe referred not only to the separation of the Pacific peoples from those of the Atlantic, but the distance taken from history of the peninsular inhabitants themselves, whose tools, habitations, and customs "have not changed since the discovery of America by Christopher Columbus." Larthe found them in "primitive" costume, living in "wooden and bamboo huts, covered with palm leaves." With interpreters from the local missions he learned of a cosmos where the jaguar is feared for incarnating the vengeful spirit of an enemy chieftain, where giant tarantulas prey on tropical songbirds (and nearly kill the author), and scavenger birds are revered for removing decay and pestilent death from the world.

With a European's fascination for these apparently "savage" peoples—especially the Choco, Kuna, and Guayami, Larthe accompanies the men to hunt snakes, tapirs, and caimans; in a village he notes that "in the hot countries, adolescence is much quicker to arrive than in temperate climates," and he observes the sexual ripening of young women between twelve and sixteen years. Panama is full of such enticements, from its oft-mentioned "immense virgin forest" to its "seductive" jungles with their overabundant fruit trees. Autigeon also combined nature and sensuality, recording of the locals, "the fruits which come from the wild practically suffice to sustain them," to which he attributes something of their character, "sweet, indolent, and *serviable*." He even maintains, "They greatly love Frenchmen, and unions are easy between the *gringos* and the young women of the country." Seeing a connection between the French project and such liaisons, Autigeon concludes, "the opening of the canal will increase the sympathies they have for the French." The meanings of "Panama" were deeply encoded in possible affections and pleasures.[46]

Not all accounts of isthmian encounter agreed with such sensual Gallic description; indeed, possible intimacies were shaped by the encounters themselves. The Kuna high chief Néle de Kantule, earlier so critical of the Spanish, left his descendents oral recitations later transcribed as "the History of the Kuna Indians from the Great Flood up to Our Time." These feature multiple passages about the misfortune brought to the Kuna lands by "a Frenchman [who] came and built his home near the Indians." The Kuna community is initially a site of possible alliance and exchange. The outsider is offered (as Autigeon might appreciate) a villager's daughter to marry, but is soon abusing his in-laws and allying not with the Kuna but with other French settlers to build a prison in the village. In Kantule's recitation, "They also built a clubhouse for dancing and the Frenchmen began to dance with the Indian women and changed the women's way of dressing. They began to mistreat and punish the Indians severely. When some of our forefathers spoke against the Frenchmen they were captured and put in the prison."[47]

Far from Autigeon's promises of friendly unions, conflicting French and Kuna politics of women, affection, and meanings of marriage here become cries of violation and finally rebellion. As the first Frenchman's in-laws suf-

*Possible intimacies? "The Canal will increase the sympathies
they have for the French."*
Types indigènes dans le fôret (1888–1903).
Source: National Library of Australia

fer his new tyranny, the man's putative "brothers-in-law," led by the angry Miguana, "set off to the mountains to meet their countrymen." There, according to Kantule, "They said to them, 'let us make war on these stupid Frenchmen.' They set off to Carti and notified the people there, 'we come to urge you to fight against the Frenchmen.'" Miguana's party wipes out the offending settlers, except for one young man who lives apart. For him, Miguana has a special task: that of witness and chronicler to the history of injustice brought by the foreigner: "Will you be so kind as to write a letter for me about everything that the French have done to us, for you have seen it with your own eyes."[48]

To reinforce the importance of maintaining local histories and wariness of the new empire, Kantule then narrates the return from exile of the chief Morgolo who never submitted to French authority. In parable, Morgolo says, "Before this happened I sang that one day you should have thunder, much rain should fall. Then there would be lightning, storms, and so on." Using aviary images for foreigners, he warns, "As before, pelicans and wild birds invaded our districts and fouled them. Some day they will come back to our places and dirty them up as before."[49]

Whereas Kantule and Morgolo invoked a plague of dirty and wild birds to caution against French encroachment, French chroniclers continued their ideological romance of empire by relentlessly transforming the traditional world of the isthmus into a place of inevitable passing, a narration that would grip most of Oceania and much of Asia. Their reports were of twilight and a certain despair, a pitiless and melancholy spirit of impermanence. Even their own bird stories were tales of thwarted love. Armand Reclus saw fit to explain the region's omnipresent vultures by recounting the incident of a young man who had fled into the woods searching for a "desperate resolution to his unhappiness" created by *chagrins d'amour*. Unable to locate the young man, searchers followed the bands of dark birds to his final resting place.[50]

Other writers fashioned tales that compounded loss and longing directly with a racial biologism. Although Larthe invoked Indians "discovered" by Columbus, they were for him also a vanishing people. In this case, the logic was not that of disease or extermination (Europeans in Panama were themselves much more vulnerable in the face of yellow fever and malaria), but notions of racial dilution. As Lucién N. B. Wyse wrote in his observations, "in the isthmus of Panama properly speaking, there are no more Indians" but, rather, a mixed population of mixed-bloods, blacks and Indians (zambos), Indians and whites (mestizos), and the occasional Indian and Chinese.[51]

Hiking and camping among the "half-savages" of the forests and jungles, through "torrid" and "pestilential" valleys, Larthe, Wyse, Autigeon, and Chio come upon Panama City, part commercial center, part lawless frontier town, an irregular plot of urban life. What attracts their attention are the old colonial structures, some tumbled down buildings, some abandoned residences of the Jesuits. Wyse prints several sketches of the crumbled edifices in his account. Larthe finds the romantic's favored architecture: ruins. "Remakable ruins," he notes somberly, observing "these cracked and blackened walls," inhaling the "perfume of mystery, resuscitating in the mind an entire past of brilliance and grandeur." Now, all that remain are "these vines and creepers which silently hide the walls, the cornices which tumble down from above the crosses and doorways, all inspiring melancholy and sadness."

Autigeon also reports that "Panama has nothing of interest apart perhaps from its hospitals and old, crumbled ramparts taken back by the sea, the weather, and the flowering vines which take root in their fissures." Idly crossing the town, Autigeon notes "the walls that remain from burned-out houses and ruined edifices," which bring to mind "a rush of vague and somber ideas." For these commentators, as for many empire writers, landscapes are redolent of European grandeur. "Old Panama" was not synonymous with the indigenous peoples but with abandoned "haciendas," the aristocratic style of the landed estates, or the ruins of a Porto Bello, "the old former emporium of trade between Spain and its South American colonies, and the principal place of warfare on the Grand Ocean." In Panama, Larthe, Reclus, Autigeon, and Wyse saw the old Spanish empire, its faded and misguided glory matched against their own, an entwined romantic sensibility of progressive transformation to be wrought by the canal, bounded by the sentimental extinctions of the past.[52]

Such nostalgia and savage romance were the stuff of Panama for French scouts and surveyors, yet unsurprisingly, these same also were part of the canal company's publicity explanations of agents and laborers dying from disease, accidents, and the generally poor working conditions that characterized the entire project. The first director general of the canal works, Jules Dingler, is best known for the destiny symbolized by the elegant house he built, "La Folie Dingler," reported by Willis John Abbot: "Before he had fairly moved into it, his wife, son, and daughter died of yellow fever and he returned to Paris to die too of a broken heart."[53]

Dingler's case stood out but was not unique among what the reporter Albert Tissander called the "incredible mob composed of the most diverse races, the black workers come to the canal site, mixed with their Indian,

Hindu, Chinese, Spanish, [and] American comrades."[54] Among the largely anonymous Panamanian, West Indian, American, and Spanish laborers, thousands succumbed to malaria and yellow fever, accidents and overwork. Despite the Euro-American acceptance of brutal conditions, criticism of the canal company slowly grew. By 1887 even the French papers reported on the "enormous mortality" of the project and "wagons full of cadavers." In perhaps the most significant single incident, Lesseps found himself defending his enterprise against charges that his agents had let die some thousands of Chinese laborers. His reply is an extraordinary bit of relative statistics and sentimental philosophy that strikingly underscores the rhetoric of the canal project. "That number is strongly exaggerated. No more than fifteen hundred have died, and of that number almost three hundred hung themselves from the sorrow of being separated from their wives."

He was drawing on a journalistic tradition handed down from alleged multiple suicides of Chinese workers during the building of the Trans-Panamanian railway in the 1850s, when American reporters wrote luridly of "the despairing Chinese," and detailed the variations on drowning, shooting, hanging, stabbing, and starvation by which the men supposedly took their own lives. Indifferent project management leading to epidemic disease, rank poverty, discrimination, and possible opium and alcohol abuse played major roles, yet what is so noteworthy about Lesseps's justification is his *chagrins d'amour* approach. Was it his fault if he could not fill the emotional wretchedness of his workers as his company controlled their bodies and labor?[55]

Supremely confident, Lesseps had not attended closely enough the ambitions or lost lessons of the Saint-Simonians, for whom social and civil engineering were synonymous. Great projects required not only excavators, builders, and impressarios but also a practical "humanitarian" organization. When the United States took over and established its own American-ruled colony on the isthmus, the new canal commission disseminated flattering self-promotion to distance itself from the former Compagnie universelle, suggesting, "It was an ideal community, from the pragmatist's point of view, that had its being in the Canal Zone, for there was no privileged class, no idlers; every adult had a part in the great project that had brought 35,000 men with their families together there."[56] Looking back on the canal initiative from the vantage point of the Panama Pacific Exposition of 1921, the American historian Frank Morton Todd ventured that any planning committee "had to do much more than dredge, excavate, and build locks and dams—it had to create a government, institute courts, administer justice, open public schools, provide water supply, organize a police department, hear the complaints of employees wives, regulate the liquor traffic, enforce sanitary regulations."

In effect, an entire semi-permanent civic and administrative order had to be created and regulated in what was conceded at the time to be a supremely inhospitable region of the earth for anyone but local Indians. More, the multiracial, multiethnic, and multiclass force would have to be kept "reasonably contented by means of schools, libraries, clubhouses, and social relaxation." Establishing a canal company meant knowing how to "run a railroad, conduct hospitals, build fortifications, and administer the estates of dead and insane employees." Clearly, thought the Americans, Lesseps's canal company never effectively succeeded in organizing such administration, even if the American company itself ran its own work teams with separate quarters for whites, blacks, and Asians, unequal privileges and pay standards for the "gold men" and "silver men," and punitive restrictions on Asian and Caribbean groups' customs and habits.[57]

Neither the French nor American canal projects reckoned with the true affinities emerging from the initiative: the fraternity of an increasingly self-conscious international workforce. Focused on fair work, pay, and work conditions from the 1880s, canal laborers did not respond to the romance of the French canal. Alexander Tissander was particularly chagrined to discover that "mixed-blood native" workers were militant about their own autonomy. Having completed a task for a negotiated rate, they refused their French supervisors' authority: "They were no longer yours . . . they no longer knew you, they went back to being free men." The worker's motto, "Yo soy un hombre libre!"—I am a free man—was expressed so regularly and vehemently that Tissander found French historical aspirations to lead the Latin world cited back at him. As he reported with exasperation, "these people believe in seizing the Bastille every day."[58]

For all the passions that swirled around the canal project, it was ultimately Lesseps himself who would require the most pointed salvation *du coeur*, and it was Philippe Bunau-Varilla who provided it by forming a syndicate to buy out the bankrupt canal company and arrange its sale to the United States. Bunau-Varilla attacked the critics of Lesseps and his associates, and the burdens "our country has weighed upon those hearts which have never beat except for her." By pressing seriously for the restoration of Lesseps's reputation and the original rightness of his project, Bunau-Varillia hoped to derail rival American plans for a canal through Nicaragua.

In voluminous works, part engineering and financial treatise, part polemic and propaganda, Bunau-Varilla transformed Lesseps's monumental failure into narratives rivaling Christ's Passion. The most pointed, *Panama: The Creation, the Destruction, the Resurrection*, frames the history of the ill-fated enterprise in a plan not unlike the stations of the cross, with corrupt advisers and bankers, poisonous journalists, and disloyal politicians filling the roles of the Lord's betrayers. Patriotism substitutes for faith, financial shares for silver, and heroism for divinity as the reconstitution of the Canal Company becomes Bunau-Varillia's vehicle for the salvation of a wasted France. Bunau-Varilla even borrows from the master of redemptive fiction, Victor Hugo, to make allusions to *Les Misérables:* "We must stop confusing the combatants who give their heart and their soul for France in an heroic battle with the Thénardiers robbing cadavers at the rear of the army."[59]

In the end, the heart and soul of Lesseps were crushed and he died a very old man a few years after the scandal. Bunau-Varilla salvaged $40 million from the Americans, and helped the Unites States arrange the gunboat secession of Panama from Colombia. For French observers, such as the foreign trade adviser Charles Lemire, it was a harsh end to the dream of a French Pacific empire radiating through the isthmus. "It is at the moment where our possessions . . . will have acquired an immense and ineluctable importance, at the moment where they become valuable by the force of circumstances, that we will abandon to others all the profits and leave the playing field which is ours."

Even more galling, it was not only profit but also a keen sense of historical leadership and destiny that was ending. "North America has become master of two oceans whose doors she will open or close as she pleases. It is her certain domination of Latin America that we—we Latins—abandon to her." And beyond the Americas, also cast away was the ancient dream of the East: "The doors of the two worlds of the Pacific and of Far Asia are about to be thrown open and our keys have been stolen." For the French, those keys had been the canal and islands like Tahiti, "an earthly paradise," the projected stepping-stone from the isthmus to Asia. To console himself, Lemire read Pierre Loti again after Panama, but concluded: "It is like the celestial paradise: it is too far away." Empire lost did not concern the historical chronicles of Néle de Kantule, the Kuna chief who had resisted Spanish and French exploitation. He subsequently wondered over Americans, Colombians, and Panamanians who came to Kuna territory, but reaffirmed a vision of his own rightful place and history: "As our great Néles have told us, we are born in here, just as if it were outside of the end of the world."[60]

The making of a saint: Pierre Chanel martyred by Musumusu.
Source: Archives des Pères maristes, Padri Maristi, Rome

THREE

WALLIS AND FUTUNA

Martyrs and Memories

Wallis (Uvea) and Futuna are small islands some two hundred kilometers apart, lying between the *grand terre* of New Caledonia and Tahiti. In 1886 a small child named Louis Wendt, son of a German trader living on Wallis, was feverish and becoming sicker after more than two weeks of illness. The local priest, Father Ollivaux of the Société de Marie (popularly known as the Marist Fathers), was asked to come and record the child's last breath, and reported that the child displayed "all the symptoms of imminent death." The priest performed his rites, but also suggested to the father to request a miracle from Pierre Chanel, a Marist priest who had been killed on the island of Futuna back in 1843. The father Wendt made the prayer, promising to go with his son on a pilgrimage to Futuna if the boy was allowed to live. Presently, the boy recovered; within three weeks he was restored to perfect health.[1]

In the Wallisian district of Mua about the same time, a six-year-old child of Sosimo Toemahi was also in agony of an unspecified illness. Father Ollivaux administered an extreme unction, yet once again suggested that the parents petition Pierre Chanel. They did; the child recovered. Both these cases were attributed to miracles, or more properly, as evidence of miracles realized through the intercession of a blessed name. In Oceania, Pierre Chanel was a name to reckon with. His colleagues labored long to see that it would be so forever. He had been one of their leaders; soon he would be a martyr and one day a saint.[2]

This is a story of good works, miracles, and love. In 1889 the French Republic celebrated its centennial. At the Universal Exposition in Paris, ethnographic exhibits featured island peoples and artifacts that demonstrated France's continuing efforts to establish an integrated national identity for its colonial subjects. The year 1889 was also a momentous year for the Church and the distant Pacific; two generations of missions had established a Catholic influence in Oceania, self-described by Marist Fathers as "the love of a priest for his flock . . . the love of the same for his child; even more . . . the love of Jesus Christ for his church." In Rome this love would become commemorative veneration as the pope agreed to declare an 1889 beatification of Chanel, thus making him the first martyr of the Church in Oceania; his beatification would later be confirmed by his 1954 canonization as Saint Pierre Chanel by Pope Pius XII.[3] Futunan chroniclers such as Petelo Leleivai also have recognized their island as "the cradle of the Catholic faith in Oceania," suggesting, "after the martyr of Saint Pierre Chanel, a veritable love story was established between Futuna and the French missionaries."[4]

Love and martyrdom were at the heart of Chanel's legacy on the island of Futuna. On April 28, 1843, he had been feeding the chickens in the garden behind his house; he was alone, his catechists having gone to the other side of Futuna to baptize some possibly dying children. A local chief, Maulisio Musumusu, appeared at the door, bleeding from the face and asking for medical attention. Chanel did not know that Musumusu had been injured while slaughtering the priest's followers in a nearby village. Musumusu was soon joined by other men, Filitika and Ukuloa. Filitika threw the priest's hamper of garments out the window where it was seized by a growing crowd. Musumusu reportedly cried out, "Why the wait to kill the man!" Filitika pushed the priest down and Ukuloa and another man, Umutauli, struck repeatedly. Chanel reportedly cried out "Malie fuai" (It is well for me). A third man, Fuasea, then speared Chanel. Musumusu apparently inflicted the last blow, striking the priest on the head and causing part of his brain to come out of his skull. Tales arose that the priest was then eaten, an important part of his story, although no evidence supports this.[5]

The killing had a powerful impact, letters between Pacific stations indicating that the Marists immediately began referring to their lost brother as "the first martyr of Oceania."[6] For the Church, Chanel's death would become a narrative of historical and theological inevitability written in reverse. To be deemed a martyr, the death would have imperatively been occasioned by his faith; as such Chanel had to die a defender of the Word to which islanders, presumably, had been resistant. The murder would not be Chanel's end, but the logic of God's love and triumph in the South Seas. In death, Chanel realized his mission.

Close reading of reports also indicate another, quite different understanding of the events for the Futunans involved. The killing appears less as irreligious savagery and more as violent reaction to a serious interference in local politics, a projection of generalized concerns about slaving and exploitation by Europeans, and an attempt to maintain a customary universe prescribed by chiefly succession. As the islands came under French protection, then annexation, the religious and historical vision built around Chanel by the Marists arguably triumphed. His death directly abetted the French Catholic advance in the Pacific, giving narrative and symbolic form to the Marist's versions of pre-Christian island life, attracting support from both Rome and Paris.

That support developed because mission work, despite its often dismal realities, had a powerful symbolic allure in the nineteenth century, part of which intersected with the domestication of exoticist and adventure narratives. Empire was fashioned and comfortably circulated into European parlors and play rooms as a printed and illustrated space of desire. Island stories were carried in France to Rochefort, where Pierre Loti remembered of his childhood, "A missionary! This seemed to combine everything—distant voyages and adventures, a life of constant peril—but in the service of the Lord and his sacred cause."

As a Huguenot, Loti's already pronounced sense of localism within France was heightened by his family's minority religious faith. In memoirs, he spoke of his grandmother's village on the island of Oléron "where many of my ancestors lay sleeping, having been excluded from the Church ceremonies for having died in the Protestant faith." Yet, although he related that "indignation filled my heart against the Roman Church," he was also frank about his Huguenot austerity, "The tedium of certain Sunday sermons; the soulnessness of the prayers prepared beforehand and uttered with conventional unction . . . the indifference of people in their Sunday clothes." His search for a more engaging faith took him, for a time, to imagine missionizing as he would empire—that is, as his own search for France. The evocation of "sleeping ancestors" was a means to tie himself to an immemorial legacy. It was a rhetorical strategy greatly popular among nineteenth century romantic nationalists for whom historical, generational ties to the soil were critical for grounding their definitions of the patrie. In Loti's hands, these were linked specifically to his childhood, the originary age of innocence and yearning; it was easy for him to present empire as an earnest, spiritual longing.

A devotee of the monthly mission newsletter *Le Messager* and its stirring pictures, Loti dreamed of "an impossible palm tree on the shore of the sea behind which an enormous sun was setting, and at the foot of the tree, a young savage watching the Advent from the remotest horizon, of the vessel bringing the good tidings of Salvation." At home in his provincial garden, Loti's formative yearnings for what would become his imperial project were gained in great part through his subscription education in spirituality, a seductive instruction in attractive images. "I was still under the charm of that huge sun half-swallowed in the sea, and of the little missionship in full sail towards an unknown land." It was thus, he claims, that when questioned about growing up he would reply, "I shall be a missionary."[7]

⁓

Loti never took up the calling, although he claimed, "It is very certain that if the Inquisition had been revived I should have endured martyrdom like a little visionary." In fact, his Protestants struggled mightily with the Catholics in territories with palm trees and setting suns—-the Pacific islands—although it was the Catholics who declared the first saint. The Marists first arrived and began establishing their missions in 1837. Wallis and Futuna were hardly major territories. The Fathers had chosen the islands in part because they were one of a few groups not yet reached by the London Missionary Society, whose influence had forced them out of attempted establishments in Samoa and Fiji. Church correspondence shows local priests complaining bitterly of "the calumnies of the Protestant ministers," Pierre Chanel himself writing of islands adjacent to his station, "The moment seems favorable to penetrate this archipelago. . . . the Methodists cover it and have everywhere arrived before us."[8] Such competition continued throughout the century; as Chanel complained of the Methodists, so Methodists in Fiji would have their faithful file depositions alleging Catholic abuses, such as that of one Atonio Tukana, who swore, "the priest from Naililili one day came into my house carrying a double barreled gun. He sat down and placed the gun near him . . . [and] said that if anyone wishes to become a Roman Catholic he may do so for no one can prevent his doing so."[9]

The rival missions also accused one another of trying to buy converts, and issues of household wealth meant early struggles were often shaped around marriage questions. A certain degree of wealth, material comfort, and prestige attended the ability to support wife, children, and servants at a mission station, and one thing the Catholic Marists could not do was compete directly with the domestic model of their rivals. Having taken vows of poverty, celibacy, and obedience to monastic rules, the priests pursued holiness but did not always impress the local peoples with their limited resources. As Father Xavier Montruzier reported from the Solomon Islands, "When we tell them, 'all the chiefs of men, all the riches of the earth are nothing compared to Jehovah,' Oh! they say, 'our stomachs are sick! Write to him, asking him to come to Murua for us to see him, and tell him to bring iron and axes.'"[10]

The notion of the comfortably pious Christian family in hearth and home as an example to islanders was strategically and ideologically reserved for Protestants, often English or American. For the 1820s Hawaiian missions, Boston Reverend Samuel Worcester had declared women necessary "to shew to the rude and depraved islanders an effective example of the purity and dignity and loveliness . . . which Christianity can impart to the female character." Later in the century, the Edinburgh missionary Maggie Paton described her own domestic role and standards with rather more unintended complexity by relating from the New Hebrides, "I often wish you could all look in upon us in our pretty Island Home . . . you would think mine a lovely and inviting Home, and you see it can't possibly suffer from comparison, as there are only the Native huts all around!" In her letters she would fulfill Euro-American domestic ideals while also giving cause to critics who saw missionary wives tending to the exclusion of their charges: "How I did appreciate the doors and windows here, after living two or three months without them! The Natives gave us, or me rather, so much more of their company than was quite agreeable." Although unflattering to the locals and her own charity, Paton's account illustrates the clear attractions of faith-as-domesticity for herself, as well as for her congregation.[11]

To establish themselves against such challenges, the Marists had worked hard from the beginning to promote an idea of a love in the company of men, a family based on the total brotherly community of the mission under a unified spiritual, and ultimately political, leadership. Allying themselves with the king, then queen, of Wallis and the kings and chiefs of Futuna, the missionaries pursued the strategy of *cuius regio, euis religio*, trying to win over the political rulers and imagining that the population would be obliged to follow. On Wallis, this was a fruitful approach, not least because the island's political rulers, Lavelua and his daughter, Amélia, found the missionaries useful: the message of faith and obedience gave Amélia prestige after her father's death, and the Marists' ability to negotiate with traders, naval captains, and other outsiders was important.

Through growing political influence, control of lands, and mission schools, the Fathers gradually established what both critics and admirers called a Francophile "theocracy." Friendship treaties with the house of Lavelua date from November 1842, and a formal French protectorate was declared in November 1889. The nature of Catholic rule was described (skeptically) by Captain Henri Rivière in 1880, who called the Marist leader Pierre Bataillon "a bishop of the twelfth century wandered into our own," and a man of "anchorite asceticism, inflexible, fearless, authoritarian." He was the supreme patriarch. As for Queen Amélia, Bataillon "raised, instructed, adopted for spiritual daughter, and continues to dominate her. He is, through her, master of Wallis . . . he has made the people carry stones on their backs to allow him to build a cathedral." Rivière did not grasp how well, in this instance, the Word was appropriated by the Wallisian monarchy to solidify its own presence and authority over the islands. Nor, in general, did he comprehend how stories from the priests' teachings might be personally understood as "wonderful tales" of love, war, suffering, and hope by islanders and native preachers around the Pacific who found them "so close to their own way of life."[12] Still, by any account, the Marists in Wallis and Futuna had found perhaps their greatest success in the Pacific. The naval doctor and writer Victor Ségalen called Wallis "the most exotic place" in Oceania to the degree that "the monopoly exercised by the missionaries . . . is absolute."[13]

⨳

As Wallis had quickly become the center of the Marist authority, Chanel had gone on to Futuna with another lay missionary to try and establish a station. There he met his fate. His death was not an inconceivable tragedy but a love story perfectly realized. Chanel had long asked his parishioners "Why does He love us so much?" and preached on "the desire for Heaven," calling out, "Do you love pleasure? It will be there in Heaven. Do you love joy? Oh, how great it will be above. Do you love glory? Oh, how it will be brilliant!"[14]

Chanel incarnated the principle of sacrificial love for his brethren, who praised him: "In the eyes of the missionary, [the native] is above all a man whose soul is worth that of a European; he loves the native with all the force of his Christian charity."[15] The founder of the Marist congregation, Jean-Claude Colin, had himself dispatched priests with the exhortation, "You are leaving your country, parents, friends—everything—to save souls and suffer martyrdom." A year before Chanel's death, Father Montruzier wrote a colleague of his passion "to be for some moments the object of the cruelty of barbarous people and after that to be able to say, 'I am going to Heaven and I am leading thousands of souls there.'" He also spoke of "the chance of martyrdom and the glory of being the first apostle of a country."[16] For the Marists, who often had little in the way of other resources, imitation of the Lord was a powerful weapon in the battle against both unbelief and Protestant heresy.

Mourning their brother yet recognizing the value of his example, the Marists wasted no time establishing Chanel's candidacy for beatification. Père Poupinel drafted reports on Futuna that were reviewed at the Wallis mission. Monseigneur Bataillon appointed an investigator to prepare a detailed report on the circumstances of the killing, a narrative fashioned through general inquests of the Futunan population. The report was formally presented at Rome on April 27, 1857, and authorized by the pope a few months later, thus beginning the intricate and sometimes generations—or centuries-long process of considering the dossier. By Vatican procedure, at least fifty years would have to pass from date of decease before any definitive judgment could take place, to insure that the candidate was not simply a figure of cultish fashion. Chanel's case went well. In 1889, Pope Léon XIII declared the beatification.[17]

What does Chanel's legacy tell us? Although papal canonization and sainthood are models for all of Christendom, beatification is a more localized affair, authorizing the celebration of the local works and legacies of the "blessed" one, or *bienheureux*. The Marists's Futunan records thus say much specifically about Oceanic Catholicism. Of particular interest is the procès-verbal written up by Chanel's colleague, Louis-Catherin Servant, a narrative resembling a legal brief which attempts to reconstruct the circumstances and reasons for Chanel's murder.

Based on detailed testimonies taken from islanders in 1845 and 1848, Servant's report places the case admirably far from the popular notion that the priest was cut down and eaten by cannibal savages. As late as 1895, Marist Oceanic missions still often encoded themselves in an almost hysterical language of sacrifice: "I was alone ... absolutely alone ... my savages could have killed me, eaten me, digested me, etc." Servant is a more sophisticated narrator; this is not to say that the report is flattering to the Futunans, but it does attribute the murder to a complex series of spiritual, political, and material motives, from fears of European slave-trading, acquiring the mission's (doubtful) wealth, and resolving a father-son split over religion. The major characters are quite conscious of how they will accommodate, appropriate, or resist the mission.[18]

In fact, unlike many general reports about "islanders" and missionaries in the nineteenth century, Servant eschews generic categories like "the Futunans" and defines specific actors like the "fanatical" chief Musumusu, the duplicitous king Niuliki, and his willful son Meitala. Servant gives the testimonies voice and presents Chanel's death in a fashion that is part Machiavellian, and also reminiscent of English saint Thomas à Beckett: death by proxy caused by the imprudent words of an unwise monarch.

✌

Servant's narrative has the shape of drama. The deposition is not merely a chronicle but also is made to accommodate the Vatican's criteria for martyrdom. A true martyr must have died in defense of the faith in imitation of Christ, presumably at the hands or orders of a tyrant. Hence, the role of Futunan King Niuliki is developed in detail. Whereas heathen-cannibal imagery may have remained popular in Western accounts of island peoples throughout the nineteenth century, the Marists recognized that savages, presumably unenlightened about the Faith rather than defiant of salvation, make poor substitutes for a Herod or Caesar. In Servant's report we find Niuliki ordering his son Meitala to "reject religion," or at very least, "to go then into the forest to practice." The son refuses. To the king's attack, "What are you looking for? You are king!" the son reportedly replies, "What is it to be king? I want to embrace religion!" The open witnessing and the defiant affirmation of belief as a rejection of worldly power show Meitala's conviction, glorifying his teacher Chanel.[19]

By reconstructing such intrigues and disputes, Servant's narrative transforms Futunan politics into a Christian parable of devotion and ultimate exaltation. When the chief Musumusu offers to kill the priest and his followers, Niuliki says nothing; according to Servant, this is not a sign of spiritual acceptance, but evil complicity: "his silence said everything." By washing his hands of the matter, the king becomes part of the Christ story, as described in an 1867 biography of Chanel by Reverend Père J. A. Bourdin: "It is not only in physical appearance that one finds Pilate in Niuliki, the king of Futuna." Rather, the Futunan ruler is also clearly the incarnation of the Judean governor in his "mask of hypocrisy," and his "weakness, injustice . . . and cruelty."[20]

The moment of Chanel's death is treated with equal care as a highly structured narrative designed to parallel the Lord's Passion. In his 1845 deposition, the chief assassin Musumusu declared that Chanel cried out, as the islanders surprised him, "Aua, aua! don't do that!" Although plausible, this would be unacceptable language for martyrdom, as it indicates an unwillingness to die for the Faith. Thus, Servant attacks the credibility of the witness, noting that his multiple interlocutors of 1848 "declared not to have heard any word escape the lips of the reverend Père." Moreover, the priest's alleged expiration with the words "Malie fuai," translated as "C'est très bien," strongly indicated that he "made to God the sacrifice of his life, that he drank from the chalice of suffering with a generous resignation. All of the witnesses of his martyrdom testify that never in his agony did any cry escape him, no complaint, no tear, no sigh."[21]

From these signs—or lack of them—Servant proposes, "He always maintained balance in his soul; he died like a lamb in the example of his divine master." Although this might appear to create sufficient analogies between Chanel and Christ, Servant concludes his major notes by observing also the moment of burial. "All the natives, the two assemblies of 1845 and 1848, report that immediately before the sepulcher there was a great detonation in the sky that was heard (on both sides of the island of Futuna and on the small island of Alofi). They testified that it could not have been thunder because the sky that day was calm and without clouds."[22]

⚜

Although Servant's formal narrative is stringently organized to serve the clear logic of Chanel's spiritual martyrdom, his notebooks and letters, and those of the murdered priest, suggest complex and highly contested political struggles behind the killing. In his earliest letters, Chanel is already observing "war is everywhere a plague," and nowhere more so than "poor Futuna." Told he must seek permission of clan elders to travel around the island, he protests but concedes, "It is an old usage in Futuna that when at war one does not let those from other regions come in indiscriminately; by 'other region' they mean the enemy party." Chanel's evangelizing quickly takes on partisan overtones. Paying his respects to Niuliki, the priest nonetheless finds himself attracted to the king's defeated rivals. Unlike Niuliki, these warriors are consciously receptive to Chanel's message, although their pragmatic sense of it exasperates him: "As soon as we are the victors, we will become Christians." Disappointed about his teaching yet hopeful of his influence, Chanel gives one warrior, Samu Keletaona, a medallion of the Virgin to protect him in battle, soon remarking, "I saw them so much more animated in combat, as they believed themselves sure of victory due to the new divinities visiting their land." In the end, however, Niuliki carries about a "terrifying slaughter," absolutely defeating Chanel's allies.[23]

Marist voices are not the unique record of the events. Futunan oral narratives also highlight the complex political struggles behind Chanel's fate. Kapelu Nau recounts an assassination plot launched by local chiefs with little regard for the king so prominently featured by Servant. "Musumusu was sent to Tu'a to advise King Niuliki that if he opposed the decision made to kill the white man, he would be overthrown and replaced by Ukuloa of Kolotai, and that the white man would be killed in any case."[24]

Assailed by rivals and pressed by nominal allies unhappy with Chanel's interference in island struggles, the king never lost his suspicions of the priest. Niuliki and Chanel were initially quite friendly, yet became set against each other for political reasons, and larger colonial questions also raised tensions. From transcriptions we know that Niuliki opened his audience with Musumusu by demanding, "Will they succeed, these savage ones who come to Futuna to make slaves?" Niuliki had real reasons to fear the coming of Europeans: "blackbirding," the kidnapping and indentured servitude of island peoples, followed a logic that propelled Europeans across the Pacific—the search for cheap labor.[25] Not as large a question in the Pacific as it was in the Atlantic and Carribbean, blackbirding nonetheless meant croppers, miners, sandalwood traders, and plantation owners aggressively pursuing large scale recruitment and sometimes outright abduction of men and women from villages across Polynesia and especially Melanesia.

Niuliki would have been concerned about slaving from rival clans or islands, especially those on trade routes from the New Hebrides visited by sandalwood boats from the early decades of the nineteenth century. Initially limited to unscrupulous individual captains, the "people trade" would develop into a large-scale traffic in coerced or kidnapped workers destined for guano, plantation, and mine work in Peru, Australia, and New Caledonia. By the 1860s, indignant Sydney newspapers could maintain, "The establishment of a slave trade in these seas has been so long proved that no one can entertain any doubt of its existence. Every class of men has borne testimony to the ruse and violence developed in this trade."[26]

The encounters could be terrifying, as the missionary Maggie Paton noted from the New Hebrides: "The boat kept in deep water just outside the reef, and some Aniwans waded out and were shouted to in Sandalwood English. They wanted men or boys, and would give a musket for everyone they got. Our Natives shouted back that they were Missi's worshipping people and did not want to go with the Traders. One of the white men stupidly (it must have been in fun) leveled a musket at one of our Natives, when the cap snapped and set the Natives in a great rage, believing that he tried to kill some of them." Here, outrage and mute apologies for the white man and protective concern for the threatened natives underscore the uneasy tensions of the labor "trade" in which local missions found themselves almost inevitably entangled.

Equally unnerving, and more reprehensible, the blackbirders at times used missionary guise to gain captives. Ordered to investigate Pacific slaving charges, Captain Albert Hastings Markham reported, "Some of the kidnappers go so far as to paint their vessels so as to resemble as much as possible the schooners employed by the different missions." He particularly excoriated one trader, "A white ruffian, dressed in a black coat and hat and wearing a pair of spectacles," for pretending to be a priest.[27] When islanders boarded the presumably friendly vessel they were thrown into the hold and their canoes set adrift.

Although nineteenth-century mission stations came to oppose the harshest forms of exploitation, their own salvation projects also may have contributed to a perceived bartering of bodies and souls. As the Marist Father Benjamin Goubin reported ambiguously from Lifou in 1877, "No more than three months ago we purchased some little New Hebrideans, two boys and a girl. She was so savage that she couldn't stand the light of day or the company of others." Goubin did not elaborate the terms or purposes of his "purchase," but the Colonial Union delegate Léon Moncelon, in commenting on the indentured labor trade between the New Hebrides and New Caledonia, did underscore the common language of "buying" an islander in the Western Pacific: "One never uses any other expression, as the alleged cost of passage is in reality considered the price of the black."[28]

Goubin's purchased girl ends up, according to the priest, "attending mass on the summit of a high mountain where a gigantic cross is to be found." Such allegiances to new authority and uncertainties about selling bodies and souls could have serious repercussions, as Niuliki knew from Chanel's turning Meitala against not only him, but also the monarchy. In Servant's report Meitala declares, "I cannot abandon religion, I've eaten my *tapu*," violating the custom of not eating yams until fathering a son of his own. To violate the tapu (taboo) of forbidden things challenges not only the king but the order of his rule. As Père Chevron posed the question, "How is it that a population, so independent, could be governed during pagan times? The only rein that served to guide the people in its conduct and its actions was that of fear of the gods and the violation of tapu. Here we see the only means which the king and the chiefs had to govern the people." More than a rebellion of individual conscience, the son's choice threatened the island's structural universe. Speaking of the chiefs, Chevron noted, "One can judge how much their ideas were opposed to the establishment of Christianity, which according to them, contributed to overthrowing their governmental system."[29]

Nothing this stark or unseemly appears in Chanel's martyrdom report, Servant necessarily emphasizing the question of individual faith for Meitala. Political conflict is effectively translated from moments of struggle into markers of historical transition from the "pagan" to the Christian. Meitala was likely a willing participant in shaping this story. The Marists made much of a letter supposedly written by Meitala, "For all the Christians of Futuna," which drew on a language of spiritual Enlightenment: "in Futuna ... the shadow has given way to light, falsehood to truth; we are Catholics."[30] With the support of the Marists, Meitala would soon become a paramount

leader, one who could instruct his brethren—and perhaps the Marists themselves—on what it meant to be an island Catholic. The Marists in turn used
Chanel's death to glorify their work and mark the transition of the islands
from savagery to Christian society, when all references to violence, pagans,
and idols could be relocated into "previous times."

To realize this change, Chanel's legacy was to be that of love—the martyred champion of Christian charity in the South Seas. Declarations of
emotion became part of the politics. At Chanel's funeral, Servant extolled
islanders' weeping and cutting themselves with shells, while dismissing Niuliki's apparent grief and shock as "crocodile tears." For the 1889 beatification,
Father M. Morel, the head of a seminary at Belley, produced *Dernière Journée
et Martyre du Bienheureux Pierre Chanel*, a drama in verse in which Marist
transcripts were given theatrical expression. In key scenes Méitala, the king's
dissenting son, engages in open debate with his father about Christianity
and political rule. Where the king warns his son that religion has shaken
the kingdom, the son replies, "among a loyal Christian people, it assures
peace and divides nothing." Where the king argues "my rights are abolished
by all you believe," Méitala intones, "Your rights, no! Your errors!" Niuliki's
position is subsumed to the Marist's power of love as the son tells his father,
"since I have loved God our holy master, I have even more love for you, I
know better to recognize this."[31] That love is no longer under the chiefly rule
of the father, but the Marist's authority of the Father.

To give this love concrete form, the Marists quickly made the site of the
murder a rallying spot for their message. Bishop Pompallier had Chanel's
body transported to New Zealand, and erected a cross on Futuna and a
chapel where he was killed. This did not go undisputed by some of the
chiefs, about whom one priest noted, "All efforts have been made to prevent
the construction of churches, above all that which was put up on the very
place where the first martyr of Oceania spilled his blood." But other chiefs
took full advantage of the Marist efforts; those seeking alliances or peace
converted to the new faith, and services and memorials for Chanel proved
popular with the new adherents. Father Poupinel, selectively drawing out
a history of Futunan clan warfare, reflected with satisfaction, "Before their
conversion, the Futunans were, from time immemorial, divided into two
irreconcilable parties, the victorious and the vanquished. Today, each part
has its king; both are devoted to the cause of religion."[32]

To strongly mark religious and enlightened Futuna, Marist teachings
formalized the evils now overcome. In their narratives, Niuliki himself aided
the growth of the priests' authority by conveniently dying of a "putrifying"
disease shortly after Chanel was interred, a fate that also befell the assassin
Musumusu a few years later. Meitala's defiance of his father became standard

lore as a tale of an inverted Eden—the taking of knowledge as an escape from ignorance, rather than an expulsion from paradise.

Whereas Marist stories focused on such markers of divine faith, conversion, and justice, Futunan narratives underscored their own maneuverings to abet or restrain the Marists' political influence. In oral accounts Vasa Keletaona has noted, "The Catholic priests at that time wanted a single king for Futuna and wanted power to be alternatively shared between Alo and Sigave," the key domains and clan centers. That is why at Niuliki's death, "The chiefs of Alo would accept the proposition of the religious authorities to anoint [Chanel supporter] Samu Keletaona as king of all Futuna." Notably, the Futunan oral tradition also tells us that Keletaona ultimately ceded part of his authority to Niuliki's son, the redoubtable Meitala. In a ceremonial pronouncement to the headmen of Alo, he declared: "As you want to have a king for Alo, go from today to Kolotai to anoint Meitala; he alone is worthy of being king; as for me, I will be king only of Sigave."[33] The political legacies of Chanel's original supporters, Keletaona and Meitala, were clearly served along with those of the Marists.

Some scholars have noted that such Futunan narratives can serve to reimagine the customary villains of Chanel's martyrdom, such as Musumusu. The erstwhile assassin, although opposed to Keletaona and Meitala, nonetheless lived to see the kingdom of Alo preserved in the person of the son of his former patron Niuliki. Odom Abba has argued that Musumusu was in this way a champion of Futunan political tradition, a great warrior and defender of his kingdom. Indeed, in telling language, Chanel's chronicler Louis-Catherin Servant described Musumusu's return to Futuna after a self-imposed exile in Wallis: "A few elders who still felt the blood of the victorious party flowing through their veins were thrilled to see him again, and gave him the name 'savior of *la patrie*.'"[34] The translation may be inexact, but the political sentiment of Musumusu's own histoire d'amour in contest with that of Chanel's is unmistakable. Notably, Servant appeared to respect this struggle—and Musumusu's conversion to Christianity while in Wallis—by relating the Futunan chief's own death in a manner remarkably parallel to that of Chanel: "He never let out any complaint, and was never frightened by the approach of death."[35]

Other markers also defined the boundaries of Marist and Futunan negotiations. The false reports of Chanel's being eaten by the Futunans, although partly obdurate stereotype, also contributed to the logic of his European apotheosis. In general, overcoming cannibalism as a legacy of Chanel's murder allowed the Marists to create historical narratives demonstrating the important progress of the missions. The key word is "progress," for as Père Chevron saw it, "the Futunans only do what their predecessors have taught them; the spark of invention is completely foreign to them." The state of anthropophagy was used as an historical gauge across the Pacific. Speaking of Hawai'i in an 1889 colonial newsletter, the journalist Paul Barré presented a favorable view of the monarchy in terms of "an advanced degree of civilization, contrasted with the cannibalism which still reigned a century ago." In his ethnological reports on the Oceanic islands, Alphonse Bertillon in 1883 argued that "the best proofs" for indications of differential historical progress among island peoples was to be found in "the phases of cannibalism" of the archipelagos.[36]

Yet Chanel's tale of Christ's love overcoming savagery had no monopoly in narrating cannibal lore; Futunans kept their own histories. Their tales illustrate Oceanic-wide migrations and struggles over centuries, and are often structured around contacts and aggressions by peoples such as the Tongans. Generations of inter-island invasion created a sophisticated body of epic in which monstrous rampaging pigs and fearsome "cannibal kings" such as Saufekai wreaked horror, slaughtering and eating Futunans such that "one saw the villages near the sea depopulated." It was the great warrior Fatumoana who slew Saufekai in classic fashion at a Kava ceremony, smashing his skull with a strong blow: "They say that the brain sprang from his head with such force that the whole house was astounded." Parallel to Christian martyrdom, local storytellers were conversant in maintaining narrations of epic heroism and salvation.

More specifically, Kapelu Nau's oral narratives suggest how Futunans could understand cannibalism not as the practice of a barbaric culture but as a commentary on tyrannical abuses of power—associated with foreign invasion. In recounting the tales of a royal house/ossuary favored by despots, Kapelu Nau gives full credit to changes in practice to none other than Chanel's old adversary, Niuliki. "We all know from the stories of our grandparents that human bones attached to the roof hung down everywhere in this house until King Niuliki outlawed cannibalism."[37] In Futuna, thinking about cannibalism was not a simple matter of overcoming barbaric practices. Marists reproached Futunans who in turn worked from local invasion tales and had their own ideas about enemies, justice, and outsiders.

Associations of cannibalism in Chanel's case were shaped by the particular logic of Marist politics and ideology. Through the transubstantiation, the Fathers well knew the power involved in the sacrifice of the body, its eating, and the drinking of the blood of the Lord. The problem, Père Chevron suggested, was that instead of joining the body of the faithful in holy communion, Futunan anthropophagy was an attack within the sanctity of ordered relations themselves, the community of man, God, and brother which the Marists extolled. When Chevron deplored "these hideous festivals" it was principally because "one sees them cutting the throats even of their own family members."[38]

Eaten or not, Chanel's death incarnated brotherly sacrifice: sowing love rather than discord, Chanel was the lamb whose spilled blood gave the Fathers a sanctified place to shape their brotherhood and found the community of their church. It was a powerful message. Backed by the Wallisian monarchy, thousands of neophytes were baptized; by 1845, just two years after the martyr's example, Futuna itself was made effectively Catholic.

Chanel's demise would become a powerful example of love in the service of religion, politics, and patriotism stretching from Oceania to Europe. In memorial services at his beatification, a *triduum solennel*—three days of pious exercises and devotions—inseparably linked the South Pacific to rural France. Sermons extolled the martyred priest, "how great was his love for his land of birth . . . leaving his family and beloved village, he carried their loyal souvenir even to farthest Oceania, from whence his heart turned frequently to Cuet and La Potèrie." Here, logically but also ideologically, France was not Paris but Chanel's home village and hamlet in the department of Ain. Chanel's memory of provincial, traditional France would be love of the faith as he carried out his mission, "how much toil and privation to carry the holy word afar and make known and loved Jesus Christ."[39]

More general evocations of France often lay at the heart of the preservation of Oceanic souls. Priests' letters praise the devotion of their charges, praying "with neither ostentation nor timidity," and for carrying off "all the liturgical chants as well as is done in the great churches of France." More pointedly, the priests admit that even though quite often, "the natives understand nothing," it matters little since any Europeans present "believe themselves transported to their *patrie* across the sea, and many cannot hold back their tears."[40]

France was never far from Wallis and Futuna. Father Poupinel, writing during the Second Empire, attempted direct political analogies: "The Futunans are perhaps more republican than monarchist; at least their monarchy is constitutional and their chiefs are elected."[41] With Chanel's beatification declared in 1889, the islands became increasingly enmeshed in the combined and conflicting interests of the republic and the Vatican. Although defiantly secular since the 1789 Revolution, France a century later nevertheless retained a strong Catholic church which was completely separated from the State only in 1905. Catholic ideologies infused movements such as the Action Française, and other movements of political and spiritual reaction against the republic. This difficult dance had seen both concordats, notably Napoleon Bonaparte's in 1804, and attacks against Catholic teaching, schools, and congregations across the nineteenth century.

In Paris, republican nationalism and Catholic institutions would not only battle but also serve each other well. The French Foreign Ministry and the Ministry of Colonies generally agreed with the radical Gambetta that "anti-clericalism is not for export." In fact, with increasing repression at home, culminating in 1901 laws that outlawed many congregations and schools in France, the church saw great benefits in missionizing abroad. The vociferous "Republican Catholic" of the Third Republic, Bishop Emile Freppel, argued for overseas colonial expansion "from the point of view of the honor and interests of France," and claimed that "it is necessary to hold on to what France possesses and not permit any other foreign power to encroach upon French domination." Such enthusiasm at a time when even the government was ambivalent about distant imperial projects caused Georges Clemenceau to call Freppel "Jules Ferry in priest's robes," aligning the bishop with the famously pro-colonial prime minister.[42]

Disdainful of the church at home, republicans saw the advantages of the Catholics around the world. Some could find political common cause with Rome, as Juliette Adam: "In my capacity as a Frenchwoman and republican I am convinced that it is not possible to have a truly national policy without having constant diplomatic relations with the Papacy." Her interests were shaped by the *La Liberté d'opinion* editor Jacques Bozon, who argued that French influence in the world was especially due to Catholic missions. "Because religion, which I envisage purely politically, and ought I say, nationalist, religion is the vehicle abroad for influences and ambitions . . . if you do not support French Catholic missions . . . you will see in their place the Orthodox pope or the English clergyman."[43]

Although nominally at war with the republic, the Marists were themselves patriotically French against the British, Americans, and Germans in Oceania. Disenchanted with his government's support for defending the New Caledonian island of Lifou against English incursions, Father Benjamin Goubin reported in 1884, "A steamship has come . . . to set up three French schools on the island . . . at last they have understood that France must be made loved in this country." Goubin emphasized the theme of French Catholic charity; others took up strategic and economic arguments. Père Bouzigue (1887) defended the French protectorate with Wallis and Futuna by invoking the "exceptional urgency" of "the coming breach of the Panamanian isthmus, the rivalry between the English and the Germans."[44] Small though the islands were, they might yet prove critical as strategic *points de relâche*. In Tahiti, where Protestants would rule, the Catholics waited until *French* Protestants took over before retreating, and the French navy provided protection.

Such cooperation, or mutual exploitation, of Catholic mission, French state, and Oceanic monarchy was solidly incarnated in the events of Chanel's beatification. With the pope's blessing, the vicariat of Oceania established official ceremonies and a special mass to honor the newly blessed. Monseigneur Lamaze was dispatched from Rome to organize the proceedings and arrived in Futuna in August of 1890; his plan was to lead a great pilgrimage of Marists and of the faithful from all over Oceania to conclude at the tomb of the beatified Chanel at Poi. The French navy obligingly helped transport mission figures and locals from around Samoa to Futuna. Although strikes on the commercial ship lines prevented any participation from Australia or New Zealand, the response and dedication of the islanders to their new *bienheureux* was beyond expectations. According to Lamaze, the kings of Futuna, the queen at Wallis, and all of the local chiefs manifested great pride in the activities and "without exception, all of the inhabitants, men, women and children, truly exhausted all of their resources for these national festivals; they would have liked to do more, but simply could not."[45]

As events of "national" importance, Lamaze intended his pilgrimage activities to unify the faithful through veneration of Chanel at a newly sacred site. Organized pilgrimages of this sort were a form of inverted imperialism. John Williams, the leader of the London Missionary Society in Tahiti at the beginning of the century, had declared the Society Islands a center for missionary expansion "from whence the streams of salvation are to flow," carrying the evangelicals' influence from "Fiji, the New Hebrides, New Caledonia, Solomon's archipelago, New Britain, New Ireland, and above all the immense island of New Guinea."[46] As a priest, Chanel had followed this standard pattern of extending Christian authority by moving from the Marist base on Wallis to Futuna. With his beatification, the faithful now flowed from distant parts *into* the mission authority to commune with the memory and miraculous powers of Chanel the national martyr.

Chanel was a national figure in other ways. The great Oceanic pilgrimage was complemented by highly organized rites for Chanel back in France, which enabled both lay and religious groups to promote different aspects of a Catholic imperialism. Chanel's body and the commemorations surrounding his death circulated through New Zealand and back to Lyon, to be venerated at the Colline de Fourrières. At a time when republican governments were organizing civil commemorations as forms of secular unity with the nation, the church demonstrated its continuing talent for using ritual spirituality to organize material and political interests.[47]

Chanel's martyrdom could be adopted to serve patriotic ideology, religious fervor, or simple commercialism—Oceania as part pilgrimage, part tourist excursion. In church services around Chanel's home region, honorific proclamations echoed Marist reports, "God called him to suffer as a martyr / he accepted with joy and happiness / they struck him / he pardoned them / he expired / I bring myself to sing his greatness." Chanel's memory was not only transformed into commemoration but also commodified and resold as souvenirs. Instructional pamphlets establishing the calendar of his beatification events offered useful information to pilgrims concerning available train lines to designated sites, recommended taverns and restaurants, and the best means for obtaining reservations to masses, prayers, and other events.

Also offered were catalogues of "objets de piété": statuettes, medallions, and images of the blessed. One guide in particular recommends "the different scale reductions of the beautiful statue created by the talent of our compatriot M. Cabochet, and the engraved medals struck by the efforts of M. Fornet. All pilgrims will want to take and give them as souvenirs of the festivities of the beatification." Those wishing more personalized memorialization were invited to contribute to a monument and have their names inscribed in marble upon a tablet at a rate of one hundred francs for benefactors, five hundred for "founders."[48]

For the faithful, Chanel's elevation, with its ceremonies and objects, was an opportunity to see the miracle of his love come full circle from Oceania back to France. One Monsieur Félix T., suffering from anemia and serious maladies of the stomach and intestine, found himself ecstatically recovering as the Lyon ceremonies progressed. Upon restoration to full health, he kept a Chanel medallion and henceforth "recited everyday three Our Fathers, three Ave Marias, and three invocations of the blessed Martyr of Futuna." A hobbled Sister M. Saint-Brune invoked Chanel's name repeatedly at mass and found "I kept standing without pain or fatigue. At the same time an indefinable emotion swept over me and delivered a joy and happiness I cannot describe." Tears and profound feeling characterize Chanel's miracles. One powerful surge grips a dying man's physician more than even his patient and strikes humbling blows against the certitudes of his medical science. A notary records, "All of a sudden emotion conquered him and two tears fell from his eyes," upon which the doctor himself exclaims "I am obliged to recognize that there is someone above me who is taking care of you."[49]

Such heartfelt humility, expanding to enclose both faith and knowledge, was broadly promoted in the presentation of Chanel's love for and service to France. With a rhetorical dialectic of great subtlety, Chanel's example to the Catholic faith and his meaning for French patriotism were especially ably intertwined in the *triduum solennel* that inaugurated his pilgrimage. The

Vatican took pride of place in these orations, intoning "Rome speaks and proclaims his glory," making Chanel "triumphant in the *sainte patrie*." Yet the holy land of faith is transfigured as the martyr becomes "good soldier of Christ," and finally "French apostle." What results is the multiple declaration of a Chanel appropriate to his political station, at once spiritual, emotional, patriotic, and defiantly imperialist. "Futuna hence is ours forever. . . . La France has conquered by your great deeds a new world where our flag, cherished by your flock, will wave over your tomb. Far from your small village, close to your flock, La France will guard your tomb."[50]

Chanel had long prefigured the adoption of these affectionate elements in letters of 1839: "It is never without strong emotion that I watch multitudes of young children run to me, all loving France and desiring to go there."[51] The collusion of faith and politics would continue throughout and after his life. When, in 1954, Pierre Chanel, *bienheureux* would be elevated to Pierre Chanel, Saint, the flag also was present, as official reporting of the ceremonies made clear: "From the previous day the tricolor was hoisted on its line next to the statue of Saint Pierre Chanel; thus July 14 was associated with the glorification of the first French saint of the Pacific." It was an association that Father Morel from Belley had inscribed in his dialogues between Niuliki, Meitala, and Chanel. Where the king complained to Chanel that "our beliefs were enough just until you arrived," the son interceded, extolling not only Chanel but also "France . . . glorious land, you are the queen of the world where you do so much good/ a people is your friend when it becomes Christian."[52]

✑

The tenuous, but real cooperation between religion and politics, islanders, priests, and administrators satisfied many of the missions. In Wallis, the alliance of Church and navy manifested itself directly in annexation politics. As the captain of the frigate *Hussard* reported in 1881, "I know from conversations with missionaries their desire to see France establish herself in some manner on Wallis," a tendency he saw leading ultimately to "a political act." Although carefully registering Queen Amelia's concern for her autonomy and independence, the captain drew on what he saw as the Wallisians's "sympathy for France" and suggested "they would accept French occupation or protectorate much more than any other."[53]

The shifting line between religion and politics is most clearly manifested by comparing the treaties of protection and annexation signed by King Lavelua in 1842 and Queen Amelia in 1886. The former document, signed November 4, 1842, declares: "We the King of the islands of Wallis and chiefs undersigned, having embraced the apostolic and Roman Catholic religion, declare our will to form a free and independent estate, and for reasons of religious community demand to be under the protection of His Majesty Louis Philippe I, King of the French."⁵⁴ The emphasis on the empire of religion and the community of church (and of the Marists) notably contrasts with the 1886 document of the queen: "The Queen of Wallis, desiring to strengthen the bonds which for many long years have already united her to France, accepts to be placed under the protectorate of France. As an external sign of this mutual engagement, she will set aside her banner for the French banner." The emphasis on religious community from the first decade of Marist influence is, a generation later, clearly subordinated to the expression of national sentiments, most dramatically indicated in the exchange of flags. Yet the Marists have incorporated, rather than ceded their political authority to ministries in Paris. Unlike the 1842 document, the new treaty also sets forth in detail the role of a resident who will be charged with "foreign relations and all affairs concerning Europeans."

With a sophisticated eye to Oceanic politics, the document continues: "The Resident will have the right to sit on the council of ministers. The nomination of the Resident will be at the pleasure of the Queen, and should the desire of the Queen be so, as long as it does not trouble international relations, the Resident will be a Father of the Mission." In this, the Marists reserve their rights to be the queen's interpreters and advisors. More, the treaty affirms, "The Queen will determine a terrain of about twenty hectares for the use of the Resident and the functions he will have to fulfill."⁵⁵ Both the queen and the Marists planned to reinforce their authority in the islands while the French navy protected a territory at the edges of English, American, and German footholds in Tonga, Fiji, and the Samoas.

What did the French Catholic imperium accomplish? The moral "civilization" of the nineteenth century and doctrinaire ordering of a Christian theocracy triumphed, the Fathers of the Church serving as educators to the islanders and key advisers to the monarchy. Still—the church's critics notwithstanding—that morality and theocracy were never seamless projects, as other moralities and love stories continued to challenge the Fathers' authority. Where early on they had struggled against the married example of Protestant rivals, and with and against the French republic, so the Marists were at times exasperated trying to enforce their understanding of Chanel's legacy in daily practices of love, community, and devotion among their parishioners. Conflicts especially erupted when the territory was annexed and the appointed resident was not the Mission Father the Marists had hoped for.

Some cases—especially those collapsing politics and marriage—are dramatic demonstrations of the willfulness of individual islanders to negotiate fractures between church and state. In the "Piho Incident" of 1910, the wife of a mission gardener was condemned by Father Fellion for picking up bad influences while in domestic service to a republican resident, particularly her habit of "living habitually separated from her husband." Worse, she accompanied the resident, Dr. Brochard, on a trip to Noumea and France, causing Fellion to warn Piho that he could no longer work at the mission if "he and his wife live apart." Stung, Piho does not demand his wife return to him but, rather, "the same day he went to the resident saying that he had been chased away without knowing why." From this, reports Fellion, "I received a letter of formal convocation, telling me that the expulsion of Piho did not only concern the internal affairs of the house; I should go to [the resident] and give an explanation."[56] Fellion indignantly refused, perhaps ruefully aware that the Marist's authority has not precluded gardeners and gardener's wives from negotiating between church and state to declare their own projects of affinity, interest, and sense of justice.

When the resident went further and tried to have the head of the mission expelled, the Marists struck back, drawing on faithful parishioners to force a confrontation. The aggrieved Superieur, Father Bazin, evoked "the direct line" of the Lavelua who knew Pierre Chanel and Queen Amelia ("who gave Wallis to France!") to oppose the resident. When the expulsion order appeared with the signature of the (albeit reluctant) king, local villagers rallied to "head toward his house to elect a new king."[57] Popular action saved the mission and forced "the Resident to make his apologies to Father Bazin." Such chronicles underscore the villagers' personal and political affinities within Chanel's legacy in the shaping of the Marist "theocracy."

Yet for those French commentators in search of a nineteenth-century Pacific unspoiled by change, or politics, Wallis and Futuna still seemed to reach the twentieth century uniquely. In 1931, almost a century after Chanel's death, the writer and administrator of the transport line Messageries Maritimes René de la Bruyère noted, "one has the impression that this archipelago is perhaps the only to not be radically transformed. . . . [E]verywhere in the Pacific civilization has deflowered nature and prostituted the scenery. It seems that Wallis has conserved its character."

La Bruyère pondered the logic of his own business—transport and movement around the Pacific—suggesting, "Our mechanistic century seeks a return to nature, and it hopes to find it in these archipelagos where there are no planes, few or no automobiles, and the populations have remained very simple." [58] Focused on the Oceanic theme of isolation, he did not consider links between Wallis and Futuna and Marist missions in New Caledonia, nor how many islanders would be sent to Noumea for education and became part of a circular migration that would see them working in New Caledonian and New Hebridean mines, households, plantations, and companies. By the end of the century, more Wallisians would be in Noumea than on Wallis.

Transport and nostalgia would leave their traces a few years after La Bruyère's remarks when the islands again celebrated the work the Marists had begun in 1837. For the centennial commemorations, eloquent sermons and particular praise were reserved for Pierre Chanel and Monseigneur Bataillon, the founders of the missions on Wallis and Futuna. One of the celebrations involved a play, *Enosi*, which dramatized the historic good works of the two men and their followers.[59] For this, the provincial leader of the Marist Fathers of Oceania came especially from New Caledonia on a boat of the Messageries Maritimes, named for a naval commander and famed writer who had once dreamed of being a missionary. Unable to wait the months for another ship, the Father was obliged to return rather quickly to Noumea on the same ship—the *Pierre Loti*.

FOUR

SOCIETY ISLANDS

Tahitian Archives

In 1878, Juliette Adam's *Nouvelle Revue* published the first installment of
Pierre Loti's Tahitian romance, *The Marriage of Loti*, setting the young
author on the road to literary celebrity. In an 1886 essay for the culture review *Gil Blas*, Guy de Maupassant, referencing Chateaubriand, commented on Loti's initial success, praising the grace of his characters and
prose: "Across the mists of an ocean unknown to our eyes, he showed us an
adorable island of love, and he remade with Loti and Rarahu the poem of
Paul and Virginie. We did not ask ourselves if the tale was true, as it spoke to
us with such charm."[1] In his belles-lettres appreciation, Maupassant unwittingly touched upon the essential points of a colonial project: if ever a part of
the world had had *love* attached to its name it was "Tahiti," a singular land
of love in a literary tradition. Tales about it were charming; one did not have
to reflect upon their truth.

Loti would later have the opportunity to invest his characters with theatrical ruminations on love, empire, and something missing from a merely
charming tale: the historical expiration of Tahitian civilization. A musical
version of the novel at the Opéra-Comique (1898) fully dramatized and
flattered the arriving empire with such choruses as "I saw brilliant French
officers come down from the Neptune," and "it is our land of love, island
of dreams." Closing with the anguish of the French protagonist's lover
"Manéhu," the play warns that while Frenchmen may come to Polynesia,
Polynesians may not go to Europe. "No Manéhu, you cannot follow him
to France . . . the flowers of our land fade in the land of exile and lose their
attraction. They need the sun, the scents, the mystery, the enchantment of
our forests." The islander may not act but must remain remote and wistfully

"Nothing must be forgotten."
Icon of authority and resistance. *Portrait of Queen Pomare Vahine IV* (1851) by Charles Giraud. Source: La Société des Études Océaniennes, Papeete, Tahiti

preserved, only to wait on the island of dreams, and ultimately despair, "Oh! To be no longer loved, to be a thing vile and without radiance! Sweet past times of light, fatal awakening!"[2]

That awakening was long delayed. Bounded as colonial territories, the Society Islands, capital at Papeete, Tahiti, centerpiece of the Etablissements Français de l'Océanie encompassing Bora Bora, Huahine, Raitea, and the Gambiers, Tuamotus, and Marquesas, would cease to have their own histories. The islands became closed to grand legacies of Polynesian navigation and migration, to kinships, exchanges, and encounters of the Oceanic world that linked the Maohi peoples to mid-Pacific islands and to Hawai'i in the north and Aotearoa–New Zealand to the south. Imperial narratives of the isles fixed upon apartness and romance, collapsing the heroic eighteenth-century European romanticism of Cook, Bougainville, and Chateaubriand into the nineteenth-century visions of sensual expiration of Loti and Paul Gauguin.

The French creation of Tahiti was already a cliché by the middle of the nineteenth century. "Why speak of Tahiti?" wondered the civil engineer, explorer, and geologist Jules Garnier on an excursion around the Society Islands in 1868. So many "eminent writers" and "illustrious voyagers" had consecrated so many long and feverish pages to this "point lost in the vastness of the Pacific Ocean." What would there be except valleys, ravines, and creeks enveloped by "a fresh and fragrant atmosphere?" What could one do except "abandon oneself along with the natives to a voluptuous repose," to follow their animated dancing and beautiful singing, to watch and desire their handsome and beautiful bodies "ornamented, rather clothed, with perfumed flowers?"[3] Even before he arrived, Garnier knew what to expect. "Tahiti": the reports of European navigators had been long known—placid bays, great chiefs, sensual women, mysteries, and mysticism. Throughout the nineteenth century, naval officers had written eulogies to the islands and peoples: "In all that I have seen in Europe and everywhere else, nothing approaches the beauty of this Polynesian race."[4]

That beauty disguised and enabled a French imperial history in the Pacific. In a detailed report of 1884, the future French president Paul Deschanel captured the complexity of imperial motivations in the islands from "commercial relations between Oceania, America, and Europe" to the threat of "being caught behind Germany and outmaneuvered by England," yet framed these strategic observations by recommending, "One must read *The Marriage of Loti*, that idyllic Tahitian sketch, work of a great painter of nature, to grasp the penetrating charm, intense poetry, and ennervating sweetness of Tahiti."[5] It was not only a popular but also consistent choice for imagining empire: the conflation, at times deliberate confusion, of sensuality and strategy.

Loti's characters established the framework for what some Pacific historians have politically called *Le Mariage Franco-Tahitien*. By marrying the Polynesian princess Rarahu, Loti's naval officer alter ego creates a sentimental strategic alliance with Queen Pomare Vahine IV, making conjugality a form of family politics. French authorities worked throughout the century to ingratiate themselves in such alliances. Where the royals themselves were the concerned parties—as with an impending 1883 marriage between Prince Hinoï and the queen of Bora-Bora—local governors sent confidential letters to the Ministry of the Navy and Colonies in Paris, relating, "It seems to be in our highest interest in forseeing our future annexations that we attach ourselves to the Pomare family, and especially the young prince."[6]

The Oceanic Empire of Love for France was both art and bureaucracy, a system of possible histories fashioned through literary and artistic works, held together by administrators, civil servants, and clerks. Within this system romance triumphed and annexation disappeared. Tahiti was "isolated": made lovely, sensual, indeed so impossibly rare that it had only one historical recourse—to perish. In all, a remarkable political chronicle is elided. "Tahiti" has been written into historical narratives of paradise and despoilment of many kinds, from Christianity and Western Civilization, to syphillis and alcoholism, to tourism and nuclear testing, yet—except for sovereignty movements of the twentieth-century postwar—rarely one of violence and anticolonial struggle. Scholars of this absence such as Colin Newbury have wondered why so little work has attempted to study "the complex reactions to European settlement in the Pacific, by comparing and analysing periods of armed revolt."[7] Where do we find chronicles of the protectorate illegitimately placed over the kingdom in 1843, French occupation, or the pitched battles and guerilla warfare between Tahitian warriors and French garrisons?

Arguably, such stories remain submerged as long as Tahiti remains—as it does into the twenty-first century—a French territory. Official French narratives still maintain that the Maohi peoples of the Society Islands peacefully ceded their authority to France.[8] This is correct if one dates local histories only to the 1880 decision of King Pomare V to surrender his authority to Paris in exchange for limited sovereignty and a salary.[9] Generally, however, such narratives elide the Franco-Tahitian War of 1843–1846, and the Leewards War throughout the 1880s and 1890s when French protectorates were fiercely resisted by island monarchs, dozens of chiefs, and thousands of warriors throughout multiple island groups.

Tahiti was theoretically annexed to the French state in 1843 by Admiral Abel Dupetit-Thouars as a strategic support to naval actions in the Marquesas Islands the previous year. There, the admiral had gained rights to establish a whaling station, military outpost, and Catholic mission.[10] Although the Marquesan mission was dictated from Paris, the admiral's actions in the Tahitian Islands were neither wanted nor supported by the French government; the ensuing conflict developed awkwardly from disputes over the ejection of the Catholic missionaries Honoré Laval and François d'Assise Caret from Tahiti by Queen Pomare Vahine IV, and disputes over French interests, trading rights, and property. Likely, the admiral was thinking less of Paris and more of London, particularly following the British annexation of New Zealand in 1840 and the Treaty of Waitangi that gave his rivals an encroaching settler presence in the South Pacific. Although formal annexation was repudiated by Paris, skillful maneuvering of diplomatic counterparts with a *fait accompli* allowed Dupetit-Thouars to have his seizure of Tahiti recognized by both the French and British governments as a "protectorate."

As the crisis unfolded, pro-British forces in the islands, up to and including the queen, waited in vain for England's support, and petitioned Victoria with anxious letters. The response was underwhelming. One British warship captain found himself firing salutes to the French flag while conceding, "We have perhaps no right to find fault with France, for Tahiti has been repeatedly offered to England and as often refused . . . the deed is done, and it's too late to repine."[11]

Unsurprisingly, Dupetit Thouars was less successful with the peoples whom France now purportedly ruled; the islanders. Tahitians, beginning with the queen, were less than enthusiastic about their putative protection. The Tahitian case is instructive as a struggle over a history that Loti's pastoral and Gauguin's images did so much to shape for the nineteenth century. In the 1840s, Maohi protests and resistance were clear, immediate—and written. In this, the power and attraction of stories and images about mute, mysterious beauties illustrate how literary and iconographic authority overshadowed the empirical qualities of the written record.

Women were the center of this struggle: for Europe's Tahiti to continue as the amorous and erotic vahine-maiden favored by Bougainville's inheritors, silence would have to be historically imposed on the vocal Queen Pomare celebrated by the Maohi. The queen was not silent during the French incursion. In furious letters, she described the terms of cessions and indemnities demanded by Dupetit-Thouars, and eloquently and indignantly complained, "In the event of my refusal to either one or other of these terms, he would, by two o'clock on the following day, commence hostilities with the view of taking my land."[12] Depositions and complaints by her council, sent out in January 1846 as an *Appeal of the Natives of Tahiti to the Governments of Great Britain and America*, excoriated Dupetit Thouars's high-handedness, declaring, "He demanded the little island called Motu uta. He demanded also the large island Tahiti." The admiral also allegedly demanded the ritualistic "exchange of names," which would give him the reputed sovereignty of a local chief. "Give me the name of Pomare; and if that is refused I will open fire upon this land at 8 A.M., and will destroy every man, woman, and child." To this the chiefs added their own assessment, "Look well at this, friends! does it look like a treaty! Where will you find such a treaty? Begin by murdering the people, and then hoist the Protectorate flag!"[13]

London and Paris were not the only sites keeping records. Maohi political strategy and allegiances assert themselves in transcripts of Pomare's formal sessions with chiefs to discuss the crisis in 1843. Detailed records of the queen's meetings with British naval officers illuminate her attempts to maneuver diplomatically between two great European powers. Meeting with the captain of the *Talbot*, Pomare had clear objectives: "I would like that you reestablish my former sovereignty—and that the government set up by the French not be left in place." Her rhetoric is impressively complex. She well conveys her sentiment ("I have always thought that England would be my salvation") as well as her realpolitik ("I do not envisage returning to Tahiti unless there is a British warship there"). Interrogated as to the presence of her signature on Dupetit-Thouars's protectorate demand, the queen replied, "I signed because if the French admiral fired upon my land, there would be no more English, nor Americans, nor French, they would be all massacred." Here she ably matches a presumed defense of foreign lives and "fear of a blood bath" with a frank political assessment: "perhaps then three nations would take my land."[14]

Although a truism that Europeans often wrote about "natives," Pomare has her own—and in this case appropriately crafted—assessment of the French and English. "The French: that is a nation that does nothing but threaten without attempting to inform itself. The English on the other hand seek through dialogue the information they lack, without haste or hesitation." Her view notably reverses the Gallic self-stereotype of affinity and attributes it instead to her English protectors. She also is not above projecting a bit of familial and perhaps deliberately "feminine" humility, telling the captain, "I am in your hands and admit to you openly my great weakness. . . . I would be like the child who goes to ask the aid of her mother."[15]

Tahiti was not ceded peacefully—it was taken in a struggle characterized by deep rancor, and an imperious French play for domination—one only supported officially after the fact. Islander protests were matched and abetted by the highly visible attacks of the English Reverend George Pritchard, who commanded the influential Protestant church and advised the queen. He wrote long and bitterly of "French aggressions" after he was imprisoned, humiliated, and then forced off the island while seeking diplomatic support for a British protectorate. Pritchard's account of the coup d'état, one of the primary sources of the written diplomatic record of these events, was not published until the late twentieth century, for fear of upsetting French-British relations.[16]

Notably, Tahitian school textbooks a century and a half after the events present, rather passively, "the difficult *mise en place* of the protectorate," and propose "the Queen, Pomare Vahine IV, who had at first signed the protectorate treaty, wished to go back on her decision under the influence of the English pastor Pritchard. Conflict subsequently broke out." Such accounts accent a vainglorious (and English) Pritchard and a vacillating queen as the sources of the war. More familiarly, official government newsletters maintain "From September 9, 1842, Queen Pomare IV and the chiefs of Tahiti decided to place themselves under the protection of France."[17] Less publicized have been the Tahitian's own words and the tenacious resistance to and disavowal of the French actions in Tahiti for more than three years and around the *Etablissements* by hundreds of islanders for a good forty more.

The early struggle was marked by the taking and retaking of Papeete by French and Maohi forces and monumental clashes for blockhouses and fortifications. Thousands of islanders supported rebel camps manned by hundreds of warriors armed with muskets and other weapons. In Tahiti, fighting concentrated around mountain redoubts and featured fierce Maohi resistance, especially at Faaʻa in 1844—an event commemorated over a century later by Tahitian pro-independence parties to the displeasure of French authorities. In 1845–1846, a naval blockade of the island of Raiatea was lifted by the massacre of French forces on Huahine by Queen Teriʻitaria. As with the confrontations involving Pomare, narratives of dusky beauties were shaken. The sensuous Polynesian vahine of Bougainville was displaced by vivid reporting about the "woman chief who is always at the head of the opposition." In his report on the conflicts, Governor Armand Bruat recognized the open challenge of the woman who declared, "In the name of all, that she would never accept any arrangement, and that the gathering would not dissuade her." In this interregnum of the Polynesian idyll, battles and skirmishes with chiefs limited French authority to Tahitian bases around Papeete, and the initial armed rebellions cost hundreds of lives. Descriptions of naked and willing bodies were male rather than female, linked to military operations such as that of "twenty-five natives commanded by Taiirii. They climb completely naked, having nothing but their rifle and their cartridges."[18]

Entire districts took up arms, some remaining strongly anti-French for generations, as chiefs moved into and out of alliances with each other and with British and American traders. Throughout the recently "protected"

Marquesas, erstwhile French allies like the chief Ioete opened up guerilla warfare against the European interlopers. As late as 1870 and 1880 armies of up to a thousand colonial troops were engaged in battle with the Marquesans. Struggles in Huahine, Bora Bora, and Raiatea continued over decades as the "Leewards War," little remembered in French Pacific scholarship.

Far from a simple protectorate, the annexation of Tahiti was imposed by brutal conquest. Stationed in Tahitian waters 1846–1847, the British naval captain Henry Byam Martin left a record of the hostilities as a litany of inconclusive bloodshed. At Mahiana, north of Papeete, "400 Frenchmen supported by the guns of L'Uranie frigate and Phaeton Steamer were landed . . . a battle took place without any result, each party losing about 100 men." Closer to the capital, "Another body of the Tahitians (about 1600) had taken post at Bunaroo with an outpost at Faa'a only 4 miles from Papeete. The post . . . was attacked about the same time by Capt. Bonard with 100 men. He was forced to retreat with a loss of 6 killed and himself and 18 wounded." And so it went. "On the 9th May, 1000 men supported by the steamer *Phaeton* started for the attack on Papenoo . . . on the 10th and 11th the first entrenchments were taken but the principal position of the natives was found too strong and after vain attempts for several days to force or turn it, the French retired to their fort at Pt. Venus. . . . In the affairs between the 9th and 15th the French lost about 100 men in killed and wounded—the natives about 20."

Months of stalemate and wretched skirmishing ensued. At the end, the French forces outmaneuvered the Tahitians at the valley of the Fautaua River with the aid of one Mairoto from the island of Rapa, whose mountaineering talents got the marines a commanding position on the mountain ridges. By this time, reported Martin, "The Tahitians are suffering from sickness, and very nearly in a state of famine, and no one can desire to see them hold out without a prospect or even a chance of success."[19]

Not charming romance, but political dissension, armed resistance, collaboration, fractured politics, and pitched combat thus characterized much of the first French history in the Society Islands and South Pacific. Not surprisingly, the military struggle and political turmoil only reinforced European notions that Polynesians were not capable of self-government and required the forces of "order" that a protectorate would bring to end the strife between the Pomare dynasty, colonists, missionaries, chiefs, and conflicting American, British, and French consuls. One correspondent for Juliette Adam's *Nouvelle Revue* conflated familiar narratives of paradise blamelessly despoiled in a piece "La France en Océanie" (1898) by beginning "The contact of Europeans has been fatal to these lands blessed by God." Predictably, this admission provokes not self-reflection, but a description of "complete anarchy, confusion of powers" in the islands, with the logical conclusion that "it was indispensable (in 1842) to create a strong authority, surveillance, and a police force."[20]

Still, "confusion of powers" would not have been a wrong description, for the French actions, while bringing new European violence, also enflamed long-standing island conflicts. Tahitians had their own interests collaborating with French forces in battling Marquesean enemies, and chiefs in the Leeward Islands also took advantage of the warfare to eliminate traditional rivals. Although Queen Pomare was properly lionized as a powerful symbol of resistance, it is well to remember that her family line had itself come to power in 1815 by defeating other islander parties, at times by ably employing arms, tactics, and ideologies (such as conquest in the name of Jehovah) adapted from European missionaries and other outlanders, including some of the original *Bounty* mutineers. The powerful chief Paraita early on cast his lot with the French protectorate against the queen and was named a disputed "regent" when Pomare went into self-imposed exile until 1847. With her own council divided, the queen frankly admitted, "I think they signed in order to take my power themselves."[21] Mairoto from Rapa was happy to aid the French marines against chiefs and villagers from Tahiti for a price. Conflicts also ran along religious and national lines—majority anglophone Protestants against francophone Catholics.

The wars were not strictly anti-European, nor should they be understood as simple imperialist versus native struggles. Yet the striking feature of this period, apart from its complexity, is its invisibility. Even French patriots—speaking only of their own imperial grandeur—lamented this historical absence almost immediately. There was no glorious "victory." Painter Charles Giraud, in Tahiti from 1842, was much impressed with the Fautaua campaign, and fashioned this account with a journalist after leaving the islands: "17 September 1846: The assault on the inaccessible fort! One of the highest feats of our national bravery and intrepidity. Search for a narration of it in books about the History of French Colonization: you will find it scarcely mentioned; not a page tells of this incredible achievement." To maintain "Tahiti," the romantic pastoral would triumph. The sort of Pacific history Giraud witnessed, was, as he put it, "almost completely forgotten."[22] As Bougainville, Loti, and Gauguin so well captured, French Polynesia would be a world fallen from grace to Christian (initially Anglo-Protestant) and commercial corruption—not one seized in the violent spasms of French empire; its story would be of love lost and languorous tragedy, not colonial warfare and conquest.

The long oblivion of Maohi resistance and the triumph of French paradise and tragic despoilment cannot be attributed to a lack of records, but to their control and disappearance into the literary and administrative apparatus of empire. Many of Pomare's letters to hoped-for allies among the British and Americans were intercepted by French agents and simply never reached their destinations. More critically, where protests could not be stolen, they could be pointedly transformed into accommodating narratives.

Here is where the work of writing the Pacific played such a critical role in French Oceanic Empire. The French narratives of the Tahitian takeover were solidly established within a generation. Charles-Victor Crosnier de Varigny's popular tome *L'Océan Pacifique* (1888) predictably relates the conflict in terms of Queen Pomare's "request" for a French protectorate—"Considering that we are unable to continue to govern by ourselves in the present state of affairs in a manner to conserve the good harmony with foreign governments"—and concludes with "Admiral Dupetit-Thouars accepted the request for a protectorate *sous réserve* of the decision of his government."[23]

France's best-known display of empire for European public consumption—the Colonial Exposition of 1931—featured a Tahitian exhibit and a published history of the islands by Queen Pomare's granddaughter, Princess Takau Pomare Vedel. Her story is compelling for the ways in which it both accommodates and subverts its own telling. For the most part, her official narrative apparently repeats the French view. "It was thus that certain native chiefs, judging the necessary imposition of a European protectorate demanded that of France. After various incidents and tergiversations of the queen, the colors of the French protectorate were raised at Tahiti on September 30, 1842 by rear-admiral Dupetit-Thouars."[24]

Pomare Vedel does briefly cite a Tahiti "divided into two parties" and a "new war" but suggests these only in terms of a battle for Fort Fautaua—with no suggestion of the meaning of the fighting. She then outlines the return of the queen from her self-imposed exile on Raiatea and moves quickly to "close this small historical summary." The story turns to Pomare Vedel's father, Pomare V, who abdicated in 1880 and died in 1891, and concludes "the island was thus definitively annexed to the colonial domain of France, and the Leewards came to be added in 1888." The last "came to be added" effectively erases the entire Leewards war from the official story. By contrast, note a British history which suggests, "Raiatea now belongs to France, but was not taken without serious opposition from the natives during which many houses were burned and enmities aroused."[25]

Perhaps most telling in Pomare Vedel's narrative is not even her words, but her framing. Her presentation is published as "Jadis" (times past); the "Aujourd'hui" (today) is written by Dr. Léon Sasportas, a specialist on eels and leprosy. Her world is that of the lineages; to him is left the real history. That history functions by displacing all Polynesian knowledge into mythology, thus transforming Tahiti into "the visiting place of God . . . it could not be other than Eden," a familiar trope. Recounting a "Maori legend," Sasportas suggests that the islands were created by the Almighty on the seventh day as a place of perfect repose for Himself. As for the islanders, "the fortunate humans who would be born and live there, most ignorant of their situation, called it Océanie."[26] That the islanders would live in apparent bliss, excluded from knowing their own past, is not completely unintentional in his ostensibly folkloric narrative.

Erasure of the protectorate and its violence was also abetted by Bougainvillean and literary-aristocratic notions of grand struggle with savages of a most noble variety. Where years of costly warfare could not be entirely ignored, popular press such as *L'Illustration* could summarize the conflicts and translate them into picturesque and honorable tales. In one report of a fierce siege of islander positions, the French commander encountered his chief opponent smiling at him on the battlefield and demanded an explanation. The warrior responded, "You would never have reached Fautaua unless I had wanted you to. . . . Remember that day when you were washing in the valley with your aide? For an hour that day I had you in my sights, and I wasn't alone!" "Ah, exclaimed the astonished Admiral, why didn't you kill me?" To this question, the chief raised his head proudly and brightened: "I would have been dishonored in the eyes of my men if I had killed, naked and by trickery, a chief like you."[27] The story is narrated in such a way as to disguise its own lack of meaning. It compliments the warrior (he is not a savage) by giving full expression to his gesture, yet simultaneously frames the exchange in terms of a warrior code of honor, a form of equanimity and respect that renders the war an almost gentlemanly air of unfortunate dispute. Rather than guerilla warfare, it is a grand battle in the mythic Napoleonic style.

Although French reporting thus attempted to fashion the battle for the Society Islands as a set of honorable aristocratic skirmishes, local voices played out the deeper sentiments of brutal—and unresolved—warfare that echoed throughout the islands. Both narrative and territorial dominion were highly unstable. In September 1849, Protestant Reverend John Muggridge Orsmond transcribed the epic *Encouagement aux indigènes Huahine qui vont aux combats* from a dictation by Apo of Atimaha on Moorea.[28] After Reverend Pritchard was forced out of the Society Islands, Orsmond replaced him as head of the Protestants in Tahiti. Less strident than his predecessor, Orsmond kept a low profile and accommodated the new authorities by continuing his ministry in Papeete and studying the local language and customs. Later he accepted a position as director of Native Affairs for the administration.[29]

Cultural translation was part of his mission, yet Orsmond did not handle the *Encouragement* epic simply as missionary ethnography; copies of the translation were kept by Commandant Charles Lavaud of the French Navy and posted to Paris, where naval officers concerned themselves with rebel movements in the islands. There was reason to worry: a French force had been wiped out in 1846 on Huahine, and sporadic warfare would also continue on Bora Bora and Raiatea for another forty years. Not until November 1897, with the capture of the Raiatean rebel leader Teraupoo, could the Chamber of Deputies in Paris proclaim "the victorious end of the last military campaign in our islands."[30]

Although Apo's tale is not specifically anti-French—it is ostensibly directed against Moorea's enemies throughout the islands, especially the Leewards—it is easy to understand why Commandant Lavaud treated it as a political rather than literary document. In allegorical fashion, Apo uses his voice in the *Encouragement* to mark the mythic birth and training of a warrior people, and to narrate their ultimate devastating destruction of foes. Allusions to both islander positions and French redoubt tactics are most evident in passages such as "let us attack their fort and destroy them . . . let our chiefs and our great ones lead us on." Yet more critically, the epic poses a counternarrative to the French story of peaceful accession to political authority in the Pacific or honorable expression of difference. Apo's language is appropriately unreconciled, "Let them be caught in the net / destroy them utterly / burn their house, let nothing remain / let our whole army unite all their ranks in overcoming and destroying them."

In spite of the forced protectorate in Tahiti, the struggle for an islander's victory clearly is not over, nor is Apo's rancor against the foe diminished. "Let us not regard the enemy / let us fight them, we are brave and do not fear them / they cannot overcome us, our anger is unabated." Apo's tale disrupts the narrative of protection around the Islands of Love. His story of the *Etablissements* even two years after the surrender of Papeete is little but a promise of relentless pursuit and conflict. "The Chief of the enemy has escaped us / we are sure to have war again / we have trodden on a slippery stone and must again prepare for war."[31] Rather than an empty history, the invocation of future wars profoundly underscores Apo's view of a dramatically incomplete struggle.

From the French side, naval reports suggest the unstable tensions of the ongoing war in the islands, yet they are inextricable from the most preciously crafted literary imagery. In 1869, Captain Michel Jouslard of the *Jules Hautefeuille* was directed by the Ministry of the Navy to make a reconnaissance of Tahiti. In his report, he rhapsodized about the "old reputation of this island, so blessed by nature which seems to make it an Eden." As we have seen, that reputation was "old" only in the sense that it relentlessly extended a Rousseauist literary past by colonizing a present evacuated of political history. Realities in the islands proved otherwise. Still, Jouslard seems almost astonished when he notes, "everything has changed . . . already for many years dissensions, rivalries, jealousies have been kindled."[32]

The Tahiti Jouslard found was divided between a settler colony protected by French military occupation and a scattered population of islanders strongly loyal to the authority of Queen Pomare. Resistance to French authority took multiple forms. Topographically, France in Tahiti was bounded by its trading and settler outposts, "beyond this enclosure our influence disappeared." For those who actually knew Tahiti, this was not news. Pomare tolerated but remained unreconciled to the French occupation, and could still stir resistance or bring local activity to a standstill. In his travel account of 1850, Jacques Arago had mocked the French governor, "You have blockhouses, forts, soldiers, cannons, and powder. Pomare, who has nothing but a hut next to your palace is more powerful than you."[33]

The French enclave defended its interests from a secure fortress, and Captain Jouslard looked upon Pomare's governance as akin to tyranny. "Foreigners are carefully kept isolated . . . all relations are subject to the strictest authorizations." The queen, he argued, was supported by a "vigorous system of surveillance and espionage; more than a third of the men act in step with police agents." Could this island really be Tahiti, the land of "penetrating charm, intense poetry, and enervating sweetness"? Jouslard's report bears testimony to disappointment and confusion generated by absent history. Tahiti, as always, seems fallen. Responsibility appears to lie with a corrupt and paranoid monarchy; "decline" from anterior Edenic states suits such narratives better than chronicles of open warfare, armed rebellion, and imperial domination.

Although he searched for the islands of love he knew from Europe, Jouslard found the Tahiti of French empire. He narrated Loti on "the breath heavy with seduction and sensual trouble which caresses this enchanted isle," yet had little choice but to report frankly on the prosaic institutions that made that imagination possible. If the French in Tahiti wrote themselves as sailors and artists craving sensuality and melancholic poetry, their privileged presence was framed by the bureaucrats and agents of Paris' system of knowledge and communication for controlling an empire.

Colonial assimilation itself appeared to be a site of contested authority. Within the French outposts, administrators and agents matched Pomare's subjects for intrigue. Jouslard reported on local civil servants educated and coopted into the regional administration and found them disappointing. In particular, he was dismayed to find that the petty *esprit fonctionnaire* was alive and well even in Papeete. Distant Tahiti was but a tedious example of the politics of a modern bureaucratic organization. Through the protectorate and annexation, the Service Indigène maintained a substantial payroll for its agents, including transcribers, interpreters, secretaries, teachers, honor guards, police, and pensioners. Many were district chiefs who benefited from colonial recognition and took full advantage of overlapping compensations, as Ariipeu a Hiro, for example, who was a local functionary and also president of the high court, or Ariituteamahine a Arato, who fulfilled duties both as a mounted escort and as a secretary.

Many enjoyed their posts while clearly keeping priorities other than those of the colonial administration in mind, evidenced by exasperated letters from the interior minister to district chiefs: "Why haven't you yet sent me the registers of the état-civil for your district? Execute the orders of the administration better," or "I am very discontented to note that you don't know how to make yourself obeyed by the inhabitants of your district." Or, on a matter of seized building materials, "there's nothing I can do. If the inhabitants paid their taxes this wouldn't happen."[34] Collaboration was both real and desultory, and locals continued to control much of the daily functioning of the territory.

Worse for the administration—going back to Jouslard's report—the mimic-like excellence with which some locals followed French procedure was almost a parody of the institution itself. "You would not believe the place in the lives of these employees which is taken up by questions of rank," the captain noted, commenting sourly on "the time they take up drafting notes and reports" about protocol and compensation while public business accumulated on desks and in stacks of cartons. In this case, becoming French seemed to work all too well. With palpable exasperation Jouslard concluded, "They have all truly taken on the administrative morals of our colonial agents."[35]

Meanwhile, the colonial agents at the Ministry of the Navy continued to fashion Tahitian history by writing and inscribing the islands into a form of administrative knowledge. As Jouslard's report indicates, even the petty squabbles that earned his ire were subject to drafts and reports. The circulation and registration of texts and documents were the life-blood of nineteenth-century administration and Empire. Naval archives stored endless messages from commanders, ministers, and section chiefs, often in the form of a "note circulaire," each stamped, numbered, and copied into departmental registers.

In Papeete, control of dossiers was the heart of French authority, an authority constantly under local pressure. When Tahiti was annexed in 1880, an official Maohi delegation demanded specific rights and protections from the former commandant Henri Isidore Chessé, Commissaire de la République en Océanie. The delegation demanded faithful execution of the annexation terms, a promise that goods and security would be respected (in particular against venal Europeans), the right to use the Tahitian language, and "the delivery to local districts of the registers of the *état-civil*, in order to mitigate expensive and annoying travel contrary to our interests."[36] Without the registers, no official business could be conducted, and no registers could be consulted without the populace making pilgrimages to the site of its archiving. As part of the demands to respect the new order of annexation in the islands, the local representatives requested minimally an accommodation in the relocalizing of the documents—a necessary part of negotiating administrative authority.

The Maohi continued to be vocal. Official representatives had specific ideas of "our interests," ranging from legal to cultural and language protections. At an 1881 legislative assembly of chiefs and deputies, Tahitian leaders expressed their frank dissatisfaction with European control over local justice. Their spokesman, Aitoa, remonstrated especially against the imposition of French legal codes. To allay tempers, the governor responded with a telling history lesson. "Our codes derive from an old society having its archives, its traditions, its needs, and its obligations; from a society of men having homes stacked one upon the other, lacking air and space, suffering from cold and hunger, living by the imperious law of work and need."[37] In seeking to justify his position the governor, perhaps unintentionally, established that it was France, an "old" nation, which had archives and traditions. Evoking the harshness of life in Europe to defend French law only reinforced the presumption that Tahiti was an idyllic place without suffering, work, or need.

In Paris, the Society Islands need not have history per se; the French possessions in Oceania could be reduced to summary information and evaluation by ministers and bureaucrats. While Loti served on French naval vessels in Tahitian waters, the land of his fevered passions and his love Rarahu was narrated as a set of administrative parameters for the naval ministry in Paris. The new Eden was divided into four rectilinear columns in ministerial ledgers, a system of knowledge shaped in ink and registers. The first demanded the origin and date of a given piece of information. The second asked for a brief explanation of the subject. The third proposed a short analysis. The fourth column was reserved for the "registration number and date of registration in the archives" of the information. For the calendar year 1872, for example, we find that "the situation in Îles-sous-le-vent is still the same." Or, "in Bora-Bora everything goes well." Or, "in Raiatea the situation has not changed."

Some disturbances are noted, usually at the diplomatic level, such as problems with abrogations of treaty agreements and with the suspicious presence of other European naval powers. Occasionally, the forgotten local history of the protectorate fitfully emerges, as one sees in some "resistance" by the locals to French jurisdiction due to inaction on difficulties with "bandits." Yet even where such documents were analyzed more fully, criticism of French colonial policy could remarkably serve the cause of improving imperialism—through love.

In his "La France en Océanie," *Nouvelle Revue* correspondent E. Watbled excoriated a pacification mission to Raiatea that, according to his reports, required the navy "to employ canon and fusillade, to kill, to wound, to sack and deport 500 rebels to restore calm." What most seemed to trouble him however was not the logic of rebellion nor loss of life, but a lack of administrators "who know how to make France loved by sympathies with which they know to surround themselves." Lauding the "successful" governance of Isidore Chessé, Watbled made clear that the navy's problems sprang from a subsequent failure to grasp imperial affection: political rule based on "a perfect understanding of the history, the morals, and the aspirations of Oceanic populations."[38]

He might have been speaking of a gendarme in the Tubai archipelago lauded in a report by his superior: "This gendarme . . . who represents our administration on this island, knew how to make himself loved by all. Intelligent, and of an upright and sweet character, he renders real service to the populations by his counsel." Such reports, as in Watbled's survey, mark empire as an alliance between power, knowledge, and sentiment, a project of rule whose mastery of local knowledge both defined and served the end "to make France loved."[39]

Colonialism itself is never called into question, only its proper expression and execution. Truly motivated popular resistance to European authorities is still absent from much reporting, and, as archival summaries liked to emphasize, "nothing has changed in the state of things."[40] Not all reports and ledgers were so vacuous, but all maintained the same imperious distance from peoples and events. As such, the islands remained as they should,

The Imperial Archive: Narrating empire in pen and ink.
Ship's log, *La Flore* at Easter Island (1872), South Pacific mission.
Source: Collection Christian Genet

in a general absence of temporality, awaiting the territorial and narrative decisions of the ministers and governors. In these reports, the only actions worthy of note seem to be those that relate transfers of authority—"French protectorate established by me at Rorotu, Rimatra, and Maria"—the part of empire that is *possession*.

One must look to personal entreaties to see the fractures in these narrations, such as that of the gendarme Auber in Rapa who wrote to his commander desperately seeking a transfer. "I regret my lieutenant, to be obliged to ask of you a change in residency," he apologizes, "but, despite all the efforts I have made and all the means I have taken, nothing has come of it." Facing disinterest in and resistance to his projects, he blamed the locals, coding the islanders "a population that, in order to succeed, one would have to handle rigorously, especially the young whose laziness makes them insolent." In this, he recognized the only true source of his authority: "the inhabitants have been awaiting ever since this report the arrival of a warship . . . but seeing none arrive until now, the little respect and fear they had for me has completely disappeared."[41] Here, the empire remained quite provisional. Likewise, instructions forwarded to incoming Etablissements Governor Morau in 1883 indicate the political and military organization behind the azure calm of the South Seas: "For a long time the most complete tranquility has reigned in the northwest group of the Marquesas. The presence of a resident and a brigade . . . is sufficient to maintain our sovereignty there."[42]

With stolen letters, ennobling battle propaganda, and administrative reduction, Tahiti's first half-century of French history was pacified. Yet these were not the only means by which the Etablissements were narrated into historical absence. The literary fashionings of Loti, Gauguin (his *Noa Noa*), the critic and novelist Victor Ségalen (*Les Immémoriaux*, 1907), and a score of journalists, captains, and colonial officials were in many ways institutional extensions to administrative procedure. Great works of art and literature functioned within an administrative network that erased Tahitian political history by conflating somber and exotic images with authority and authorship. Ségalen was a naval doctor, Gauguin a French colonial. France dominated by the force of Dupetit-Thouars and Chessé, and by the authority of its production of love, mystery, and beauty.

Well into the twentieth century, Loti especially remained a singular voice for things Tahitian. One writer, Pierre Benoit in 1933 exclaimed, "Tahiti seems to have risen from the Ocean solely to justify the vision of a poet of genius . . . at Angkor, at Brousse, at Nikko, I have understood the difficulty of describing a landscape already evoked by Loti. But, in Tahiti, this difficulty becomes a complete impossibility."[43] What literary production and reputation produced were not only the author and his texts but the author *as* text. As Loti wrote his islands into being, his own life story became the template for local history through the labors of his biographers. In 1926, Edward D'Auvergne's *The Romance of a Great Writer* reiterated Loti's attraction to "the spell of the South Seas" and proposed an unintentional truth, "The islands have no history, or none, rather, has been transmitted to us." Other biographies detailed the travels of Loti and his brother to Polynesia, while marking a Tahiti "which had become a French protectorate in 1843 at the request of Queen Pomare IV, who feared annexation by the English." Such casual misinformation, so incidental to the centrality of a distinguished author's life, is rendered almost invisible as imperial consciousness. These accounts were clearly unable to consider documents from the queen's chiefs and advisers, as Tati and Utami's joint declaration, "The French consul did truly dictate and write the letter said to be written by Queen Pomare and her governors requesting the protection of the King of the French."[44]

Loti and his literary influence were inescapable throughout the extended colonial struggles. As anti-French resistance spread from Tahiti in the 1840s to other islands and to the Leewards long into the 1890s, some French reporters took to attributing their own lack of military success precisely to the dominance of his literary narratives. About the Raiatean rebel leader Teraupoo, René La Bruyère commented, "Why don't we force him by main strength of arms to give up? It is because the officers of the Naval Division are repugnant to shed the blood of a race as sympathetic as the Malayo-Polynesian." La Bruyère clearly did not consider French military field reports that boasted, "a few discharges of repeating fire produced a very murderous effect." Rather, he suggested, "For a long time, in accord with the custom described by Loti, the officers have contracted unions with the women of the country . . . nothing is more charming than this sensual and sentimental idyll."[45] Dominant narratives not only described but also shaped, abetted, and restrained the possibilities of history in the islands for both islander and European.

The conflict with Teraupoo was indeed heavily invested with and finally concluded on marital notes. In his personal journal, the governor in Papeete mused about the rebel leader, "It is not he, what's more, who has created the most trouble for us on Raiatea. It is [his wife] the queen . . . who demands, orders, and menaces." Political writers called her "even more fanatic" than he; upon capture, both were exiled to Noumea. Such reports fixed on the notion of married couples for their meanings; the clan and kinship networks that had sustained the rebels were ignored. For the wives of rebels in the Marquesas who had a choice about exile, French communiqués noted with some satisfaction, "The wives were consulted to know whether or not they wished to accompany their husbands. But the reception they had to this proposition was rather cold, only twenty (out of several hundred) leaving with their children."[46] With such indifferent spouses, it seemed, this had not truly been a common struggle of devotion and sacrifice.

Marriage" and liaison as sentimental idyll à la Loti triumphed. Armed resistance faded and sensuality and sentimentality were transmuted into an ascendant narrative of togetherness. Kept from the restricted political realities of the Tahitian monarchs, what other than a love story could one make from the official rhetoric of King Pomare V, ceding his final authority to France in 1880: "I transfer my rights to France, that is to say, all the guarantees of propriety and liberty which you have enjoyed under the government of the protectorate . . . our resolution, I am sure, will be received with joy by all those who love Tahiti and who sincerely wish for progress. We have all already been French in our hearts, now we are in fact."[47]

The cession was at once a statement of affinity and resignation—joy and love framed by surrender to French and Oceanic "progress." This narrative trajectory of change—and necessary loss—haunted the islands, swallowing up the Tahitian history of the nineteenth century. Through their own investiture as culture producers, even sympathetic chroniclers such as Gauguin and Victor Ségalen manufactured and complemented a created longing for a corrupted race and its destroyed traditions. Gauguin's heavy-handed journalistic polemics to protect Tahitian and Marquesan islanders from colonial abuse barely register against the high visibility of his paintings of mystery and melancholy. Within a cultural and administrative dialectic, "Tahiti" was narrated into and out of existence. Ségalen's own Tahitian tale, *Les Immémoriaux*, is told through a Polynesian character, Terii, who loses his role as keeper of clan memory to written texts and encroaching European Christian "civilization." *Les Immémoriaux*—the title suggests "those without memory"—gives center stage to questions of broken oral narrative and signs of collapsing tradition and heritage. In Paris, *L'Illustration* presented such sentiments as the end of Tahitian history: "The memory of men, and especially that of princes and of priests was the only vehicle through which their past could come up to now. As far as the language which conserves these traditions, the savant language of Tahitians, it becomes less and less understandable every day for the natives themselves." A dying orature was a fault and tragedy of Europe itself. "It is to the Europeans and especially to the French that it is necessary to attribute the weakening of this sentiment of which we can just barely recover what remains."[48]

By simultaneously recording and enclosing subject peoples, such reports followed an exquisite logic of conquest that allowed putative destroyers to take upon themselves the historical burdens of "dying" peoples. In this, Europeans became champions and keepers of testimonies to regrettable demise—witnesses to history passing from a state of enchantment to one of corruption. Evil emanated not from colonial violence and struggle, but contact itself. Such melancholy tales were transposed to the places of love Bougainville had made famous: Polynesian bodies and faces. Captain Jouslard only reiterated stereotypes by lamenting "this Tahitian race at one time so beautiful, already fallen," thus conflating a narrative of erotic charm with that of historical extinction. No wonder the "melancholic" look was so powerful in the imagination of the French Pacific—as Loti had done with Rarahu, talking about it was a sensual and beautiful way of saying "doomed."

The constant return to the somber beauty of the race thus says much, and Gauguin's languid, searching faces and earthy bodies were only the most famous French records of Tahitian physiognomy. Most significantly, the Polynesian *regard* interested the clinical anthropologists at the Paris École d'Anthropologie, who worked from skulls, reporting, "the front of the face is elongated, oval, and well-proportioned," and, despite a primary interest in measurement of the cephalic indices (average 88.4 for men, 92 for women), they couldn't help noting, "The physiognomy has something particular about it which strikes all who see Polynesians, and especially Polynesian women, for the first time." Measurements aside, the École published a report as poetic as a Gauguin canvas, lingering over "the expression of a calm melancholy that carries through the entire expression, a certain softness of regard and of the voluptuous in the lips of the women. It is difficult to define this *expression sympathique*, but one recognizes it right away."[49]

The attention to the "calm melancholy" of faces was rooted in the nostalgic beauty of extinction: expiration of the loved one. The resulting litany of regret was almost unbearably formulaic. François Guillot, a gendarme posted to Papeete, lamented, "What now for the happy ones? Surely before the arrival of Europeans, the Maoris lived in perfect happiness, being without ambition. Civilization has destroyed their happiness." The explorer and geographer Jules Garnier suggested, "We can attend the rapid invasion of the entire Earth by our race and our civilization; already in Oceania the first inhabitants are leaving their place to us and vanishing." The future French president Paul Deschanel intoned equally about "the decadence which our appearance in these waters has singularly hastened, which we may be able to contain in certain times and places, but not stop." As for the Polynesians, "[the race] is condemned to die, and it is Europe that will inherit its vast domains."[50]

The Polynesians did not die out, and they and the Europeans assimilated each other. French authority continues in the Society Islands, yet a century after Deschanel's dire predictions it is the notion of "French" itself that is redefined within the boundaries of a "Tahiti métisse" of Polynesian, Asian, European and *demi* communities. There is a monument to Loti along the Fautaua River outside Papeete; another for the twentieth-century nationalist leader Pouvanna a Oopa sits in front of the Territorial Assembly. Both the exoticist and the anticolonial activist are celebrated and have unresolved legacies in the islands. Polynesian navigation, art, and custom are promoted under the purview of French territorial administration. Tahitian has been an official political language since 1980.[51]

A century and a half earlier, a short account of Polynesia, *O-Taiti*, by one Henri Lutteroth, had proposed "the printing-press, which we only had after a thousand years, they've had after a thousand days, and the *Evangile* was the first Tahitian book." Strikingly, yet consistent with the making and unmaking of modern Tahitian history, he continued, "But after growth comes decadence, and as everything comes to [the Polynesians] on ships, the good as well as the bad, it is also the sea which brings corruption, intrigue, controversy and conquest."[52] Lutteroth published his work in 1843, as Dupetit-Thouars was landing.

Another story of words and memory, spoken in the same year, poses another narrative to consider. Here, in a meeting with Queen Pomare, the Tahitian chiefs, led by Arahu, themselves ponder the history come to their shores. "My dear friends, I ask you to be attentive to the words of the queen, to that which the admiral has said in his letter, and to the instructions given in strong voice by [British representative] Sir Thomas Thompson and the captain of the queen's warship, the *Talbot*; also to the terms of the threatening letter of the leaders of France." At stake is an *Immémoriaux* variation: "Nothing must be forgotten . . . listen attentively to what these letters say; no reflections out loud, no misplaced words. Do not express any opinion—listen now to the spokesman for the queen."[53] It is a moment of configuration: speaking and silence, remembering and imagining consequences to come, writing the history of Tahiti and Tahitian archives.

FIVE &

NEW CALEDONIA

Prisoners of Love

In 1900, the French had been in New Caledonia almost half a century. They had established a notorious penal colony, agricultural settlements, and the largest industrial nickel-mining concession in the world. They also had opposed revolts, a major rebellion against the indigenous Kanak in 1878, and political and economic strife with the British and Australians. Yet, for one Clement Wragge, an English meteorologist out of Brisbane, New Caledonia was less a stronghold of strategic and economic power than of a certain idea of France—and Frenchness. On a tour of the Caledonian Islands to establish weather data collection, Wragge's first observations focused on the deported denizens of what he rather artfully called "The Prison Island."

As he came ashore, a convict band played mournful tunes down at the Place des Cocotiers, and their conductor captured his attention. Forbidden by the gendarmes to speak to the prisoner, Wragge simply invented the man's life history for his readers. Drawing on an inference that the prisoner was a renowned music teacher in France, Wragge proposed "an affaire d'honneur, a fit of passion and presto! He shot a paramour, a lover of his wife." Maddened by her dishonor, he would say, "I did it. In blind fury and with reeling brain I killed that man, cut out his treacherous heart, cooked it as an entrée over a slow fire, and forced my Babette to eat the morsel for supper. . . . Pity me, you who reck of the power of Love; I loved her madly, and madness seized me."[1]

Wragge contrasted his British heritage ("'Duty first,' that is an Englishman's maxim," he offers) by describing something he thought profoundly Gallic. Even at an antipodean remove from Europe, the logic of his New Caledonia was that of an assuredly French sensibility—crimes and punish-

Uncertain sympathies: "Here is what you have left us."
Kanak families, French colonials.
Source: Archives de la Nouvelle Calédonie, SANC

ments of love; passionate, treacherous, ferocious, and mad love. Perhaps he also thought that Frenchmen condemned to the South Pacific should have cannibal tendencies, even while crediting the murderer with a typically thoughtful attention to his cuisine. Wragge's reliable and enthusiastic stereotyping reminds us of the complicated exoticisms that marked the European presence in the Pacific, of which "the French" were one.

How can we disentangle the assumptions behind this penal-administration version of French *amour*? One familiar with the inseparability of love, power, and New Caledonia was Juliette Adam, whose close associates, like the dramatic leftist deputy and journalist Henri Rochefort, were exiled to the penal colony following the Paris Commune of 1871. Although resigned to her friend's sentence, Adam interposed herself directly in deportation politics, using her political connections and the sentiment of her "most persuasive voice" to remind the supervising Commander Launay "how it would be serious for you if our friend should die en route." Greatly moved by Madame's grace, attention, and importance, Launay promised her "my total devotion." Adam and Rochefort kept an extensive correspondence throughout his exile and imprisonment.[2]

In her long editorial career at the *Nouvelle Revue* Adam also presented many critical pieces on love and literature, philosophy, history, and politics, which go to the heart of Wragge's imaginative story. One she edited for a *Revue* of 1899, Louis Proal's "Les Crimes d'amour," is an essay with a striking set of definitions. "In the majority of crimes of passion, the love which is the decisive factor is not other than the desire of possession, the failure to not have gotten, or the rage of having lost. The ferocity of murderous love arises not only from the violence of passion, but also the exasperation of offended pride [amour-propre]."[3]

Unlike Wragge's merely pathological romance, Proal frames his crimes of passion within a language of French imperial ideology: the desire for possession and the exigencies of pride. Colonies, like Loti's collections, were French possessions, and military imperialists like Admiral Du Petit-Thouars and Francis Garnier claimed territories for glory in responses to "insults to the flag." Read as an implicated tale of French Pacific empire, Wragge's passionate French murderer is a truthful stereotype—the criminal whose own love story is a recapitulation of his jailer's project: to act out the "desire of possession" and to declare his honor.

The counterpart of Wragge's delirious love was its mad cannibalism. The parallelism of the two is an amusing take on what was, in fact, the dominant French representation of New Caledonia throughout the nineteenth century. The naval officer Victor de Malherbe remarked on Kanak "cannibals" as he made a tour of New Caledonia in 1859, and said of the local chiefs, "Justice is swiftly rendered; the only penalty is death . . . the most frequent crimes are adultery and murder, the second often as consequence of the first."[4] The conflation of love, sex, and murder was already a transposable French narrative by the time of Wragge's melodrama. As the historian Alice Bullard has keenly argued, such violence, tied to notions of cannibalism and hence "savagery," were constituent discourses for the Melanesian Islands, widely employed to frame the local Kanak peoples as degenerate and bestial, qualities also attributed to members of the Paris Commune who were deported and exiled there.[5]

In fact, not only Kanaks and Communards but also debates about Pacific possessions in general were framed by elaborating savage love stories. In an 1888 survey of South Pacific islands, Charles Victor Crosnier de Varigny argued, "Each of the European races has its own mode of colonization . . . the battle in Oceania is between England, personifying the spirit of conquest, the substitution of the white for the native race, and France, in which is incarnated a profoundly human genius that allows two distinct races to live side by side on the same soil." Empire itself provided the opportunity for defining "Frenchness." Denouncing the crass force of England and its lost colonies (they destroyed the Australian aborigines and the Americans revolted), de Varigny presented the superior fidelity of "our most beautiful possessions": "In which of its former colonies does the name of France raise such rancor and inimities? The name still makes the hearts of loyal Canadians and grateful Indians beat faster."[6] Compared to the "brutal conquest and systematic destruction" of the British, France, he claimed, forged an empire of civilization and devotion.

&

Love and savagery were the twin powers that defined and inscribed the French imperial project through narratives of possession, pride, and defense of civilization in the territories. Henri Rochefort related the impact of these assumptions in his letters to Juliette Adam—although, as a restricted prisoner, he was somewhat skeptical about who the true savages were: "Today they declared to us that if we have not been sent to the main island it is because we would be eaten . . . leaving us the unique alternative of dying of hunger, isolation and sadness, or of ending up in the belly of a cannibal." A more spirited Rochefort also jokingly boasted, "My beauty, my youth, and my freshness provoked such a passion in a young girl of eighteen that I had to call on all of my principles of father and wise man to resist."[7]

In New Caledonia, the policies of governors and functionaries were organized around Rochefort's twin evocations: the management of savagery and the fashioning of love—even to the suggestion of fatherhood, ultimately in the name of the French nation. Specifically this took two complementary forms: the remaking of local Kanak peoples into workers, and transformation of base European men and women—convicts or poor whites—into colonists and patriots. A diligent Kanak labor force and European farming plots would develop Noumea as the "center of economic attention for the French islands of Polynesia," while materializing "the dream of creating, at the antipodes of Europe, a small New France, peopled, like the great one, with small property owners living from the fruit of their land, their prairies, their vines."[8] Policies of expropriation and "cantonnement" of the Kanak on reservations were central to these intentions. Transferring expropriated lands to European colonists would realize the governors' projects of supporting the key institution in which, presumably, heartfelt loyalty overlapped with economic production: the French peasant family household.

Weaknesses of the plan were legion: inexperienced cultivators, lack of capital, restricted markets, unproductive terrains. The obviously poor quality of support—and more than a few of the participants—doomed many farming plots. Impoverished immigrants, released convicts, day laborers from other Pacific colonies were, and had perhaps always been, a wishful base for evolving a new civil community.

Still, the legal privilege of even hapless white concessionaires dictated that basic explanations for failure ultimately turned to unsuccessful labor integration of the Kanak peoples. With familiar exasperation, an 1885 colonial bureau report complained, "The Canaque of New Caledonia is naturally indolent and resistant to all work of long duration. His desires are restricted and he has no need to work to satisfy them." Europeans thus faced a regular shortage of laborers for farms and mines, and governors worried over instability in the colony. "Every day the *demandes* are addressed to an administration that cannot satisfy them."[9] Economic policy is here clearly framed by attempts to manage "satisfaction," and based on practical assumptions that the "désirs restreints" of the Kanak, which allowed cavalier independence, would have to be reconfigured into economic and moral need forged from necessary work, debt, and compensation within a commercially viable labor system. The administration of desire would be integral to colonialism.

For the intents and purposes of the administration, both the rude colonists and the Kanak could be savages, yet both were capable of civilization and had to be instructed or coerced into proper values as subjects. The governor's task was to outline the boundaries and possibilities of each. For white settlers, the model of instruction was a moral community of work.

Perhaps the best-known articulation of this philosophy as policy was the "phalanstery" of New Caledonian Governor Charles Guillain (1808–1875), who established himself in the islands in June 1862 under the sign "to civilize, to produce, to rehabilitate." A devotee of the utopian socialist Charles Fourier and of Saint-Simonian principles, Guillain promoted an enlightened technocracy, establishing offices for native affairs, bridges and roads, civil documents, land surveying, and the first official journal to report government business. Guillain's zeal for innovation illustrates the role of New Caledonia as a testing ground for projects and fictions of transformation that might have been impossible to realize back in France.

Guillain's most famous work remains the phalanstery he championed at Yaté in 1864, three hundred hectares of farms and workshops populated by small cadres of miners, ironworkers, mechanics, papermakers, stonemasons, carpenters, merchants, bakers, and agricultural workers. Under the direction of farmer and brickmaker Narcisse de Grasville (called Leloup) in the role of "father of the family," the colonists were intended to become a self-sufficient community of work, charity, and abundance on the model of Fourier's utopian socialism. No breakaway group, this was a project of French bureaucracy itself, as Guillain made a bit overly clear in his opening harangue to the colonists: "And so, pioneers of the association in New Caledonia! The government has taken measures to facilitate your establishment and will applaud all of your progress. Go on! The colony accompanies you with its wishes and exhorts you, Courage!"[10]

At the beginning, ideals seemed realized, with even the Kanaks getting good press. Wrote one lieutenant of the infantry Mariene Bourgey, "The attitude of the Canaques is very peacable . . . the natives enthusiastically bring the colonists fish, vegetables, pigs, and chickens . . . understanding and harmony preside over all social relations." Such reports were colored by what one Guillain scholar has called "the assimilationist ideal of Saint-Simonian colonization, hostile to brutal conquest." Guillain himself stated the clear conflation of politics, empire, and love in 1863: "It is not the policy of expedition and military occupation I plead here. It is simply the policy of organization and civilization, that pacific policy which consists of good relations with the natives, making us known and loved of them while advising and guiding them in their own interest."[11]

For the European colonists, labor, community, and abundance were to be their rewards, and, at least initially, "stimulated by the richness of the soil granted them, they work with an uncustomary ardor." Time did not bear out this idyll. Lack of investment, organization, and a series of disasters, including a major fire, shattered the community. The geographer Jules Garnier would be among the later visitors to write Yaté's epitaph: "Within one or two years they harshly separated, filled with defiance, bitterness, and hatred against each other, not only ruined, but in debt." The abandoned community became a sort of pilgrimage site for melancholy. In 1878 Charles Lemire reported on "the orange trees and blackberry vines and rose bushes, the ruins of shacks and brick ovens that recall the phalanstery attempt," while another writer pondered "the miserably perished sort of communist phalanstery founded under such strange conditions."[12]

Despite these setbacks, the government did not give up. In its role as the nation, the French state continued to take upon itself the task of creating the households it wanted. If a voluntarist social utopianism was impractical, perhaps an obligatory family-state model fashioned on ascendant bourgeois ideology might yet succeed. This would require moral and patriotic instruction in domestic values centered around matrimony, private property, child-rearing, and small-scale production. Capitalizing on the islands' status as a penal colony, colonial ministers mandated liaisons, partnerships, and marriages to convicts and ex-convicts, seeking to create families and thereby engender paternal, maternal, and domestic affection and solidarity in the name of patrie and empire.

The archives of ministries serving the Caledonian project are rich with the evidence of projects to entice, coerce, and otherwise barter women in the service of colonialism. Communications from 1872 between the Ministry of Interior and the Naval Ministry observe that "the number of the transported to New Caledonia provisionally released with authorization to establish an industrial or agricultural employment increases day by day. It seems . . . indispensable to second the efforts of these men and to allow them even to be able to establish a family." To this end, the ministries concurred with a directive "that new convoys of female prisoners be directed to the colony." A report from the director of penitentiary administration neatly summarized the issue: "This is our solemn hour; let us with every means at our disposal put women on the farm and children in the house. We can have no more illusions: women, or no colonization."[13]

From Louis Napoleon's Second Empire through the Third Republic, the state directly involved itself in creating matches and families, working assiduously even with French communal governments. The Naval Ministries in Paris sent orders to local mayors and councils asking for their cooperation with the colonial project. A letter to the Mayor of Vernon in 1867 read, "I request that you let me know as soon as possible if the woman Barat agrees to go and rejoin her husband. In this case, she will be transported free of charge from her domicile to New Caledonia and will receive before her departure the sum of fifty francs for herself and twenty-five for each of her children."[14]

Departments kept files on all recipients of such largess, made reports on other likely candidates, and looked for the sort of ideal family groups that would make successful colonists out of redeemed deportees and transportés. One separated woman was judged "robust, full of energy and health. Living in the country, she knows all the details of agricultural life." Better yet, she could apparently bring an entire industrious brood with her. "Her stepson . . . is a journeyman mason of the first order and very hard working. Her young son, aged fifteen has just finished his apprenticeship as a locksmith." Even her youngest daughter, although still being schooled, "works very ably at sewing." The government set up deals with the railways to make reunification of families even easier. An order of July 1869 from the *Service général* to the stationmasters of the Charentes decreed, "From the 15th of this month, the families of prisoners on their way to join their head of household in the penitentiary colonies shall be transported at half-price. To obtain the benefit of this reduction, the families of the prisoners should present a certificate [from] the Ministry of the Navy and Colonies." Family history was shaped to administrative visions of a carefully articulated household.[15]

Every aspect of policy related to confirming future colonists could be subjected to some management of affections. In July 1873 the Ministry of Colonies at Paris consulted with the governor of New Caledonia on the standing policy of forbidding family members from accompanying condemned husbands, sons, or brothers to the docks. Seeing that prisoners tended to become despondent at the moment of exile, he suggested, "It could be that the presence of the family . . . keeps up the courage of the transporté better." These last moments, if well managed, might encourage prisoners to think of themselves as colonists building new lives, and to entice loved ones to follow. To test his theory, the minister noted "I authorized a certain number of women to attend the departure." Whether the minister's experiment succeeded is unknown. We do know that Juliette Adam obtained such special permission to bring Henri Rochefort's children to see him at the moment of departure, and that Rochefort's final words to them were, "I promise you that I'll escape."[16]

In fact, Rochefort kept his promise, making a sensational escape by boat to Australia with other members of the Commune and the collusion of an English ship's captain. In a popular account of his weeks in Australia (he vied with fellow escapee Paschal Grousset to publish first) Rochefort retained an oddly sentimental view of the South Seas; he never tired of retelling tales of local history as amusing love stories. Port Jackson, for example, was purportedly first seen by a young, crazed mariner chasing a native woman to a hilltop. Whereas Rochefort's host considered this origin tale a "grand humiliation for the crown of England," Rochefort himself demurred, "It is probable that another great power [that is, France] would close its eyes to the indiscretion of this sailor, and would declare that, to have Australia at that price, is really not much at all." The 1845 gold rush is brightly related as having begun with the shepherd MacGregor engraving the name of his sweetheart on what he at first thinks is a rock. And, in keeping with his "French" self-image, Rochefort described his prison-ship crossing an Australian reef having "the flattering aspect of a corset whose cords are lovingly cut by the prow of our vessel."[17]

Rochefort's journalistic vision was supported by his well-connected friends. Records of the inquiry that followed the escape show that the costs for hiding the stowaways and subsequently gaining them passage to Fiji, the United States, and on to London were not borne by sympathizers in the antipodes. The colonial entrepreneur Higginson noted that twenty-five thousand francs had been sent to Rochefort from Paris by the banker and senator Edmond Adam. "Rochefort telegraphed from a (Sydney) bank to Monsieur Adam, and the money arrived by intermediary to a branch office. The amount was provided, it appears, by Madame Adam, Perrin, and V. Hugo. Madame Adam is the guardian of Rochefort's children."[18]

With such friends, Rochefort never had to imagine bringing his family to the Pacific. But over decades others would. Before New Caledonia was annexed in 1853, political prisoners also were sent to Polynesian islands. The sensual mystery of Paul Gauguin's later "escape" to paradise contrasts with such cases as that of Edouard Bellmare, relegated to the Society Islands with the government's injunction, "this individual should not be allowed to return to France and should remain interned in Tahiti" for an attack on Napoleon III. Some cases strikingly capture the strategic deployments of affection in colonial policy. One M. Longomazino, condemned for plotting against the government at Lyon, was exiled to the Marquesas. His wife's remarkable plea to the Interior Minister to rejoin her husband shows her sure grasp of the administrative vocabulary of love and family. "Aware of your well-known humanity and above all your paternal love, [I] dare to hope that you will grant my request, because you will not fail to ignore how much the love of family influences the opinion of a miserable prisoner." The Ministry happily granted her request, and its own reports of the family's subsequent internment, are in turn, Oceanic idylls: "The gendarme accompanies the children on a walk. He distributes fruits and fish. The gendarme accompanies the son on a walk. He distributes bananas sent by the commandant."[19]

What is certain is that in Pacific empire, emotion and administration were tightly intertwined. At times, views openly conflicted. One Admiral Ribourt filed reports to the Ministry of the Navy and Colonies in Paris suggesting that "the transported [prisoner] should not be able to write but once a month to his family. Correspondence suitably controlled will have a good influence." But other records indicate that, although prisoners may have been the condemned of the French state, prompt delivery of communications and sympathetic satisfaction were important to the bureaucracy. Prisoners called letters from France their lifeline and only hope. Undelivered mail and checks resulted in pressure from the minister of colonies at Versailles in his dispatches to the governor of New Caledonia. "I have received numerous reclamations concerning the tardy delivery of letters and postal-orders addressed by an intermediate of my department to the prisoners in New Caledonia. The families of these individuals complain. I would be very obliged for you to give orders that each prisoner receive letters and packages addressed to him as quickly as possible."[20]

⚘

Where communications alone were unsatisfactory, or families resistant to emigration, the French state would manufacture new couples. Condemned women were sent to the South Pacific as prisoners, not just to serve out terms but as prisoners uniquely targeted for marriage with liberated male former convicts. The governor at Noumea filed regular reports to Paris, such as an 1873 memo indicating "all of the female prisoners have been received with all the precautions demanded by their sex and their position." The important part of the report is however the governor's obviously proud declaration that "of fifty women come to the colony, thirty-four have already contracted marriage, two more are authorized to do so, and the majority of these households live rather comfortably." In establishing its plans for housing the female convicts transported to New Caledonia, the Ministry of Colonies envisioned "about one hundred women and ten to twelve Catholic sisters to watch over them. Although this penitentiary ought to be absolutely isolated from that of the men, it is useful that it be as little distant from the locale of the released prisoners working concessions, in order to facilitate marriages."[21]

The project was never terribly successful. As Johannes Caton, deported communard to the Isle of Pines, wrote in his diary, "Poor girls, to be thus sacrificed without having committed any crime except to lack family or to have been abandoned. The government hopes that a good number of deportees will offer to marry them and try to constitute families of colonists who will stay definitively. This hope will be disappointed."[22] No deportee, he believed, would marry under such conditions and most still dreamed of returning to

France. He was generally correct. Although couples were formed, prisoner marriages never had a great impact on the colony, and governors still looked longingly to successful free immigration to fulfill their projects.

When prisoner marriages did not work, there was always the possibility of Frenchmen trying to appropriate local women. Proponents of colonialism through intermarriage openly decried the distance taken by male prisoners from Kanak women and vice versa. Part of the savage and backward reputation of the Melanesian islands directly followed from constant comparison with Polynesia, where the Bougainville legacy inscribed women of open and easy sexuality. In his detailed 1895 study of New Caledonia, geographer Augustin Bernard noted, "Melanesians and Polynesians . . . the former regarded as degraded, the latter covered with praise. The origin of this prejudice is not difficult to see: the Polynesians are very sociable and libertine; the voyagers to whom they offered their women could not avoid thanking them with a few words of eulogy."[23]

Tahitians were especially attractive for appearing eager to couple with European men, even if this was primarily based on establishing claims of social and political alliance with the outsiders and within complex Polynesian status ranks. Locally based Melanesian clans had no such general system for circulating women politically, disappointing the erotic imagination of the French. One commentator particularly lamented that such behavior would "deprive our colonists of resources available in other countries," and New Caledonia developed as a territory where women, as opposed to Polynesian beauties, were "ugly" and "bestial."[24]

Circulation of women, if not Melanesian, was certainly colonial policy, and female bodies were made equivalent commodities across French empire. Colonial development projects around Noumea could be rendered commensurable as local expressions of an empire-wide politics of sex and sentiment. Thus, imperial ministries tied Caledonian policy to projects in other colonies, especially penal institutions in Algeria and Guyana, where the reluctance of local populations did not exhaust the possibilities of the colonial governments for forging matches.[25]

Noting the multiethnic populations of prisoners under the empire, the minister of colonies in 1878 opened discussions with the director of colonies in Paris about the introduction into the colonies, where appropriate, of "women of Algerian, Cochinchine, and Senegalese origins in order to contract marriages with the prisoners of these different countries." The correspondence even noted, "This is not the first time that this department has taken up this question which touches both Arab and Annamite. Already in 1875 and 1876 this subject was raised about Algeria and Cochinchine."[26] At Guyana in particular, the Ministry of Colonies requested from Paris special action on the Senegalese population. The director wrote, "I would be very obliged to you for seeing whether in the free population or in prisons you could not find Yolof women who would agree to go to Guyana to contract marriages with their compatriots."[27]

Similar arrangements also were proposed to stabilize the male populations of New Caledonia, although, for non-Europeans, a logic of limited contract was often enforced. New Caledonian governors came to depend upon the close relation of their islands to the New Hebrides, and satisfied bureaucrats reported, "New Caledonia recruits immigrants from the New Hebrides and neighboring archipelagos . . . her inhabitants are active, intelligent, and adapt quickly to different sorts of work." The Hebrides, they thought, would provide the *main-d'oeuvre* to build the southern oceanic empire. Yet, although colonial reports concurred that "everyone uses the *Néo Hébridais*: the bureaucrat, the trader, the farmer, the coffee grower," Eromangans and Tannese were regularly engaged by bosses precisely because migrant or indentured recruit workers could be paid minimal sums, had few clan and family obligations, and—unlike the Kanak—had no home village to which to flee if discontent.[28]

For Europeans, by contrast, creating "home" was exactly the point. The supposed salutary responsibilities of child rearing, secure familial love, and property ownership were strongly encouraged as the administration continued to weave its hopes for colonial settlement principally around creating peasant farmers with bourgeois values in the bush. For Europeans, this project had been established as a primary assumption of the penal colony from the beginning, as one deputy noted in 1854, "the legislature offers to the condemned the recompenses to provoke his return to a better condition. The convict will be able to have a land concession, to marry, to become head of a family, to exercise certain civil rights. In exercising these rights, he will learn to respect those of others. Head of a family, he will find his dignity as a man; Christian, he will find touching consolations in religion."[29]

Redeemed, the convict and family would establish themselves like resourceful free colonists, of the sort so glowingly embellished in Caledonian memoirs by Hélène Lainé: "The bush cleared, land is ploughed ready for corn, while coffee is planted in shady places and a herd of cattle imported which quickly seems to acclimatize itself. The courageous women set themselves to brighten their primitive homes, making them as comfortable as circumstances permit."[30] Lainé's burnished tale makes clear a critical point: the domain of the household and the role of the woman were all-important as indicators of true colonial success.

It is fair to say that Lainé, a third-generation immigrant Caledonian, or "Caldoche," very much imagined New Caledonia in registers of domestic romance. In introducing the governorship of Admiral Amédée Courbet (1880–1882), she proposed, with frank simplicity, to "set aside the history of events to plunge into the history of hearts." The sentimental recounting of the admiral's arrival and flirtation with the author's mother as *jeune femme* is overtly charming and deceptively ideological.

Best known as the commander of the French naval squadron in the Gulf of Tonkin during the height of colonial debates in Paris, Courbet was widely admired by the left for his duty to republican policy, and the right for his famously devout Catholicism. When he died of fever during the Tonkin campaign, his body was sent on a long, reverential pilgrimage back to France on the flagship *Bayard*. He was the first colonial figure to be given a state funeral by vote of the republic; it featured dual rites: one an official ceremony at the Invalides in Paris, and a second religious service in his hometown of Abbeville orated by Bishop Freppel.[31] Courbet's untimely death in 1885 allowed both republicans and royalist conservatives—especially Catholic mission supporters—to rally around French colonialism even while bringing down the government of Prime Minister Jules Ferry. The admiral's image as a man of rigorous honor, heartfelt passion, and unshakable devotion made him an imperialist whom all parties could find attractive.

For a man who carried out the directives of Jules Ferry, was adored by Pierre Loti, and died during a campaign with Chinese naval forces while seizing Tonkin, the Courbet of Lainé's sketch is genuinely trivial. A story replete with a local dance, flowers offered to a blushing girl, and a brief rivalry with the author's soon-to-be father, the "history of hearts" is about as profound as the admiral's epigram, "Without . . . the world and the women in it, a sailor becomes blunted and coarse."

Yet, as an articulation of imperial politics, Lainé's tale is strikingly astute. From his first appearance, the admiral reinscribes the necessary civilizing role of women in colonial projects as the counterparts to the raw action of *militaires* like himself. More, the admiral's flirtation, while flattering *mademoiseille*, gives him full opportunity to demonstrate the civility and sacrifice of his position among men. Admitting to his deputy Commisaire Lainé that "it is not only you who feel the charm of this young girl. I love her myself," he nonetheless resigns himself to his station and his duty. He is the paragon of a passionate, yet honorable colonialism.[32]

The two men, posted from New Caledonia to Tonkin, forge an intimacy and "talk together like old friends" about their political assignments: "I guess Mr. Jules Ferry would pass a disagreeable half-hour if he came to Kelung. Talk wouldn't save him as easily as it does in the Chamber." Yet, although arch, both Courbet and Lainé carry out their duties. Clement Wragge had imagined his Frenchman through an "affaire d'honneur" and a maddening dishonor; the men of Lainé's story are colonialists whose honor is their dedication to service and mutual respect. No wonder Loti would write the admiral's passionate epitaph for *Le Figaro*; in Hèléne Lainé's words, Courbet was at the end, "the man disappointed in love and disgusted with politicians, crying 'Good luck!' and then bursting into the refrain, 'without hope, it goes better.'"[33]

As the state arranged Courbet's apotheosis, his erstwhile confidant, Comissaire Lainé, moved ahead with marriage plans, a set of prosaic family encounters that expose the subtle tensions of empire as effectively as the admiral's funeral. Upon returning to France, Lainé encountered imperial ideology at home in Brest, where his aunt tried to match him with the daughters of her friends; she was opposed to his marriage on the grounds that "a colonial can in no way compare with a French girl." Lainé's mother also was strongly skeptical, but she was persuaded by a reassured notion of status through family lineage, shaped by blood and culture. "She realizes that the girl of his choice, daughter of distinguished and honorable parents, cannot but be worthy of her race."[34] The satisfaction of race here refers not to color but to the maintenance of culture and status distinctions.

In sardonic memoirs, the teacher, provocateur, and ex-colonist Marc Le Goupils wrote of being taken from his farm to Noumea by a driver who "very much wished I was at least a cattle breeder, the one who reigns over thousands of hectares, impressing the populace. But my driver knew . . . as he said, the entire aristocracy of Caledonian planters, and I did not belong to this aristocracy."[35] If planters and farmers could be lords over their workers, they still struggled within the deeply hierarchical and conservative order of their fellow colonists. Pierre Loti had sought out his own noble status abroad by seeking privilege where none was available to him in France. The Caledonian planters were a paramount example of a successful landed gentry, deeply invested in social distinctions on an unstable frontier. It was this "race" of status that Lainé, like many colonialists, would take back with him from France to New Caledonia, his part of the struggles and negotiations to establish the order of the Empire of Love.

That empire, always partly fiction, regularly verged on collapse. From 1873, Admiral Ribourt had warned of building a colony on "the most perverted men and the most corrupted women," and Governor Paul Feillet (1894–1902) would have appreciated Madame Lainé's attention to race-worthy spouses as he lamented the poor quality of his own household subjects. In 1897 interviews with *La Calédonie* he admitted, "The successful concessionaires have been exceptions." Putting aside hopes of virtuous reform of convicts and ex-prisoners through family, land, and work, Feillet staked his hopes on free colonization and railed against "deplorable marriages which unite depraved natures," declaring transported women—far from Admiral Courbet's civilizers—"corrupt, former prostitutes."

The reform dream of hearth and home at the center of the colony was not to be. "It was necessary to take the children from their parents. It was strongly felt that by leaving children in the hands of the concessionaires, one created a detestable population." At the turn of the century new measures were called for. Domestic bliss and the hope of naturally inculcating bourgeois work values and familial affection through concessions was derisory; the administration turned to direct intervention. "Thus the necessity of creating boarding schools with the blackmail of a free education."[36]

Such imperatives undergirded not only recommendations and reports on white convicts and colonists but also French Kanak studies. The geographer Augustin Bernard's descriptive accounts are typical of such studies, assessing the status of the locals by focusing on the horrors of Kanak marital arrangements: "The Polynesian sees in his wife an instrument of pleasure, the Canaque a beast of burden. She is truly a slave, carrying heavy loads, cruelly punished for the smallest mistakes." In a perversion of the conjugal model, the woman "does not even live in the same hut as the man." To these miseries, add the barbarism of a society in which "abortion is regularly practiced and infanticide of girls is honorable."[37]

With a clear view to the violation of all French civil, emotional, and religious values in the domestic realm, Bernard included in his account a pithy judgment about Kanak child-rearing practices by relating observations of "children who alternately take the breast and the smoking-pipe of their mothers." Such ethnography was inherently concerned with absent values and practices. Child mortality was a direct function of "the abusive length of breast-feeding, poor hygiene, poor nutrition." As colonial administrations developed formal education and hygiene programs by the turn of the century, the identification and reform of the "native mother" would become one of the centerpieces of colonial rule.[38]

Appropriate marriage statuses and domestic sensibilities were a dominant part of colonial planning in New Caledonia, but they could not be effective without land concessions to grant the new households. After all, if "to make honest men, it is necessary to make property owners" or "who makes one love the countryside makes one love virtue" were to be more than platitudes, large scale cultivable terrains were necessary.[39] Whether attached to free colonization or penal concessions, instruction in French work, hearth, and home was only half a plan whose other strategy was the necessary seizure of Kanak lands. Countless reports detail French perfidy and frustrations with "the Canaques who know nothing but the collective property of the tribe," and who refuse to divide, sell, and cash-crop their territories. [40]

Land expropriation had been official policy from the beginning of the French presence. As one 1860 government report advised on settlement projects, "The first of all conditions is to render the land accessible to every newcomer, rich or poor; [he] inspired by the American pioneer, arriving in a country shovel and pick on his shoulder, has the right to demand a piece of land and it must be provided immediately, because there is no time to waste." As for the local peoples, "It would be necessary to dominate the indigenous populations with the aid of imposing force" and to convince them of their newly subordinate status with "persuasion and patience."

The parallel invocation of force and patience is typical of Caledonian policy. Destruction of common lands and taro patches, overgrazing by European cattle, and cession of fields through legal chicanery and violence characterized a struggle that decimated local populations and forced the Kanaks onto reservations. The "pioneer" evocation was not the only lesson taken from the American experience. Yet a French empire of affection and devotion could not simply reconcile itself to outright expropriation. Consistent with imperial humanitarian ideology, "indispensable means of military repression" were to serve not only expediency but also the credo "though we are the masters, we are not tyrants."[41]

For general French audiences, policy justifications about land tenure struggle were thus translated into another kind of appropriation—that of Kanak history by reassuring, racialized narrative. Jules Durand's two-part "Among the Ouébas of New Caledonia," serialized in the glossy armchair traveler's journal *Le Tour du monde*, is exemplary of this strategy. Seeking a "lost" tribe, Durand proposed "the spirit of individual property which one notes in certain Caledonian tribes is not yet generalized in the land of the Ouébias."[42] Writing in 1900, Durand's travelogue allowed him to reinforce a benign history of French imperial interests—land and family—by projecting their nostalgic absence onto a sympathetic people not yet expropriated.

Durand achieved this by framing New Caledonia in the familiar Pacific narrative of race-based extinction: "By a law, fatal and all too real, the tribes in contact with civilization have disintegrated, their members corrupted; the vast "native reserves" have no more inhabitants."[43] Durand, of course, did not explore the French policies which have resulted in this disaster; what makes his particular piece so striking is that he turns the calamity to his ethnographic advantage. The displacement of the great Kanak landholdings and the decimation of the peoples is an opportunity to create adventure.

With the coastal tribes gone or near collapse, "it is necessary to travel further in order to study the savage up close." Thus, Durand seeks out the Ouébias. "It is to the land of the Ouébias that we must go to know in our time what the Canaque family is in its primal state. The Ouébias occupy a land which the interior mountains of the central chain enclose and hide." The adventure narrative takes over, as the brave European treks off into the unknown. At a mountain pass, "my black companions would not go any further . . . it only made me more resolved." Seeking a hidden valley, clambering down vine-covered slopes, Durand's narrative replicates explorer tales in general and specifically Herman Melville's 1846 *Typee*: an interior valley, unknown tribes of unsettling reputation, encounters of astonishment, and a reckoning with savage but ultimately peaceable peoples living in harmony with nature. On tumbling in among the Ouébias, Durand plays the demi-god discoverer: "We found ourselves surrounded by young Canaques who regarded us as if we'd fallen from the sky. They appeared horrified by the color of our skin and I produced the effect of a phenomenon."[44]

Although his compatriots had been decimating the Kanak peoples for almost half a century, what Durand sought and found was, unsurprisingly, the confirmation of French principles in the structure of Ouébian life. When the politician and Oceanic propagandist Charles Victor Crosnier de Varigny wrongly argued "we have not oppressed the weak, nor dispossessed the legitimate owners of the land; we have respected their rights, their traditions," he was expressing the self-evident role of French principles in any culture. Durand carried this to a logical extreme, projecting strong self-congratulatory analogies upon the clans he met. "The Ouébias do not live in anarchy, but under a sort of republican regime. The chief . . . cultivates his lands with his men and shares with them the fruit of hunting and fishing."

In imperial-ethnographic guise, a Rousseauist ideology of unaffected emotion remains untouched at the heart of the French colony. "The more one pushes into the interior, the more primitive and hospitable are the natives. The spirit of familial cohesion is preserved . . . they have for each other a natural affection."[45] By finding the Ouébia, Durand exposes his readers not to French history in New Caledonia, but his, and ultimately the administration's, own ideal of a colony: communities of landed households bound by sharing and love.

Such communities of natural affection had a harsh history. Durand's peregrinations in search of natural beings were directly shaped by the forced expropriation of almost two hundred thousand hectares and resettlement of all Kanak away from the coasts and plains, especially after 1878. There was almost nowhere else for free Kanak to live except in the valleys and hills. In that year, Captain Rivière noted, "For two years that I was in New Caledonia, there was so little question about the Canaques that I could have thought that they did not exist at all, or that they no longer existed."[46] Suddenly, the Kanak presence was more strongly felt than at any other time in the nineteenth century—at the explosion of the 1878 Great Rebellion, a violent conflict that extended from June until January of the following year and took the lives of nearly fourteen hundred Kanaks and two hundred immigrants and settlers.

In a famous report investigating the events, General Arthur de Trentinian levied profound blame against French colonial policies, naming as his first three causes of the violence "successive invasion of territories indispensable to the natives for the crops necessary for their existence"; "invasion of cattle belonging to farmers, not only on lands reserved for the Canaques following surveys, but upon their harvest which were almost everywhere devastated"; and "irresponsibility of colonists in the presence of these considerable damages."[47] Other unofficial reports had suggested as much, one frigate captain writing to the Ministry of the Navy and Colonies, "The New Caledonians are man-eaters it is true, but they also have the sense of just and unjust; it should therefore not surprise us that they have revolted against the dispossession which has followed our arrival." But reports from the governor, while acknowledging the "very tense relations between natives and colonists," put aside damages to Kanak lands by European cattle by arguing that, while barricades were necessary, "one needs time, money, and manpower. This can't be done in a day."[48]

Trentinian's 1879 report was suppressed for a century and, on the verge of retirement, he was sent on a new tour of duty to Saigon, where he died. The general's account did not adhere to important French evocations of New Caledonia as a colony and empire of love and family. Yet, notably, it was a contorted drama of exactly such questions that sparked the rebellion. The first sign of the coming storm was recorded in the journal of M. J. Mauger, a bureaucrat at the internal affairs bureau at Noumea on June 21, 1878: "We learn of the drama that has just taken place at Bouloupari. An ex-convict living in the area had taken a woman from a Canaque village. To escape the consequences of this act he left that part of the country, but he came back after some years. The Canaques have long memories. The day before yesterday they slaughtered the former prisoner, his wife, and their two children."[49]

Although an attack on a guard post on June 24 is generally regarded the beginning of the insurrection itself, the family massacre immediately became an outstanding symbol of French reporting. Journalists quickly ascertained that the man's name was Jean Chêne, he had a Melanesian wife, Mendon, and two children, and he was, at the time of the attack, sheltering a young woman named Katia from the nearby Dogny people. The massacre was an atrocity, and the family made attractive victims for writers. Katia presumably was escaping from the evils of Kanak female servitude. The wife and children demonstrated the possibilities of métissage. Chêne himself was a model reformed convict, prisoner turned concessionaire, and family man.[50]

Journalists also learned that the man leading the attacks was the Great Chief, Ataï, who for years had confronted and challenged the French presence. Feared and labeled "bestial" by some writers who believed all Kanak were cannibals, he was famed for his pride and for giving the governor a sack of earth and one of rocks with the mordant declaration, "here is what you have taken, and here is what you have left us."[51]

Notably, Ataï also used the family model in launching his revolt; no mere European propaganda device, its contested meanings also lay at the heart of Kanak understandings of the violence. Through oral tradition the intellectual and priest Apollinaire Anova Ataba has recounted Ataï's summoning exhortation to his gathering of warriors at the beginning of the insurrection. The significance—and contest over—Anova Ataba's work has been its larger implications: to see in Ataï's rebellion "the symbol, the incarnation" of a movement to construct an anticolonial order. Read this way, Ataï's proclamations are counterparts, indeed counternarratives, to European rhetoric of nationalist solidarity—family, forefathers, divine favor: "We will be victorious, because the ancestors are with us . . . you women, encourage the warriors; you children, you will carry the sacks of stones and you will be beside your elders; you warriors, prepare your arms and invoke the favor of the gods."[52]

Even circumscribed as a more localized event, the logic of family—and of declaring honor—are the centerpieces of Ataï's discourse. "The White is the ruin of our people. Katia, a daughter of our village is in one of their hands. We must save her. We must avenge the honor of the village of Dogny, outraged, ridiculed. All of our lands are in their hands. Their horned beasts trample the graves of our ancestors. Can we stand much longer such outrages, such infamies? No." Ataï frames the coming violence as an act precipitated by the stolen Katia.[53] Trentinian's report correctly outlined the long-term and large-scale depradations of land and custom leading to the conflict, yet in Ataï's words—which should be familiar to "the French"—outrage and satisfaction of honor are the sparks that will ignite the rebellion.

Letters between New Caledonia's Catholic fathers in December 1878 also worried over the "stealing of women" from villages as "the massacre began with Chêne and his concubine." The most singular cause of the violence, as Anova Ataba suggested, was "the taking of a native woman."[54]

≈

The "native woman" and her place within the struggles was at the heart of many histories as the rebellion highlighted the intertwined nature of conflict, families, emotions, and politics. On November 6, 1878, one Adele Take, a "native woman" according to her dossier, delivered a son at Païta and named him Joseph Antoine Charles. Some time afterward, one Charles Gérard Weyckmans "manifested a desire to recognize the child in question." The official in charge of the dossier noted that the couple was "not married," and that the proper certificates had not been filed within the time delay prescribed by the law. Hesitations followed. All of this was recorded as a form of colonial history by a notary who determined that these matters had not been attended to properly because of "the state of the insurrection in which can be found the territory of this jurisdiction, and also of the ignorance of the mother of the formalities relative to the act of état-civil."[55]

Putting the matter in order required fulfilling colonial imperatives: instructing the mother as to her legal duties, recognizing the authority of the father, and resolving the interruptions of administrative procedure. A series of letters between districts finally formalized the case, which was sent on to the proper bureau in Païta—a mixed liaison against the background of 1878. One thing notaries could not resolve was the violence itself. By December 1879, the government was printing standard forms announcing "the difficulties of every nature resulting from the state of insurrection found within the colony," and filling in names where required under the legend "it has not been possible to complete, within the legal time period, the act of the named _____, massacred by the revolting natives." Entire family records, including lists of names, were created from reports by military commanders, whose records became testimonies to "the cadaver named____, found at Poya."[56]

Such official documentation of the rebellion was later detailed by reports from settler points of view. Among the French colonials, Hélène Lainé dramatically related narratives of domestic invasion and evocations of family and honor. In Bouloupari, a Madame Porcheron was alone at home and surprised by "tomahawk"-wielding warriors. Struck repeatedly on the head, she fell and was left for dead, yet "fortunately she is the possessor of a beautiful head of hair twined in long thick plaits, so her wounds though they bleed abundantly are only superficial." She awoke to find herself saved by troops. In Pouembout to the north, a Mr. Schmidt wondered "why his natives have not come to work." One arrived warning him to escape an approaching clan. Running for his life, "later on he finds that the faithful native who warned him of his danger has been slaughtered." Most poignant and classically rendered is the fate of the warder Leca who, "surrounded by the corpses of wife, children and mutilated convicts . . . holds at bay over a hundred natives." He escaped as the Kanak set fire to and ransacked his lodging. "Returned to France, he is decorated with the Legion of Honor. But he is inconsolable, brooding on the tragedies he has witnessed, on his mutilated wife and children. His mind becomes deranged and he does not long survive them."[57]

Such harrowing accounts were part of a literature that typologically distinguished French domesticity from Kanak treachery. Similar stories constituted much of the news in the local press during the violence of the summer months in New Caledonia. Madame Porcheron is the woman assaulted in her home by savages, whose attention to style inadvertently preserved her from violent death until troops come to the rescue. Mr. Schmidt is given life by the ideal Kanak, the faithful servant who is martyred for saving his master. Leca is the inverse of Clement Wragge's mad murderer: he is the anguished family man, besieged in his own home, surrounded by the slaughter of all he loves. The Legion of Honor reunites him with the patrie in both soil and public acclamation, but his fate is already sealed in the overseas life he made and lived. Collapsing Trentinian's report on colonial expropriation with Ataï's quest for restored honor with Lainé's accounts of violated sanctity, Leca is the tormented, and now deranged victim of a riven Empire of Love.[58]

After nine months of fighting, the insurrection was put down by French military forces and alliances that pitted Ataï's clan and the Dogny against the Canala and the Bourindi. Ataï himself was speared and decapitated. Telegrams reporting his death described him "this energetic and intelligent chief who never wanted to entirely submit himself to French authority." [59] The colonial Marc Le Goupils wrote of the vicious fighting in terms of parallel moments in the history of France and New Caledonia. "The year 1878 and the Canaque insurrection is for the Caledonians what 1870 or the year of the war is for French people. The old Caledonians . . . speak of every historical event which they relate, 'it was so much time before or after the Insurrection.'"[60]

The year 1878 did indeed mark a break in the history of Kanak and European in New Caledonia. For Kanak, hopes that the French would be driven away or leave were broken. For settlers and prisoners rallying to French authority and protection, harsh suspicion of the islanders was followed by expropriation of almost all coastal lands, an 1887 "native code" that restricted travel and customs, and a series of formalized labor obligations on coffee plantations and in nickel mines, one last effort to make workers of the Kanak. In the free colonization project, immigrants turned their attention to other lands.

Local newspapers such as *La Nouvelle Caledonie* tried to explain the great break: "They are black, We are white; They were the first occupants of the land; We arrived later; Formerly the vast land was free; Now the stations move closer together and the colonists increase to crowd the natives out; They revolt."[61] It was an apparently sober balance sheet that disguised stringent assumptions about race and history. The geographer Augustin Bernard would later articulate them: "The withering away and extinction of savages . . . once they find themselves in the presence of the white man, is a fact about which much has been written. Civilized life and savage life seem incompatible on the same soil."[62]

Captain Henri Rivière, who commanded a gunboat off the islands and helped put down the rebellion, elaborated the same sentiment by writing, "the great cause of the insurrection, the only one it could be said, is the antagonism one always sees between a conquering and a conquered people. It is necessary that the latter be absorbed by the former or that it disappear." On the "black or brown races" he specifically suggested "they differ too much from the white race by their morals and instincts which have never progressed." Yet, at the time of the rebellion, an anonymous writer also observed, "above all it is the natives who are most familiar with our customs and most civilized who have been the leaders of the massacres and pillages." Unlike Rivière, this voice played out the vexed logic of the colonial project, precisely enunciating not so much the impossible divide of civilization and culture, but the real unease and discomforting horror of finding in former trading-partners, allies, and servants an enemy a bit too much like oneself.[63]

The writer might have been referring to Ataï, who well knew such familiarity, and in his own way shared a joint Caledonian fate for the politics of love, violence, and family—whether created by governors or destroyed by colonialism. In Rivière's writings, we find a portrait of an anonymous Madame X (Fournier), an "intelligent, active, very courageous" colonial widow and her encounters with an Ataï unfamiliar to most journalistic accounts, yet one who so perfectly captures the islands' hopes and dilemmas. "He was her neighbor and came often to see her. He brought her fruits and she offered him coffee, bread, and wine. He smoked his pipe on the veranda." The two apparently talked quite a bit, and, "One fine day, he proposed, suddenly and serenely, to marry her." Madame, stupefied, refused the offer. "Ataï repeated the proposition several times and was not pleased." Garnier goes so far as to suggest, "His resentment, perhaps, had something to do with the revolt. There is almost always a female reason determining great projects." Madame's house was untouched during the violence; notes Garnier, "Many times I told Madame X . . . that she should have surrendered herself and she would have prevented the Insurrection. She did not disagree."[64]

Disputed legacies: Whose ruins?
La Tour aux quatre visages, Angkor.
Source: Collection Christian Genet

SIX

INDOCHINA
Romance of the Ruins

Two tales of ruins. In his "pilgrimage" to Angkor, the ancient site of Khmer civilization, Pierre Loti trekked determinedly through "vegetation of a drowned forest . . . extravagant tropical flora spreads in all sorts of palms of great green tails and plumes." As his party came into a clearing, they were confronted by great stones, a scale of the "gigantic" all under "a sun of death, definitive silence." Loti had awaited this moment since he had read of Angkor in old colonial magazines and dreamed of its temples as a child. Now, at a remove of thirty years, "I had not the emotion I would have expected. It is doubtlessly too late in my life, I have seen too much of these great debris of great pasts, too many temples, too many palaces, too many ruins."[1]

A dozen years later, the Vietnamese music and theater teacher Bui-Thanh-Vân made a trip to Angkor to see the famous temples. Like Loti, he was taken by "curiosity, mystery, and the marvel" of the ancient ruins. Yet, his account detailed what Loti's essay related only as a solitary journey into the jungle. As Bui's boat landed near a small river station, he noted, "I disembark with a Frenchman, some Annamites, Cambodians, and Chinese in a sampan." Upon reaching the riverbank, distinctions assert themselves: "The Frenchman takes an automobile, some voyagers and I climb on a horse-drawn omnibus; the others crouch in ox-carts." More, he wished to stay at a hotel near the site of the ruins. "However, the French hotel, though not having but a single French guest, will not take me, because I am yellow."[2]

Two tales of ruins: those ancient and colossal, taken by the forest and memory, those recent and pained, marked by an Occidental presence. The writers, French and Vietnamese, in search of a way to capture something of

Indochina—or, rather, their place in the "Indochina" of their own creation. For his part, Loti was consistent with his mordant vision of a world lost, the seeker after the "eternal nostalgia" of his love for his childhood France. Bui-Thanh-Vân was a naturalized Francophile, founder of a classical music school at Huê, and a man rankling from the indignities of daily life and a status denied him as an Asian.

Loti's project is familiar: empire as collection—domesticating and enclosing the world. "The ruins of Angkor, how well I remember a certain April evening, a bit veiled, how they appeared to me in a vision." Secure in Rochefort, the young Julien Viaud dreamed of possessing Angkor as a fantasy. Yet, as the writer and naval officer Pierre Loti stationed in Southeast Asia, he regretted, "The first curiosity past, I do not like this country, nor any creature of this sad yellow race, it is truly the land of exile . . . there has never been but love that could attach me in a somewhat durable fashion to certain places on earth."[3]

Loti's faraway childhood Angkor failed, for the love and attachment he evoked always remained for home and France, where the "old sitting mother" waited for her sailors and soldiers "far away on the sea or in lands of exile."[4] His grandiose, melancholic vision reinforced his reputation as master of imperial nostalgia. Reflecting on "our yellow empire," in 1917 Indochina, Ligue Maritime et Coloniale Française Director Maurice Rondet-Saint groused, "Do not expect from me another description of the ruins of Angkor. The subject is already exhausted; it came to be so while being popularized by *Le Pèlerin d'Angkor* of Loti."[5]

Yet, as we learn from Bui-Thanh-Vân, the subject was not exhausted. Bui saw something quite particular in the ruins at Angkor. Loti's oppressive meditation carries his decadent burden of history, the enervation of the soul. At Angkor, the temples were characterized by their mute incomprehension, their weight and decay. Bui rather found the temples alive with messages and meanings: "They have spoken proudly, and not without justice, to succeeding generations of an ancient power of an Oriental people. This testimony will be carried still to the eternity of future centuries." Where Loti saw "colossal, cyclopean blocks of stone, invincible somnolence," Bui related a living culture, "diverse sculptures and refined carvings representing subjects and scenes from the four reigns of nature, from political life, as well as from arts and industries."[6]

Loti's morose tone is unsurprising: "Indochina" was always for him a place of death. His other connected writings, such as his 1883 accounts from Tonkin and Huê, detail French military assaults in which "Annamites fell in groups," trying to escape naval fire by "running on all fours." Tumbling into the river, royal soldiers were likened to bobbing seals to be picked off by

French sharpshooters until "there is no one left to kill." At the same time, he railed loudly against the government at Paris which sent "to die far away the bravest and best of the nation . . . may the blood of our sailors be on the hands of our miserable politicians."[7] Bui was the successor to this era of military conquest, the Francophile Vietnamese observant of both Asian heritage and Occidental prejudice, one who embraced Gallic culture and administration yet who also saw something deeply proud and "Oriental" in the ruins at Angkor.

What draws the two accounts together is their romance of the ruins. For Loti, it is an evocation of his childhood France and the beloved sailors serving in her name. Bui's response, although bitterly critical of life under colonialism, is astonishingly similar, betraying the complexities of the Empire of Love in Southeast Asia. As Loti referred his journeys back to the domestic sentimentality of Rochefort and the patriotic maternal nationalism of Juliette Adam, so, too, did Bui imagine himself the (perhaps unappreciated) son of a loving French mother. "It would be naïve to think that France has crossed seven thousand kilometers of ocean to come in good will, extending us a hand, without expecting anything of us. She perfectly has all the rights that justice confers upon an adoptive mother." Bui even asserts a parallelism between naval officers and motherly love: "The policy of our affectionate adoptive mother is the same as that applied by a generous ship's captain regarding strangers stowed away on board." He also finds common cause with "our good adoptive brothers . . . they honor their mother as they make themselves honorable; they love all as they make themselves loved."[8]

From Loti's beloved sailors in gunboat conquest to Bui's adoptive mother and brothers, tales of love frame a chronology of France and Cochinchine, Annam, Tonkin, Laos, and Cambodia as they were protected, possessed, and colonized into "Indochina." From the middle nineteenth century, military men such as Loti and Captain Francis Garnier declared missions of passionate fraternalism become patriotism, adventures transmuted into the "Conquest of Hearts" of the diplomat and geographer Auguste Pavie at the turn of the century. The "possession of the native" promoted by colonialists was realized in civil policy of the early twentieth century through state-approved mixed liaisons and colonial marriage fictions of writers such as the novelist Clothilde Chivas-Baron. The possibilities and limits of this imperial romance were tested and constantly renegotiated by generations of Vietnamese like Bui or writer Trân Van Tung, who accepted France as affectionate mother, brother, or lover, or the anticolonial essaysist Nguyên An Ninh, who reversed the romance, saying, "It is not for a sentimental project that France has gone to Indochina. . . . One would have to be the most stupid sort of colonial to believe in 'the Civilizing Mission.'"[9]

~

As a colony under a French governor, "Indochina" was the heart of an empire that extended from the Mekong delta to Panama. The combined territories harbored the only substantial French settler population in the Pacific and the only commanding landmass. Official bulletins highlighted the sheer scale of the territory: "Our colony has a surface area of 680,000 square kilometers, about 150,000 kilometers more than France."[10] As the jewel of French overseas empire and her "balcony on the Pacific," Indochina also shaped the Oceanic colonies through the leverage of the Banque de l'Indochine, and through the Tonkinese and Annamite workers sent to labor-poor settlements in New Caledonia and the New Hebrides.

The French navy first intervened in the Southeast Asian kingdom of Annam in the 1850s, establishing a protectorate over the adjoining territory of Cochinchine ostensibly to defend the work of the Catholic church. This "time of the admirals" was characterized by complicated military and diplomatic maneuvering between French governors and Annamite rulers at Saigon governing Cochinchine, the emperor at Huê in Annam, and mandarins in Tonkin at Hanoi. A series of celebrated military conflicts under Francis Garnier and Henri Rivière—both of whom were killed—was succeeded by armed colonial rule under governors including Paul Bert (1886), Jean Louis De Lanessan (1891–1894), Paul Doumer (1897–1902), and Albert Sarrault (1911–1919) who administratively bounded the regions into the Union of Indochina.[11]

Cultural and political confrontation lay at the heart of developing colonial narratives—both French and Vietnamese—which built upon and underscored for effect the differences between peoples, while also courting their loyalty and association. In one 1922 novella, the colonial writer Clotilde Chivas-Baron has the Annamite emperor compare "positive and organizing France, practical France . . . and Annam, the delicious country of immobility and dreams." In the same tale, another character praises the emperor as one who "understands the French, or at least tries to understand them . . . it is necessary to understand them to love them."[12]

From the middle nineteenth century, many of the stories that shaped France's presence in Southeast Asia were recorded as variations of *histoires d'amour*. Successive governments in Paris took up the colonial imperative, most significantly the ministries of Jules Ferry, whose stormy tenure ended in 1885 when he was voted down during a series of military setbacks and sovereignty debates branded "The Tonkin Affair." During that period Ferry himself was famously branded "le Tonkinois" for his pro-colonial policies. His supporters, such as the Saigon mayor and Cochinchine deputy Jules

Blancsubé, defended him with political love stories, arguing "there are ten million souls . . . wishing for nothing but to give themselves to us." To Ferry's proclamations of empire, Blancsubé wrote the prime minister of "the sweet tears that you have made me weep upon reading these lines where resonate the purest patriotic fiber and vibrant accents of energy and sentiment . . . to see so noble a cause defended by such a noble heart . . . to raise oneself reassured, moved, loved!"[13]

Love—patriotic, spiritual, or sexual—was an infinitely adaptable language of empire. From the contested colonies came the kind of stories on which Pierre Loti made his name: military men in erotic liaison with exotic, often subordinated or prostituted females. In his memoirs of service in Tonkin, the former naval officer Jean Léra praised Governor General Paul Bert for sagely balancing sex and danger by instituting regulations cautioning, though not forbidding, Frenchmen from visiting the "native women . . . similar to poisonous plants." Within Bert's imperium, gushed Léra, "Eros alone reigns as master and Mercury remains outside the door." Citing Bougainville's imagery of Cythère and promised paradise, Léra thanked Bert's "patriotic direction" for keeping Frenchmen in their "amorous pastimes" while also healthy and robust.[14]

A bit more subtly, M. Brenier, a colonial undersecretary, recounted the taking of the Mekong in a sexualized language. Glorious memories of French conquest "come rushing into the mind at the view of this Mekong of powerful and deceitful waters which have not responded to the hopes of patriotic sailors, who hoped to find in them [elles, the French feminine] one of the greatest routes of penetration in the world—two thousand kilometers—toward fecund and unexplored regions."[15]

As seen around the Pacific, the church is repeatedly invoked as a force whose mission is to spread the love of Christ, and at times, church and military are conflated. Upon dying in the Tonkin campaign, the commander Berthe de Villers managed to expire while evoking narration, marriage, faith, and profession: "Write to my wife that I die as a soldier and a Christian." Biographers of Captain Francis Garnier—who dreamed of opening the Red River all the way to China and was killed in combat—sympathetically trace a turbulent career in languages of religion and affection. Paul Antonini's partisan history begins, "The flag of France floats in Indochina side by side with the cross." Antonini then cites Garnier as a man whose mission was driven by love of France and family. As the officer ponders a bleak moment in his career: "My discouragement in this regard is great enough for me to decide to quit a career which I love but which is more honorable than lucrative, if I find another that will assure the survival of those I love."[16]

In his own official address to his troops, Garnier deliberately invoked a politics of love to frame his conflation of civilization, force, and colonial hierarchy. "Sailors and soldiers, in sending you to Tonkin to protect the interests of French civilization, the governor-admiral has granted you the favor of showing proof of his trust . . . you will therefore abstain from any act of brutality, and you will by all of your efforts make loved and respected the flag which you bear." Jean Baptiste Eliacin Luro, Garnier's comrade and director of the Collège des Stagaires de Saigon, rhapsodized in 1877 about his friend's fate by extolling those who "have loved Cochinchine unto death . . . happy are those among us who will have had the honor of dying after having so long suffered and worked for our country."[17]

Recalling the fates of such expeditions, the adventurer the Duc de Montpensier reiterated, like Loti and so many imperialists, the logic of grand emotion as an integral component of nation and empire. Paying homage to "valiant naval officers," Montpensier insisted to his readership that "my sailor's heart imposes the duty of according a moving remembrance . . . I love Indochina, and I feel the need to glorify, even if only with a brief memory and modest mention, the valiants to whom you are indebted." In imposing a settlement at Huê on King Kiên Phuc during the Tonkin campaign, French diplomats drafted the monarch's pronouncement, "I love France greatly, and I will do all that is possible to please the French."[18] To *love* and be loved by Indochina was the articulation of French empire: the shaping of the nation and its conquests.

Perceptions were modified by the long history of struggles and domination. Reporting on an early 1861 Cochinchine expedition when French forces were still tentative, Léopold Pallu de la Barrière organized this writing around metaphors *du coeur:* "The Annamites have . . . a certain bravado, even an occasional courage, because their passions are from the heart." In the same report he encoded such strength as a form of savagery by suggesting a "terrifying superstition": "When one of them is killed, they open up his body, tear out the heart, devour it still beating." During the invasion of Tonkin, 1883–1885, the campaign's early chronicler Dick de Lonay reported, "The Annamites hold their positions and keep up their fire, they are most assuredly brave." Yet by the era of formal colonialism after 1885, such images are heavily modified. In 1886, the historian and geographer A. Paulus said "The Annamites are sweet and docile, capable still of resistance, reflective, timid, cheerful." As will befit a chief administrator, Governor General De Lanessan's 1889 view is completely pacific and concerned with productivity: "The Annamite people are sweet, hard-working, peaceful, attached to the land that they water with their sweat."[19]

This transition to the docile and rather "ethnographic" Asian was abetted by a new French romance with Indochina, one shaped and widely popularized by editorials, essays, and travel accounts by highly visible colonial figures such as the politician Jules Blancsubé and the diplomat and geographer Auguste Pavie. If the period of direct military conquest was marked by tales of bravado and fierce, patriotic passions, the decades of administrative territorial expansion and mapping were characterized by stories of benevolent protection.

As Saigon mayor and delegate to the Chamber of Deputies in Paris, Blancsubé was one of the most forceful voices for colonialism as a politics of love. A long-time resident of Cochinchine, he rooted his family romance there: "I adopted it for my own, I created my family there, I owe it my existence. And it is because I love it, that I have tried for so long to make it known and to conquer for it a place in the patrie and to become the loveliest possession of the republic."[20] His ability to evoke family, conquest, possession, and patrie within the context of "I love" was exemplary, although not unusual. Such talent was critical in parliamentary struggles for budget credits against eloquent colonial skeptics such as Georges Clemenceau or Léon Renault, who warned, "France should greatly hesitate before engaging great expenses, of running the risk entailed by the pursuit of colonial possessions."

Blansubé's lobby of supporters, by contrast, played up his good colonial image as "head of a model family that has raised eleven children," presenting him as a "passionate servant of his country." Pro-colonial ideology revolved around establishing "a union necessary and fecund" with the mother country. The colonial newspaper Le Saigonnais even proposed a vocabulary that would have done Juliette Adam's maternal nationalism proud: "Let us see if by these diverse obligations we could substitute ourselves for the mère-patrie and become what in recent debates has been called a mère-colonie."[21] Le Mé-Kong thundered, "Should we abandon . . . this Tonkinese population that is persecuted because it has faith in us?" To be emphatic, the editors insisted: "The Tonkinese people love us, they want to give themselves to us."[22]

This vision of amorous surrender was most widely and effectively developed by Auguste Pavie, one of the major figures in the post-conquest age of French control in Southeast Asia. Following stints with the navy and postal services, he was a minister plénipontentiaire based in Siam at the turn of the century, and leader of the eponymous Mission Pavie that mapped and detailed much of Indochina for French governors. With his maps, natural histories, photographic collections, and ethnographic studies of Indochina, Pavie, noted one admirer, "long worked at her territorial enlargement, and has given so much at helping understand her." One colonial archivist and historian even argued that Pavie's work provided the basis for "the map of Indochina and the administrative structure of the country." In 1885, France, "solidly fixed to the south of the peninsula possessed nothing to the north but a few precarious bases . . . in 1895 French Indochina had become a political and economic reality."[23]

In his political correspondence, Pavie was very much the expansionist, writing to the Ministry of Foreign Affairs, "France would commit a great error in contenting herself with the Mekong as the limit of our Laotian possessions . . . we should wish that the Mekong be a French river." But he made his reputation by assuming the persona of benevolent explorer and special protector of Cambodia and Laos: "As much as the resistance from Siam is violent, our advance should be calm and firm. We have the populations . . . they await our deliverance."[24]

Pavie's own notebooks, preserved at Aix-en-Provence and still lined with the occasional seedpod or fragment of butterfly wing, trace the strategic and sentimental itineraries of a man who chose as his motto "one most have heart!"[25] Not surprisingly, Pavie's best-known book, based on his journals and oral histories, was his *A la conquète des coeurs* (Conquest of Hearts), a work particularly worth detailing for its wide impact. Georges Clemenceau himself wrote the preface to the 1921 edition, calling it "the best colonial book that I know." What the "Tiger" of French politics so admired was not a tale of ferocious adventure but of one man, "barefoot, without provisions," marching though Southeast Asia "toward that ideal to make the lands you crossed French with the assent of their inhabitants." What Clemenceau particularly fixed on was Pavie's ability to relate stories of "populations you have seduced . . . and which you love; you have dedicated yourself to inspire in them the sentiments for France that you yourself have for her." The result of this was a particular kind of empire: "Having given birth to devotion, you have, in gaining their hearts, conquered lands that, morally, give themselves up upon knowing you."[26]

Clemenceau was only reveling in Pavie's own self-fashioning as imperialist as protector. The "barefoot" Pavie of Clemenceau's reading contrasts with Pavie as minister at Bangkok greeted by the unfurling of the tricolor and "thirteen cannon shots from the forts at Paknam." Pavie's own reports from Cambodia detail him selectively as a man in a canoe taking the hands of villagers and insisting, "The French are good, they will love you as I love you and will take you to their hearts." Local chiefs apparently told Pavie they have "loved him already" even before his arrival in their region, "after all of our misfortunes, we have a chance, you are here, seated before us, you smile at us, and we touch you!" Pavie used his influence to obtain freedom for captives in disputed territories between Laos and Siam, and the out-pouring of devotion and gratitude are recorded as "eloquent testimonials of love."[27]

Pavie's is not the only voice advancing these testimonials; his protégés also adopted his vision. One, Deo Van Tri, addressed Pavie "Cher Protecteur" in his letters, and was given a French education and even a trip to Paris with his family. Unable to ever repay such debts, he wrote his master, "We will work for the good of the country and will guide the inhabitants on the road of progress, and we will make it understood that France loves us greatly and wishes that we become one day an equal people."[28] In such recognition Pavie realized intimately what Jules Blancubé set out schematically by outlining the "perfectly defined civilizing role" of French imperial policy: "The goal of our interventions was not conquest, but to protect the country . . . the Annamite being still too weak to protect himself."[29]

The grandest popular expression of this affectionate protection and tutelage was in Parisian colonial expositions where reproductions of "great pagodas" housed discreet presentations of prosperous and grateful colonies. A replica of the grand pagoda of Cholon in Cochinchine became, at the 1900 Paris Exposition, a warehouse for abundant rice, sugar, bamboo, cotton, cacao, wax, and honey. "Equally," notes a program, "there are in this pagoda . . . models of great iron bridges and works of Indochinese art commissioned in France by the governor general."[30] The Palais des Arts displayed parasols, fans, and works in bronze and ivory; the Palais des Forets a selection of bamboo constructions and exhibits of fishing and tanning of animal skins. Perhaps most fascinating was a series of dioramas in the grotto of the "Pagoda of Buddhas," which juxtaposed images of tradition—the tomb of the Emperor Tu-Duc—with French modernity—the construction of the Doumer bridge, "one of the most important works of art undertaken in the colonies." A cinema projection completed the simulacra of the colony by screening "the illusion of Indochinese life with its animation and particular character."[31]

Unsurprisingly, Pavie played a major role in such expositions. His notes for public presentations in 1900 are initially framed in a language we recognize from Loti's Southeast Asian lands: "I had dreamed of their distant antiquity in solitary walks among ruins, in the woods, along the waters." Pavie's work also is reflexively modeled on the collection. Among his achievements for the exposition was the materialization of "thirteen life-size wax figures representing types—men, women, and children of the least-known populations." Despite Pavie's "men, women, and children" pronouncement, according to the program they were overwhelmingly female: "A group of inhabitants of Muong-Sing, north of Laos, a young Meo girl, two women of

Laos, a Pou-Thaie woman, a woman of Luang-Prabang, a north Kha-Kho woman, a young Lue girl of northern Laos, a Laotian woman."[32]

Pavie's displays quickly evolved into narratives of ethnography as love story. The discourses of passion and possession asserted themselves as Pavie eschewed formal scientific language to assert, "I love the Cambodians," a people he defines as "simply good and open-hearted." In an elegant summary, he clarified the ways in which his love was a form of historical understanding, one that rendered his subjects both appropriately glorious and nonthreatening. "I love them also for the mystery of their past in which an instinctive memory of glory, joined to the knowledge of evils that have made them forget, gives them all at once a nuance of pride and renders them timid."

Pavie loved the Cambodians in their surrendered present. Writers often employed or adopted such an aesthetic of Indochina as collection—bounded and securely held in the past. Essayists for Juliette Adam's *Nouvelle Revue*, such as Albert Savine, traveled in Cambodia, concentrating on festivities that followed "the immemorial usage, the triumphal processions of knights, chariots, and mounted elephants." The people's martial spirit is now strictly ceremonial. "[They] live for the circumstance, to take out of the arsenals and the palaces the arms of long ago, such as one sees in the Khmer section of ethnographic museums or the galleries of the Guimet museum."[33]

At Angkor, French savants eventually did declare themselves the saviors of Khmer patrimony. As one archaeologist put it, "Khmer civilization has finally taken the place it merits among the great civilizations of antiquity and the Middle Ages . . . henceforth, the Ecole française d'extrême orient is prepared and outfitted to restore temples formerly lost in the bush, ruined, and absorbed by vegetation. Wherever teams of coolies in archaeological service have come to work, the monument presents to our eyes its silhouette of another time." Asian labor under French authority shaped remote past as well as present and future.[34]

In like fashion at the colonial exposition, Pavie detailed the means by which he became the protector of his beloved Cambodians. His transcription of a historic tale "is the first which, translated entirely in French, was printed in the Cambodian language, as the author had promised the people of the village who furnished him the text." In presenting the work to the villagers, Pavie became a narrator of Indochina. "That day things did not go as usual; everyone declared that I surely knew the little that was known and that I myself should be the storyteller [conteur]." The elders of the village effectively transferred their history to the Frenchman: "What we would be happy to hear, is what you think from your voyages, your studies, of the unknown past of our old Cambodia; what you will later tell to those of your own country."

In this tale of affection, Pavie, whose works were lauded as imperial instruments by his government, resolved his passion by preserving the history of the conquered as folkloric tradition. His motto engaged the past: "I know how passionately the Khmers love to retell the legendary eras." Indeed, the Khmer seemed to look to him for their history. "We believe our hearts remain open more than those peoples who have crushed us; why then haven't we been able to bear the weight of our old glories? We return to these subjects over and over again; will you tell us about it?" Inflections of meaning are small but telling; where Pavie spoke of the "legendary" eras, his interlocutors showed their appreciation by engaging the present. "We will take up your idea, happy to be able ourselves to tell again of these old times with greater confidence."[35] Whereas he preserved their past as past, they sought the authority to recapture their own history.

This also was what Bui-Thanh-Vân described when in the stones and reliefs at Angkor he saw not melancholy ruins but proofs of the "ancient power of an Oriental people," and evidence of a testimony "carried still to the eternity of future centuries." Proud of the heritage, he nonetheless also acknowledged that it was a French savant behind "the teams of natives scattered across the jungle" who were doing the restorations, and he praised this work, "an undertaking worthy of a leading nation. She saves the celebrated Khmer vestiges which the universe contemplates with ecstasy."[36] Angkor was one of Bui's cogent figures for Indochina in the early twentieth century; it was not a silent monument but a product of collaborations and contested meanings. His romance of the ruins is important for its recognition—if at times bitterly so—of the depth of interaction between the cultures and the realities of an inescapable common destiny.

At the Angkor site, Bui contemplated with some irony the hotel-keeper of "Chinese and Cambodian blood, correctly speaking French, dressed in European style," carrying out "by order of his boss the exclusion of passengers of color from this establishment." Yet he simultaneously defended "ideal, generous, just, humanitarian" France, "mother of forty million children." His reality was inescapably entangled with the powerful ideology of the Empire of Love. It was in grand principle that he lauded his French brothers: "They share the joys and pains of the people whose mission they have to guide along the road to progress . . . they devote themselves it every way to improve their condition. They have love for France, and for the France of Asia."[37]

In the early twentieth century defining love within this "France of Asia" became a recurring figure in colonial contemplations. Bui's contemporary, constitutionalist activist Nguyên Phan-Long, dedicated a 1921 novel to Governor General Maurice Long "with the hope that my modest work will contribute to helping him better understand and love the people over whose destiny he presides." Love in this case took on a specific configuration. Advising a young woman wishing to marry an Annamite, Nguyên counseled, "I would wish that many of your compatriots would follow your example. Marriages like yours will achieve the indissoluble unity of the Great France of Europe and the France of Asia."[38]

Such projects—common destiny realized in marrying the empire—were abetted by the size and complexity of Indochina as a colony. Although derided, like Oceania, as isolated and thus backward, the France of Asia did not overtly suffer from the dominant narrative of smaller possessions—the extinction of the natives. The many peoples of "Indochina" were not simply going to die off. As the geographer Augustin Bernard theorized, "the Annamites of Indochina are not tending to disappear. This is because . . . Annamites are not savages; they are in certain respects barbaric, but that is quite different."[39] As Loti's fatal exoticism gave way to colonial administration, the dynamics of empire and authority in Indochina were not those of the gradual expiration of the Annamites, Tonkinese, Khmers, Laotians, and other peoples, but the assimilation of their history.

Auguste Pavie's missions and colonial exhibitions aptly illustrated this process in the later nineteenth century: France sought to produce and searched for in Indochina gratitude, affection, loyalty, and thus identification and compliance with the imperial project. Jules Blancsubé, arguing for intervention in Tonkin, specified "the only policy we will follow, the only which is truly French and truly republican" would be to see the Tonkinese as "our natural friends," a "brave and sweet population," in need of support against the aggressions of mandarins in Annam. As one A. Bouinais, a naval captain of infantry put it with verve, "After the conquest by arms, it remains to us to effectuate the more difficult act of possession—that of the native."[40]

Such possession required another shift in the Empire of Love. Loti and Garnier had loved in the name of France and fellow sailors; Pavie and Blancsubé were partisan "protectors" of colonial interests and native populations. As the military adventurers of the 1870s and 1880s became the administrators and colonists of "Indochina" at the end of the nineteenth century, so in the twentieth the notion of "natural friends" became more complex and intimate. The "possession of the native" developed formally and was widely explored through civil policy and the possibilities of colonial marriage and mixed liaisons.

Tales from earlier periods fixed upon basic commodity transactions. J. L. Dureuil de Rhins's 1879 travel ethnography of Annam, for example, included an almost obligatory exchange in which the author, upon being offered lodging along a river, inquired, "Can't one also purchase women?" His interlocutor readily riposted, "Certainly. A woman costs 100–150 francs," though he cautioned, "but the toilette, the jewels, will cost ten times more."[41] Women could always be appropriated to the status of congaï—like poupée or vahine in Polynesia, or musumé in Japan, the role of the European man's mistress.

In the first decades of the twentieth century, civil court cases and "colonial" literary pieces engaged with much greater subtlety tales of marriage as highly visible figures for expressing love of Indochina. The writer Clothide Chivas-Baron mastered this genre in works such as *Three Annamite Women* and *Confidences de métisse*. Chivas-Baron, winner of the Grand prix de littérature colonial in 1927, author of a patriotic and jaundiced advice manual, *La Femme aux colonies,* and many popular works of folklore and history of French Indochina, created in her tales strong and willful women, weak, boorish, or tragic men, and Indochina as a female principle. Her stories revolve around the negotiation of intimate relationships, from Thi-Vinh, who holds aloof from the French, to Hoa, who marries them. Possessing Indochina is manifested in these narrations as the characters struggle with survival, spiritual strength, and moral purpose within shattering calamities of history—including the French presence and colonial domination.

The French "authoring" of empire is prominently featured in Chivas-Baron's novella "Madame Hoa's Husbands," which traces the life of an Annamite woman married to three successive Frenchmen. Early on, the young Hoa neatly pronounces on the narrated nature of French Indochina, "In France, it seems, those who don't travel want to know what is going on in other countries. They read for their instruction books written by [Hoa's husband] Jacques Viellis and his friends." Chivas-Baron's consciousness of the power invested in colonial writings is evident in Hoa's anger when she comes across a particularly unflattering reportage on Annam: "The author sees my country with an ill-natured eye: 'hideous flat stretches, mud; ignorant natives, no art, no poetry, no history, no literature, no legends.' 'How,' I asked M. Viellis, 'can the French like Indo-China after reading such books?'"[42]

Even Viellis admits that the work in question is prejudiced, but not all cases are so easily resolved. More subtly, Chivas-Baron narrates in literary form the affectionate and sympathetic colonization of history we saw in Pavie's Khmer ethnographies. This is manifested in Hoa's unworldliness, as she frankly admits, "I have never been away from Hanoi except to make a trip to Haiphong . . . the life of Annamite peasants is absolutely unknown to me." As French savants sought to preserve Angkor, and Pavie became the keeper of Khmer epics, so "M. Jacques made fun of my ignorance; he was amused that a Frenchman should inform me about these things."

Nor is Hoa's story limited to a Frenchman having authority over Anna-mite culture. By reading French studies, Hoa is educated about her home-land, yet the consciousness arrives through the language and habits of her husband, a colonial bureaucrat. While giving his wife riding and carriage lessons he exhorts her, "Yes, little Hoa, always farther, higher! That's the essential characteristic of the French! Is your heart becoming daily a little more French?" Here Viellis manages to instruct Hoa and assimilate her to Frenchness, both within a context of marital affection. Viellis's marriage *is* his colonial project, a means of expressing the authority of European empire in the dynamics of a sentimental relationship. As he tells Hoa, "Admit that the French are making efforts to understand and love your country, which they think of as a new France."[43] The "France of Asia" described by Bui-Thanh-Vân and Nguyên-An-Long is fully expressed in conjugality.

Under colonialism, such marriages were ideological as well as affection-ate acts, and as such of great interest to the Hanoi administration. Civil records show how the governor general's office involved itself directly in validating or invalidating French and Vietnamese liaisons and marriages, particularly those of administrative and military personnel. The residents in Tonkin and Annam regularly sent reports up to the governor general's office apprising the administration of "French citizens desiring to contract marriage in the colony," along with files detailing requests of a "M. Jolly and Mlle. Hoan-Thi-Kiêt," or a "M. Riberiro and the native woman Nguyên-Thi-Lily, called Lucy."[44] In such cases "understanding" a potential spouse often meant a police report.

Legitimate unions obeyed established criteria. In the case of a proposed 1918 marriage between a Captain Derepas and a Madame Duong Thi Mo, the court at Hanoi sent the Attorney General a report favorably recom-mending the union, considering "Derepas has lived ten years *maritalement* with Duong Thi Mo; from this union have come four children." The report fixed upon the respective duties of the couple: the woman's moral behavior and reputation, and the man's financial support: "The best information has been gathered on the morality of Duong Thi Mo, who has received, by the way, a monthly stipend of 250 francs."[45] In this context, the court found no reason to object.

Other cases did not sit so well. In the case of a Mademoiselle Cousy who planned to marry one Quach Van Giai in Toulouse, a police report from Cochinchine maintained that the proposed husband "possesses, in effect, a deplorable background: accused several times of theft and complicity to theft and for assault and battery." Worse, he "is not engaged in any work, and frequents houses of prostitution." To this the colonial administration appended its advice, "the marriage he has projected with a Frenchwoman cannot but cause misfortune if it is allowed to take place; I therefore have the honor of requesting that you intervene on behalf of the department . . . and to prevent, if there is still time, the marriage that this native [indigène] has projected with Mlle Cousy."[46] By the end of the report, only Mademoiselle Cousy had a name. The administration frankly expressed its desire to intervene in what it deemed unfavorable marriage projects, particularly where a Frenchwoman was involved.

Bui-Thanh-Vân also recounted the case of a young Frenchwoman journeying to Tourane and Faifo in 1921 in search of her Annamite husband while bearing "the fruit of his love." Although sympathetically received by the "yellow race" village and townspeople, "she came up against the intrigues of her own compatriots who engaged themselves energetically to make it impossible for her to achieve her purpose, essentially for the honor of prestige." Beaten down and without resources, she returned to France. According to Bui, "in the colony, the French marginalize their sisters who live under the roof of a native person." Apparently mindful of his French audience however, Bui then softened his report by concluding it as a timeless meditation on love: "Love . . . has always been alone and unique in its singular domain across the centuries. It has lived, lives, will live by its own eternal breath."[47] As Bui knew, there were limits to how much colonialism might actually be expressed within the Empire of Love.

Europeans also explored those limits. Frenchmen might love Indochina and have their congaï, but the role of a Frenchwoman in the colonies was to love France. In her critical essays on colonial living for *la femme*, Chivas-Baron plainly stated from experience what she saw the Frenchwoman's role in empire to be: the domestic reproduction of Gallic civilization. "She is . . . the one who, everywhere, creates France around her, with the habits of France and the visions of France, with small objects and grand sentiments, with a silver tea-service and Louis-Philippe lamps, with the grace and morale of France, her goodness and courage."[48] The great allegorical drama of civilization would be most effectively realized at the moment of its investment in daily meanings and everyday objects.

Such a presence was met with reservations by some colonials for whom such domesticity had little role in their schemes of privilege. The scholar Albert de Pouvourville articulated what would become a well-worn argument about empire as it became formal colonialism in the twentieth century: that European women had spoiled it with their excessive material and moral refinements. "Comes the French feminine element bringing to our summary interiors and to our once-again uncouth souls the enveloping charm of her elegance and her preciousness." After this came the matter of the men's "lost girls" and Frenchwomen's strong dislike of them, a hostility "ignoring without doubt that in the traditional laws of Annam, temporary unions, with repurchase, are valid." Chivas-Baron noted, "White women . . . are not kind to métisses. Some of them display a ferocious jealousy in this regard." Invoking the loss of the "possession of the native," De Pouvourville bemoaned that "an entire part of our work, and not the easiest, has been wiped out. Between the white and yellow . . . a deep trench has been dug, everyday aggravated by the zeal of our pretty women."[49]

De Pouvourville's "white and yellow" receives airing when, in "Madame Hoa," Jacques Viellis is confronted by a French friend for paying too much attention to his "congaï." He merely replies, "You alarm yourself friend; you are mistaken. For me a Frenchwoman is always a Frenchwoman; an Annamite an Annamite. I'm not yet in my second childhood. Don't get excited." Hoa, overhearing, is astounded. "I listened no longer . . . my heart is broken. I can still hear the mocking voices laughing at our race. Oh, these Occidental people. They talk of Liberty, Equality, Fraternity. Even their kindness is disdainful."[50]

Directly invoking the term *race*, Chivas-Baron once again deftly displayed how "marriage" obeyed the logic of ideology, and how affection circumscribed the bounds of such race. In a practice directly familiar from Loti's writings and liaisons, ideals of union and affinity flattered notions of propriety while obscuring the double coercion of male to female and colonizer to colonized. Here, romance delivers itself as a constituent element of French authority in Indochina.

In a complementary fashion, an anticolonial activist like Phan Bôi Châu (1867–1940) could lament in 1907 the French presence through his own country's lack of a national romance. "It is true that Heaven has not been kind to us. That is because our people have no mutual love or trust. They treat one another as people from Qin and Yueh. Although of the same race they treat each other as enemies." As the fictional Hoa, he excoriated the colonizers, "They despise us claiming that we are weak; they lie to us because they consider us stupid. . . . The moral prestige of hundreds of our officials does not prevail over that of a French woman." Calling for a Vietnamese nationalism, Phan pitted his patriotic solidarity against the haughty charm of the foreigner: "When the people of our country have reached such a mutual trust and affection, will our eyes still see any French gentlemen around?"[51] Playing out the promises and deceptions of political romance, Phan, like Chivas-Baron, deftly underscored the conceits of a character like Jacques Viellis, with his unstudied—and as yet unchallenged—romance of cultural and racial superiority.

What such contests ultimately disrupted are certain and essential notions of racial difference operating under European authority. What Ann Stoler has called the "tense and tender ties" of empire are extended in complex ways to Madame Hoa's mixed-parentage cousin Ginette, who will have a prosperous life married to a European, yet will also rage, "I am not an Annamite, I am not a Frenchwoman. I am a half-breed . . . that means a creature held in contempt by both races to which I belong."[52] Again invoking race, Chivas-Baron gives fictional and dramatic form to what, administratively, became a critical cultural and civil status dilemma within the Empire of Love, a theme she elaborates to tragic ends in *Confidences de métisse*. In this novella, a young woman, half Asian, half European, searches for her place in two worlds, neither of which will accept her: "I am one of pride, whom life has humiliated." Daughter of a Vietnamese woman and a French public works engineer who has since completed his duty "in the colonies," she sadly relates a "childhood unrolled at the edges of paternal existence," and as a young woman carries out a plan to find and torment her father for marginalizing and abandoning her.

Tracking down her father Lauzebert on a sea voyage—he unknowingly tells her "no madame, no, I have no métis on my conscience"—she reveals herself with bitter satisfaction. Stricken by guilt and the intensity of her hatred, he staggers deranged before her, then falls "headfirst into the waves."[53] The Ligue Maritime director Maurice Rondet-Saint assayed the "marriage" results of France and Indochina with no more optimism. "The métis, born of the unions of Frenchmen and native women, require their own discussion . . . their situation is assuredly, infinitely false." Such children were "fatally brought to be incorporated in one or the other of these two societies, within which there is no place." Colonial marriage, thus empire, were hardly sites of Viellis's essential eastern/western dichotomies but of endlessly produced conundrums and anxieties.

The secure "type" of the congaï, or the writing of the "Annamite" colonial subject were as unstable as topographical boundaries: earlier contests over the marking of the Mekong or Red River were now transposed to the sentiment and authority of intimate relations. Was the woman who bore a métis a wife, mother, or servant—and what of the child? What if the parents were unknown? When Charles Henry My attempted to claim the status of a French citizen from his mixed parentage in 1919, the Ministry of Justice issued an opinion on this "very delicate question," denying the citizenship and arguing "the Court of Appeals of Indochina will have already pronounced upon this in a judgment of May 28, 1903, by which it has refused to recognize the status of French citizen to a métis for the reason that the mother is a native [indigene]." The Ministry then asked for clarification on whether "in Indochina the natural child doesn't belong to the mother when this is known in fact, even when she does not expressly recognize her child."[54]

For the "native" and woman, status hinged upon the notion of "l'enfant naturel." For the colonial and man, it rested upon the legal status of recognition, declared in formal administrative documentation. This was underscored in cases in which the man died, leaving his "congaï" and children without claims to any of his French legal privileges. In the case of a petition brought by one Hai-Lôc after the sudden decease of a Captain Poirot, the court declined her case, noting "no declaration of birth in the name of the woman," and no trace "of an act of recognition drawn up at the request of this officer." In similar cases in Annam, the father's lack of recognition made the mother's "nature" determinate and found that "the child legally remains Annamite."[55] Rondet-Saint made clear the dissonance involved in imagining that nurture and right could be the same under colonialism: "Is it suitable to leave [them] in the maternal milieu, or should the father educate the children in such a way that they become members of French society, playing for their rights as citizens?" Such uncertainties and questions in colonial distinction would come to dominate twentieth-century and postcolonial policy.[56]

Even when marriage was not the key figure for the romance of France and Indochina, the production of "métis" identities was one of its most striking outcomes. This was particularly true where vehement declarations of love were the political currency between high levels of the colonial administration and Francophile Vietnamese.

For key French administrators, "romance" was as much policy as personal sentiment. Governor General de Lanessan lobbied directly for an empire of sincere loyalty and understanding: "We respect the religion and institutions of these peoples we attempt to colonize. There we find a double advantage: we thus gain their sympathies and their affection." In essay after essay he repeated his point: the best way to "solidly seat the influence of France in Indochina," was to literally "pacify" the country—not through conflict, but by gaining "the sympathies of the population."[57]

Governor General Albert Sarrault pursued a similar line. Letters from colonial advisors led by Lê-Van-Trung at Saigon praised the governor for his promises to protect and "elevate" Indochina, and offered, "these words have entered into the hearts of all natives who have conceived for you a true gratitude." At Sarrault's recall from the colony in 1916, local newspapers such as *La Cochinchine Libérale* and the *Midi Coloniale* printed headlines citing the displeasure of the Nghi-Viên delegates to the government, claiming "Demonstrations of Love in Tonkin in Favor of Albert Sarrault." The papers attacked Cochinchine deputy Ernest Outrey for his criticism of Sarrault's "pro-indigène" policies, citing the popularity of Sarrault's approach, and insisting that "few can boast for themselves to be so loved by the natives as Monsieur Sarrault. Yes, Monseiur Outrey, *loved* by the natives, who are, after all, in the millions."[58]

No governor ever gained the affection of millions but, within particular groups, the message and alliance worked effectively, creating political and cultural métis with overlapping attachments. Annamite and Cochinchine councillors implicated in the colonial administration were especially enthusiastic. During the Great War in Europe, one such wrote to his son, "We have still one non-equivocal duty of testimony to make: that is the affirmation to the metropole of our respectful love and our solidarity." Nguyên Phan Long would fictionalize such sensibilities in characters like his M. Minh who tells a friend, "I love France as a second patrie." Among the mandarins, the message of love and association was also well received and repeated. One such mandarin, Trân-Tan-Binh, gained a trip to France and returned to make a lecture in Hanoi in 1907 where he admonished his fellows, "The French have come here to assume our protection; they live among us on the same land . . . they love us, they are our masters and friends, they undertake all reforms to guide us toward progress and we do not seem to have put our hearts into it."[59]

One who certainly did put his heart into it was the essayist Trân Van Tung, whose *Rêves d'un campagnard Annamite* traces the self-conscious sentimental education of a village boy longing for a French identity. Governor General Jules Brévié wrote a preface describing "the obstinate ascent of a little Annamite peasant toward what might be conveniently called Western Civilization." The governor could hardly have asked for a more laudatory text, for here love and ideology are remarkably aligned. As Trân put it: "The France I love is that of all the Great Men . . . how could I not love her when she bears me all reasons to live, when my head is full of her thoughts, when my heart is full of her sentiments?" This perfectly realized subject of the Empire of Love further avowed, "This love that I have for you, for your people, I want to keep it in all its purity, in all its freshness to communicate it to my brothers, to my friends, to my readers . . . to engrave in fiery letters your well-loved names in the memories of all children of Annam." To this enthusiastically pedagogical project Trân exulted, "O my France, you will never know how much I admire, respect, and love you. You will never know all the depth of my love." This astonishingly romantic reverie even had the author confessing, "My France, will you believe me now, if I tell you quietly that I love you more than my own country, more than my little Indochina?"

But, still, the colonial shadow falls "between France and Indochina, between dream and reality, I have hours full of melancholy and sadness." Like a scorned or ridiculed lover Trân anguished, "I want to speak of my love with men of my country, but no one listens." Worse perhaps, "I want to speak of this love with my French brothers; they also, they do not wish to hear . . . this love I have for you . . . it weighs so heavy, so heavy upon my heart." Like the hybrid lives recorded in Chivas-Baron's fiction or French legal archives, Trân found himself a sort of métis, struggling between worlds. "I owe to my Indochine the shape of my body, the color of my hair, the tint of my face . . . but my consciousness, my thought, and my future, I owe them to my beloved France." His sadness and frustration were not assuaged by attempted reflections on his homeland of "numerous and beautiful pagodas, beautiful monuments, the many picturesque landscapes." All he could think was "Thank you my Great France with all my heart and soul for your precious and generous gifts."[60]

Such extraordinary declarations of love for France did not, of course, go uncontested. The colonial critic, writer, and pamphleteer Nguyên-An-Ninh derided the French "sentimental project" in 1925 and asserted, "Only a band . . . of former office boys raised by the colonial government to the highest ranks, and Annamites detached from Confucian doctrine sing the praises of the French domination." His work neatly complements Trân Van Tung's, for he also reveres the Great Men of French letters, yet the lessons he draws are strikingly different. Where Trân effervesced "my dear France is that of writers, poets, and philosophers," and wished to sing his fervor to the youth of Indochina, Nguyên claimed of the young generation, "they have received from the hands of the French themselves the act of condemnation." The colonials, he said, could not prevent young Vietnamese from reading Montesquieu, Rousseau, and Voltaire, "who preached the demand for basic liberties which protect human dignity." It was these for which the young people of his time yearned, "battling openly, in the name of humanitarian ideals and the principles of 1789."

In response to attacks that he was anti-French, Nguyên countered that the supposed "force of love" between French and Vietnamese was in reality a "force brutale" expressing the "pride and egoism" of a conqueror. As for himself, he could make a distinction between his attachments: "Annamites shaped by French schools no longer have . . . hatred of the conqueror, but almost all are anti-colonial."[61] Such contests would be most famously manifested by Nguyên Tat Thanh, who in 1911 sailed to Paris to study, and spent subsequent decades writing, agitating, and negotiating between the French, Chinese, Russians, and Japanese. Along the way he adopted the alias Nguyên Ai Quôc, and finally took the name Hô Chi Minh.

Vietnamese nationalists had some common cause with the inverted romance presented by the writer and colonial critic Félicien Challayé, who traveled in Indochina in 1901. Enraged by the insults and beatings delivered by Europeans upon the local peoples, the Frenchman discovered that "to protest against the cruelties one sees committed is to give proof of a naive humanitarianism . . . to be dishonored, even treasonous." Guardianship presumed neither equality nor justice; demanding them was indulgence, the wrong kind of humanitarianism. Challayé noted the frequent outrages committed "with no motive, no pretext, simply for pleasure, or better as they say, to 'maintain white prestige.'" Calling on the republic to end the brutalities, he concluded, "Only on this condition will cease to appear ironic, ridiculous, and cruel the motto posted on the walls of the native schools: Love France who Protects You."[62]

Challenging that motto and those schools would not be easy. History lessons in particular were tightly controlled in the name of the Empire of Love. Professor Chau Kim Dang's 1930 textbook *Leçons d'histoire d'Annam* showed no overt concession to Nguyên-An-Ninh's anticolonialism. The text was, after all, approved by supervising history instructor Lieutenant Colonel Bonifacy, whose preface announced, "I do not doubt that upon reading it, your young students will gain from your lessons sentiments of love and of recognition . . . for those who, in the past, have prepared the present, and that they will be fair to the France whose benevolent role they will appreciate."

The subsequent details of dynasties and chronologies of military actions suggested an aggrieved France disciplining disobedient charges, as in 1862 Cochinchine where "at the end of his patience, Admiral de la Grandière was compelled to resort to armed force." Yet intentional or not, Chau made clear a logic of history that could resonate differently to different ears. As Nguyên had claimed French *philosophes* and the legacies of 1789 for himself, so Chau ambiguously advances: "The study of history develops above all patriotism. In sharing, in effect, the joys and sorrows of one's ancestors, one loves them; in loving them, one is attached henceforth to the land they inhabit, which is our patrie."[63]

❧

Whose ancestors then, and love for what patrie? In 1913 *La Dépêche Coloniale* published a letter of "an Annamite from Hanoi" with a striking and ambivalent announcement. Beginning "I love this country to whom I owe life and death," the author gave the colonial government its due, yet warned of a romance gone sour: "After so many promises not kept, so many acts of kindness without result, the mass of the population, whatever one says, is disappointed." The following year, the anticolonial leader Nguyên-Chi-Binh took up arms against the supposedly well-loved Governor Sarrault and paid with his life. Reports of his capture related that "he pronounced, along the entire route from the place where he was interrogated to the execution site, patriotic words to prove that he truly loved his Annamite country and his compatriots." His final utterances directly confronted the loving mothers and devoted brothers of French empire. "You, French, you come to our home to take what I and my compatriots have for ourselves. You chase use away, you kill us in order to assure your own happiness and that of your own family."[64]

❧

Other stories return us to the figure of ruins. Charles Lemire, one of the first Southeast Asian scholars of the Ecole Française d'extrême orient to argue for archaeological preservation in Indochina, suggested, "It is in the traditions of France . . . to attach herself to the historical memories left by the peoples whom she dominates or protects." To him, protection and domination were indivisible projects.[65] In an 1891 survey of the French Indochinese empire, the geographer Charles Meyniard reiterated sentiments we have seen repeated across the Pacific—the notion that French empire was uniquely heartfelt in nature: "What other people has ever left such memories to subjugated races? . . . they have kept for their first conquerors their sympathies and their admiration." More, "what other has left in the hearts of its former children a memory more devoted to the mother country, a more solid attachment to its language, its spirit and its morals?" France alone could provide enough history for her charges, those who would be devoted children to her loving memory.

The Duc de Montpensier, interested primarily in hunting and adventures, also could not escape the essentialized rhetoric of a benign and compassionate empire. Ruminating on the Moi peoples: "The important thing is that these savages are penetrated by this thought, that the French are goodhearted people who don't wish them any harm; on the contrary, they've come among them to protect them from the persecutions of the Chinese and the Annamites, and have no other desire than to improve their lot."[66] Rounding out the Duc de Montpensier's paternalism in historical time, Charles Lemire concluded "'protection' does not apply only to people, but extends to the genius of disappeared or fallen races." He, like the Ecole Française d'extrême orient, like Auguste Pavie, would keep the ancestors. This brought the question of romance and ruins full circle: Indochina would be taken unto love, as with Bui, Nguyên, Pavie, or Chivas-Baron, or unto death, as with Garnier or Loti. But as she was created and possessed, so she could always and henceforth could only live through France.

In an 1879 ethnographic study of *Le Royaume d'Annam et les Annamites*, J. L. Dureuil de Rhins had suggested such a trajectory across the millennia of Southeast Asia unto the coming of the French. The Annamites, he pointed out, had themselves been conquerors of the local peoples, and it was upon their conquest that the very kingdom of Annam was founded. Yet, notably, "the conquests left nothing in the landscape but ruins, upon which they raised not a state flourishing by commerce and industry, but their domination." In surveying the ancient remainders of their triumph, the Annamites were unaware that "each nation seems to have an unconscious role to play in the general development of progress, and that of Annam will have been to prepare the road for new conquerors who would extend, upon a more unified land, the benefits of modern civilization."[67]

The conquerors wrote of monuments while creating blackened landscapes. In the novella *Thi-Vinh* by Clotilde Chivas-Baron, a young heroine on her first voyage to the capital is filled with strange visions of the roadside, of the passing landscape littered with "rusted cannons," and "abandoned pagodas whose stones are blackened by fire." In measured and melancholy tones, her father gestures out over the twilight visions, "these ruins my daughter are the work of the French, and one of these encampments is theirs. In our faraway province you have had no contact with this great race of the West. You will see in the capital many things that will surprise you, others that will amuse you, and others still that will bring suffering to your Annamite soul."[68]

At Angkor, Pierre Loti described ponderous Khmer temples taken by the jungle. Chivas-Baron disdained such exoticism and displayed the ruins of the Annamite kingdom as the deliberate carnage of French occupation and gunboat firepower. Loti himself underscored this common project in his other writings—his journalistic reports of French attacks in Annam: "The shells have caused another fire, a magnificent one, this village, pagoda, everything burning with immense red flames . . . all along the coast can be seen the glare of Annamite villages, which burn in the moonlight until morning." Fleeing the French attacks, Huê regent Tôn Thât Thuyêt wept, "one looks back toward the palace ruined in the hour of the snake. The French have raised their banner."[69] J. L. Dureuil de Rhins's ethnographic tale contained no traces of irony about historical succession, and none would likely have occurred to him from his privileged colonial vantage. Still, he might have known that the new conquerors would bear not only the romance of civilization but also their own purposeful talent for ruins.

SEVEN

JAPAN

The Tears of Madame Chrysanthème

"You didn't believe in my love . . ."

The Pacific, evening, a black canopy of sky filled with stars. A seaman is reading a letter as his ship leaves the coast of Japan; it contains the words of the woman he has just left, his contract wife, now weeping inconsolably at the papered doors overlooking the sea in Nagasaki harbor.

> I want you to know that when you are far away
> from me, very far
> That in Japan also there are women who love
> and who cry[1]

The scene will resonate with familiarity for admirers of *Madama Butterfly*, but it is not taken from Puccini's classic. Rather, its origin is the lesser-known French opera *Madame Chrysanthème* (1893), based upon the tale by Pierre Loti.[2] The two works share common dramatic premises: a Japanese contract wife, a charming Western mariner, and in particular a conclusion in which a shattered woman loves with desperation and futility a man who will leave her. In this, however, the French opera shares more with Puccini's vision than with its own literary source. In Loti's original tale, the final encounter between the seaman (named Pierre) and Chrysanthème does not result in tears and is curiously devoid of drama. As he comes to bid a final farewell, Pierre does not find Chrysanthème weeping; she is counting the coins she has received from him for the now-concluded marriage contract. Far from tormented by this final encounter, she is surprised and a bit annoyed by his appearance, hastily hiding the coins.[3] Messager's opera imposes the sadness

Fictions of marriage: "There are women who love and cry."
Pierre Loti (right), Pierre Le Cor, and Oyouki in Nagasaki.
Source: Maison de Pierre Loti, Rochefort

of the final letter, as a spectacle of grand emotion in the theater plays out against what Loti reported in his writing: a flat, dispirited, and craven love, not the pleasures of affection, but its disillusions.

Loti penned his tale in 1887. The strongest legacy of Japan in France from the 1850s and 1860s was in the realm of *beaux-arts*—hence the tendencies in French studies to emphasize the fashion for *Japonisme*, which profoundly affected painters such as Manet and writers such as the Goncourts. By the later 1870s, important contacts were developed by scholar-artist-adventurer Orientalists who actually went to Japan, such as the industrialist Emile Guimet, who founded the Museum for Asiatic Arts in Lyon and later Paris. Guimet's painter companion Félix Régamey became a serious student of Japanese culture and famously rewrote Loti's story—which he hated—from Chrysanthème's point of view, investing her, like Messager, with a heartbroken romantic spirit. His 1893 version presents Chrysanthème as the daughter of a once proud noble family, brought to ruin by rapacious "foreigners."

The Loti-Régamey split throws into relief Loti's familiar self-concern as man, mariner, and instrument of French imperial designs, and his disinterestedness in trying to comprehend Japan through his "wife." Yet the controversy also illuminates the more generous Régamey, who makes Chrysanthème a real "woman" at last—that is, a creature of pained and strained sensibilities, defined by the delicacy of her sentiment, ruled by the desire to let another know of her capacity for romantic love. In both cases, the authors used the emotional life of a Japanese woman to define their assessments of Japanese civilization.[4] The Japanese case is particularly arresting, for it forced important redefinitions of imperial ideologies. Although the island nation was subjected to unequal treaties and political concessions, it was never a European colony. The marker of Chrysanthème was not solely that of an encroaching Europe but of two empires reading *each other* for affirmations of progress—or decadence.

"You did not believe in my love." What did it mean to believe or not believe, to affirm or deny, to accept or resist the possibility of love in another? Chrysanthème's grief—or not—narrates a moment when French and Japanese writers redefined their places among the world's empires. From the middle of the nineteenth century, Japan was for Europe a curiosity, a land with an apparently continental heritage yet also an Oceanic history of "isolation" from the great currents of modern history. As the writer A. S. Doncourt put it, "But from where has she come, this race apart from the history of Asian peoples, living so long isolated on her archipelago, satisfied in herself and not asking anything of anyone?"[5]

The year 1868 saw the Meiji Restoration in Japan and the decline of the Shogun's retainer system in favor of an imperial, centralized state. In the preceding decade, Frenchmen had been prominent military and commercial advisers of the Shogun. In 1870, a disastrous war for France against Prussia and the confederation of the German Empire took place. With the restoration of the Japanese emperor and France's own loss to the Prussians, French advice fell out of favor. In 1892 one French journalist lamented, "We had, twenty-five years ago, the primary place . . . today the Germans have taken the best situations in Japan." As another reviewer for the Japanese press later put it, "Japan wanted to learn everything from France; lately, French influence has slipped away little by little . . . it has become, strictly speaking, nonexistent." Unlike their Pacific colonies or as in Indochina, the French found themselves judged wanting by their erstwhile protégés, as Germany, England, and the United States became new models for Japanese policy.[6]

As it had been around the Pacific in registers of faith, sensuality, or common purpose and patriotism, love became central to French readings of the Japanese. Unlike other Pacific islands, however, Japan at this time began industrializing and developing a formidable military challenge to Euroamerican domination in East Asia, thus earning comparisons not to Oceania but to Europe. Sentiment, passion, and noble emotion became geopolitical discourse against both a "Teutonic," rigidified Europe and a newly threatening Japan whose reputation, by the Sino-Japanese War of 1894–1895, was reimagined by French newspapers loudly warning of East Asia's "yellow Prussians." By the turn of the century, not only novelists but also policy makers needed to somehow renegotiate and narrate the meanings of Japan's claim to a forward place among nations.

No French work had such an impact in shaping attitudes toward Japan at the turn of the century as *Madame Chrysanthème*. Noting the enormous popularity of Loti's tale, the journalist Félix Martin observed in 1898, "Many of the French hardly know Japan except through *Madame Chrysanthème*." In a report to the naval ministry, one French sailor in 1911 warned of "our sentimental point of view" toward Japan, following the line of a Lieutenant Colonel Péroz who in 1906 had published a work clamoring that "our sentimentality has been awakened in their favor by a writer taken by Madame Chrysanthème, and more . . . by charming descriptions of fresh and delicious landscapes." Focusing on Loti's precious language, one literary critic even averred as late as 1926, "I believe that the contempt for the Japanese expressed in Loti's books in some measure influenced the Russians to refuse Japan's requests and led to the [Russo-Japanese] war of 1904. The Russian court was open to French influence, and many Russian naval officers of high rank, following Loti's example, had discovered *Madame Chrysanthème*."[7]

Japanese commentators felt compelled to respond to Loti. The newspaper correspondent I. Hitomi asked French friends not to take Madame Chrysanthème for "a specimen of Japanese womanhood," any more than "a public woman from Marseille who sells her favors to sailors represents Frenchwomen in general." Moreover, in a pointed remark on Loti's beloved Bretagne, Hitomi said that "the singularities collected from a Breton village should not be regarded as an image of the morals of all of France." Visiting in Paris, the diplomat Baron Suyematsu debated with his hosts the identity of the "true Chrysanthème," remarking that in the shadow of this tale "very few Westerners have any idea what Japanese women are."[8]

In his novel, Loti presented Chrysanthème as a superficially splendid, marginally charming woman of no great importance. Through her, Japan was small and precious, an amusing trifle of a country. With affected weariness, he exclaimed, "I really make a sad abuse of the adjective *petite*; I am quite aware of it, but how can I do otherwise?"[9] His Japanese were incomprehensible and "small" in every way: a false, self-interested people destroying their "traditional" society through greed and idiocy.

Artists such as Régamey imagined Chrysanthème quite differently: humiliated by the West, tormented by the foreigner, yet possessed of a rare and brilliant culture. Unimpressed by American claims to have "opened" Japan to trade in 1853, Régamey wrote of the "brutal" Yankee, "voracious and rapacious."[10] These views produced divergent narratives of a Japan that could or could not love, either a refined civilization like France violated and tragically shattered by barbaric invaders, or a materially progressive yet empty land like Prussia, seduced by industrial modernity—and soon—patriotic militarists.

What Loti denied his Japan was the capacity to suffer a broken heart, to anguish at separation, to know sentiment and intimate feeling; he called Japan "this tiny, artificial, and fictitious world."[11] Régamey, like Messager and Puccini in their operas, restored a grand, anguished femininity to Japan. In literary terms, Loti was fin-de-siècle, while Régamey was romantic, the one mordant, the other passionate, while Messager followed operatic conventions of emotional display. But Chrysanthème also was part of a "historiographical operation" that created a double narrative: a widely held view that Japan was a devious and heartless land, somewhat like Germany, yet also a sympathetic "romance" of Japan, clinging, like France, to its refinement and dignity in an age of social and political shocks.

Through the question of "love" French writers organized their versions of themselves and of Japan, inscribing ideologies of emotion and sensibility. *Chrysanthème* was deployed in a politics of emotion to critique religion, social structure, marital relations, and labor practices. Favorable or unflattering, these views were ideologically linked to making love, and the possibility of a woman's tears, the measure of Meiji Japan's—and France's—place in history.

❦

Madame Chrysanthème is the story of a liaison, not a love affair. What the author discovered in Japan during his naval sojourns were not the cultural and artistic beauties so profoundly extolled by Japonisme and instant Japanophiles like Régamey. Loti's story is one of disappointment and disillusion. He captures in literary images the Japan of teahouses and geishas, of "the land of musumés" (young women), yet the tone that suffuses his temporary marriage is that of weariness, boredom, and incomprehension. The tale is unsettling in its relentless antiromantic tone, in its insistent portrayal of a Japan of spurious charms, of idiocies and self-interested principles—both Oriental and Occidental.[12]

Loti was of course a true imperialist, showing the flag from North Africa to East Asia. By contrast, Régamey drew robust portraits of women rebels during the Paris Commune and taught at the École des Arts Décoratifs. His brothers also were lithographers and painters, and his father had worked as a printer with Juliette Adam's old nemesis, the mutualist-socialist Pierre-Joseph Proudhon.[13] The differences between Loti and Régamey, politically and temperamentally, were many; perhaps one of the most telling distinctions was their relations to *Japonisme*. Many writers who championed the *Japoniste* aesthetic, such as Edmond de Goncourt, were vehemently against popular movements like the Commune. Goncourt called the people of Paris "la canaille" and thought them savages, "something exotic which voyagers will search for at the cost of a thousand sufferings in faraway countries." He adhered fundamentally to a belief in an aristocratic society where the cultured elite and the true artists would be synonymous.[14] Loti was the supreme expression of this dual vision, obeying the aristocratic principle of the *littérateur*, actually pursuing exoticism on his naval missions around the world, and later joining Goncourt in the Académie Française.

Like almost everything in Loti's universe, his ideal Japan would have been aristocratic: the noble samurai, the exquisite geisha of his woodblock-print dreams, now sullied by a modernizing Japan. Régamey championed an identical early modern iconography, yet his appreciation of worker's politics, craft-training, and teaching, and *atelier* career turned his *Japonisme* toward inspiration rather than ennui. Like many "applied" artists, Régamey saw Japanese craft technique as a means to revive moribund traditions in French painting and illustration in the fin de siècle, and he adopted Japanese practices as demonstrations of the resilience and adaptability of French spirit and artistic genius in an age of political setbacks. Publishing the craft and culture survey *Le Japon Pratique*, Régamey exclaimed, "In Japan . . . art is everywhere, as if mingled with the air one breathes." In part, Loti's soured vision of Japan stems from his littérateur's sense of decline in a materialist, popular age, while Régamey's enthusiastic view springs from the patriotic-aesthetic possibilities of a revived artistic tradition.[15]

As a serious student of Asia, Régamey faulted Loti's egotism and arrogance as a writer and naval officer, and his superficial knowledge of Japan, gained largely from ports of call. Although cursory, Loti's knowledge of Japan was firsthand, and oddly appropriate to his literary project. Loti did not seek out "authentic" Japan, for his interest was not in understanding Japan, but, as always, in expressing his disaffection with change, with the extinction of his childhood dreams of the marvelous and exotic at the end of the nineteenth century. As one 1887 reviewer put it, "*Madame Chrysanthème* is not a novel, it is a page of memories." Loti's idea of home, never urbane Paris, once again returned to the rustic comforts of his Rochefort on the Atlantic coast, where he entertained, collected curiosities, and built his fetishistic chambers—including a Japanese pagoda—to replicate fantastic visions of the Orient as a place of ancient knowledge and timeless pleasures.[16]

Against this desire to escape to the East, the real Japan of the 1880s was a disappointment. From the 1850s colonies of French, British, and Americans (along with the centuries-long established Dutch) were implanted in Nagasaki, Yokohama, and Tokyo, with multiple Japanese missions already traveling to Europe and France. Fukuzawa Yukichi in 1862 and Narushima Ryuhoku in 1873 both visited and later wrote detailed accounts of Haussmann's Paris and of the governments of Napoleon III and the Third Republic. Japanese students in Paris and Lyon filed reports on military science, mechanical engineering, mining, agriculture, political economy, and physics. Tomii Masaki studied law and became a professor at Tokyo University and Nakae Chomin—translator of Rousseau—read politics and led a People's Rights and Freedom Movement in the 1880s while Loti was still dreaming of flowers and kimonos.

In 1887, the same year of Loti's *Chrysanthème*, Chomin published *A Discourse by Three Drunkards on Government*, an ingenious set of propositions for Japan's political future, much of it based on his studies with the philosopher Emile Acollas. In contrast to Chrysanthème's submissive, trifling silences, Chomin's characters had much to say about *French* character and history. Notably, a Gentleman of Western Learning displays his mastery of national stereotypes—self-fashioned and otherwise—by expounding, "The British are rational and the French emotional; the British are calm and the French turbulent . . . the spirit of Great Britain, logical and coherent, is that of an accomplished man. But the French spirit is that of genius; it ignores logic and soars dramatically." The French were easily "intoxicated" by the new, borne by passions and fervors released by their revolutions, eternally desirious of grand spectacles: "While Great Britain is a school textbook, France is a drama."[17]

That drama played out in the success of Loti's vision. At the Paris Universal Exposition of 1867, Shibusawa Eiichi had described the enthusiastic attention paid by visitors to the exotic promises of a Japanese-imported teahouse and the "first Oriental women who have ever come to Europe," while he preferred the industrial galleries and a huge steam engine.[18] Loti and much of Europe, in many ways and evidence to the contrary, never recovered from the Japan of the teahouse. In the French case, part of this may have been Gallic historical character à la Chomin, and part can be directly traced to the diplomacy of Ambassador Léon Roche, who backed both the Paris teahouse exhibit and the collapsing Bakufu government until its demise in 1867, stranding French influence in the late Tokugawa era. An aesthetic drawn from woodblock prints and Emile Guimet's concentration on religious art and sculpture additionally reinforced a "traditional" vision of a timeless, isolated Japan while simultaneously deploring—subtly or not—the changes that defined the "modern" Meiji state.

As the steam engine crowded out the teahouse, the romance of Japan became the disillusion Loti captured in his writings. Some of his sensibility carries over into Messager's opera. From the opening scenes, the sacred and profane are indistinguishable. Western ships come not upon the land of serene Buddhas but upon vulgar hawkers in boats singing over one another: "Buy vases with the images of Buddha / and those of the Gods of Japan / Buy them for two piastres."[19]

The situation was made worse by the unsettling familiarity of the changes. One French traveler described Meiji Japan as marked by "the most striking similitudes with that which derive from our own civilization." If the first impressions of Japan were the stuff of picturesque traveler's tales, "the woods which cover the tiny islands, the bamboos, camellias, azaleas, the original spectacle of a crowd of sampans," a step away from the coastline revealed the quick disenchantment of shabbily dressed men with awkwardly worn bowler hats, stiff, uniformed police rather than samurai, and "horrible brick and stone constructions, heavy and without any style." Here was a Japan not only despoiled, but one whose ugliness was European in inspiration.[20]

Japan in the 1880s was a Japan too late for love, too late to pursue the idyllic pleasures of an uncorrupted East. A mysterious or sensual Orient could be presented only sarcastically. As he leaves Chrysanthème, Loti's Pierre is barely regretful, noting, "The fear that I might be leaving her in some sadness had almost given me a pang, and I infinitely prefer that this marriage should end as it had begun, in a joke." For her part, Chrysanthème returns the sentiment by scrupulously manifesting the appropriate signs of a woman facing separation. "At the outer gate I stop for the last adieu: the little sad pout has reappeared, more accentuated than ever on Chrysanthème's face; it is the right thing, it is correct, and I should feel offended now were it absent."[21]

For Loti, any joy or sadness radiating from his "wife" only indicated her adherence to signs and custom, her acting out of emotion she could not feel. In Messager's, Régamey's, and Puccini's versions of East, West, and convenience marriage, Madame is crushed by despair when her man demonstrates his faithlessness to her poignant delusions of love. Yet Loti wrote passionate, if condescending, tales. In his earlier novels, *The Marriage of Loti* and *Aziyadé*, he marries and leaves native women in Tahiti and Turkey, then sails away in the end from the wreckage of their lives without him. He was capable of imagining and describing female anguish, if not his own.

Perhaps he was fatigued by this narrative; or perhaps Japan was simply not a setting where it could take place. Loti had a colorful palette and imagination, and was greatly responsible for imitator's tales which, according to one contemporary, revealed Japan as a land of "young women, tea houses, pagodas of love, districts without night."[22] Yet his soured enthusiasm is not simply fin-de-siècle spleen, for the Japan of astonishing temples, serene Buddhist monks, and proud warriors was a Japan already receding by the time Loti's story became a sensation in late 1880s Europe. In fact, Japan in many ways had become a site to mock Europe and European ideals.

Although famed for its elegant style and poetic descriptions, *Madame Chrysanthème* is, oddly enough, a startlingly harsh and realist portrait of Japan. Loti always insisted it was drawn not from his imagination but from his notebooks, and in this he subverted his own myths about romantic imperialism. He was certainly no Emile Zola, but he recorded the Japan he saw: the Japan of treaty ports. He fictionalized the men and women, the merchants and traffickers of those environs, those most affected and exploited by the breaching of closed ports and the widening of foreign imperialism. One English critic, Reginald Farrar, typically denounced *Madame Chrysanthème* as a "poor portrait of typical Japanese womanhood," then, unwittingly, made Loti's case: "but of course, Loti's Kiku (Chrysanthemum) was never Japanese at all. She was born, bred, and practised in the debased and brutalising life which grows up in any foreign seaport town, whither our sailors from the West carry our enlightenment and our desires."[23]

Primary among those desires was a search for the East from within European privilege. Loti indulged his special distinctions in rank and law even as he lamented their decidedly unromantic shaping of his supposed marriage.

> They gave me an extraordinary document, a sheet of rice-paper which set forth the permission granted me by the civilian authorities of Kiu-Siu to inhabit a house situated in the suburb of Diou-djen-dji, with a person called Chrysanthème, the said permission being under the protection of the police during the whole of my stay in Japan.[24]

False and formulaic, the marriage maintained certain appearances of the sort travel writer Edmond Cotteau described in 1885: "One would have rather taken them for good young bourgeois girls than for courtesans." Yet what Farrar observed ironically was what Loti would narrate so sardonically: the corrupt imperial modernity of the West. Chrysanthème's counting of her contract coins only underscored an imperial relation stripped of any values save that of commerce. From within his "marriage," Loti recorded Japanese readings of Europe, and American, British, and French versions of Japan; in "wife" Chrysanthème, in her shallowness, dreams, and romantic hopes, he saw the West and he saw himself.[25]

What Loti saw was a Japan framed within a version of what the French enemy, Bismarck, had in another context called a "struggle for civilization." Within a generation Japan astonished Europe with an industrializing economy, rational administration, and medical and educational advances. Deputy Paul d'Estournelles de Constant demanded, "What has become of the legendary Japan of our youth, the privileged land of chrysanthemums and of azaleas, the homeland of rare flowers and refined masterpieces?"[26] For decades the "teahouse" imagination had defended France, but no more.

The new Japanese nation appeared to become suddenly "Western," openly defying the laws and logic of nineteenth-century universal historical progress and "the impossibility of sudden transformations" as described for the *Revue de Deux Mondes* by political writer G. Apport. By the 1880s, Japanese development not only impressed, but challenged the West. The "imitator" was succeeding all too well, inverting the authority of its masters. In his reports from Yokohama, Admiral Bergasse Dupetit Thouars noted, "One thing which strikes me above all in Japan is that far from falling into decomposition upon contact with Europeans as other societies . . . on the contrary the people of the country know how to assimilate what they find convenient and useful of our habits." Where Europeans often looked upon colonized peoples as children, Dupetit Thouars observed, "The Japanese . . . pretend to amuse themselves like children with insignificant details; we would be played for fools and led into a trap."[27]

In 1868, the last of the Shoguns had been overthrown by clans loyal to the imperial house. By 1894–1895, war between Japan and China over the fate of Korea and Japan's military triumph forever altered Western opinions of the old land of paper houses. Japan was now a military, naval, colonialist nation, the regional power of Asia, fitfully entering into the ranks of Western imperial states. By 1904–1905, increasing tensions with the tsar and the Russo-Japanese war only confirmed this trajectory. The stunning defeat of the Russian Empire (and France's diplomatic ally) and the advent of American mediation meant that Japan was now not an Orientalized picturesque land, even less a Westernizing concatenation of Confucianism and toy locomotives, but a "peril jaune" (yellow peril) whose ruthless ambition required a rethinking of its historical position vis-à-vis the West. In the year of the Russo-Japanese War, the journalist Charles Pettit wrote that Japan had somehow become a country "dangerous and ferocious, populated by little men both ruthless and energetic." He was only copying Loti, who years earlier had warned of "a little people which will be, among the family of yellow races, the breeding ground of hatred against our white races."[28]

As Japan quickly closed the military, administrative, and technological divide with the West, shaken French journalists and critics sought to restore distinctions to their ambivalent authority. Physiognomy and "progress" were resituated. A flood of new studies argued that racial advance would not be a triumph of geopolitics or economics, but of a redefined "civilization," a civilization that was not technology, nor even armies nor tax and legal codes—all of which could be copied and imitated. Charles Pettit noted that it was important not to confuse civilization with material progress that was in fact only one of the results of civilization. The French had been down this road before. The 1789 Revolution had presumably established France as the universal center of liberty, equality, and fraternity. The fallout of the Franco-Prussian War in 1870, fears of *degénération* and German *Kultur* had then sharpened French criteria for Gallic supremacy.

The political theorist Ourel Reshef has noted that the war for the French was more than a shocking and sobering loss; it had become a clash of "two principles of humanity . . . might and right, the quintessences of two civilizations, German and French."[29] Although Japan did not come into large-scale military conflict with France, the terracing of the road to progress and dignity was similar.[30] Pettit rhetorically kept Japan at bay: "Civilization is above all made up of moral ideas . . . it is greatly mistaken to think a people civilized in our sense because they have adopted our artillery pieces, our railways, and our electrical apparatuses." In *Chrysanthème*, Loti insistently encoded the threat of Japanese manufactures as "imitative decadence," while commander Roncière le Noury reported from Yokohama, "they have created nothing, perfected or improved nothing, and have remained always inferior even in their imitation."[31] The Japanese had the trappings of the West, but were not a truly modern people. In aesthetics, administration, and economics, the Japanese were merely a race of imitators, forever trying to keep up with their betters.

As imitators, the Japanese could never truly threaten the cultural hegemony of French civilization. The journalist and critic Victor Bérard commented, "Japan is not a people as the French people are France; it is the Mikado, the chain of gods and of spirits that link the Japanese nation to the eternal powers." In this, he invoked a subtle yet clear distinction between a fixed subject bound to tradition and a self-willing citizen. Watching Chrysanthème pray in a temple, Loti mused, "Does she possess a soul? Does she think she has one?" Her actions were for him charming and mechanical, a faith held merely "out of respect for ancient customs."[32]

Chrysanthème's mannered performance as "wife" was equally splendid yet empty; it composed a role but lacked a person. For the French, defining that person was tied up in French history. In 1868, the Japanese had restored an emperor as the French in 1870 were casting off their own. A society of manners and masks was redolent of the ancien regime. As Bérard put it, "The Japanese will never arrive at the state of man as we understand it when we see 'un homme fait;' he remains always the son of a father who is himself the son of another father." At the moment of her final separation from Loti, Chrysanthème's good manners in refusing to continue counting her coins only earns the mariner's scorn. "I expected as much; to do so would have been contrary to all her notions of politeness, hereditary and acquired, all her conventionality, all her Japaneseness."[33] By remaining tied to form and obligation, the Japanese bowed to authority in indifference to the great historical achievement of the West, the liberation of individual expression and sentiment.

The French loss to Germany only exacerbated this distinction, as French writers took on Prussian discipline as definitively symptomatic of cultural inferiority. The writer M. L. Gagneur characterized the enemy across the Rhine in 1873 by its solidity, regularity, "absence d'élan," and described "the natural inertia" of the German.[34] The French thought both the Japanese and Germans highly disciplined, but after 1870, found this discipline suspect. In his endless sarcasm toward Chrysanthème, and the Japanese in general, Loti intoned, "in speaking of them, we say, 'our little trained dogs,' and in truth they are singularly like that." Carrying this theme into other writings, Loti described scenes of Japanese dancers, "like automatons, without the slightest personal initiative."[35] Japan was not a culture empty of talent, sophistication, or the ability to develop itself in political economy, but—like Prussia's Germany—one lacking the richness of individual volition and sentiment.

One sentiment in particular interested the French—love. Specifically, individual romantic love between a man and woman, shaped by a courtly tradition. In his journal of 1870–1871, Edmond de Goncourt had denounced the new Prussian Germany precisely on this point. The innocent, "sentimental nest of platonic love," from which had sprung "the ideal, fictive worlds of Werthers and Charlottes," now only produced "the most hardened soldiers, the most perfidious diplomats, the most rascally bankers."[36] Without love, no country could seriously claim to be home to a truly civilized people.

So it is that we also find a great deal of attention to questions of "love" in French Meiji-era writings about Japan. In fact, interrogations of love might even explain Japan's successes in political economy. Ludovic Naudeau's *Le Japon moderne* suggested that Japanese men were quick to build up the "grandeur of Japan" because they were unencumbered by the demands of intimate relations and *la vie amoureuse*. The idea of romantic love was presumably nonexistent in their lives. In a detailed study of *La Société Japonaise*, the scholar André Bellessort, a solid contributor on Asia to Juliette Adam's *Nouvelle Revue*, remarked how both the Japanese and French were fond of what seemed to him theatrical farces and swashbuckling heroics (musketeer and samurai tales) yet concluded, "To be sure, one must not push the comparison too far! I know how very much our conception of life and especially of love distinguishes us from the Japanese." In fact he argued, "The idea of love . . . hardly flowers among the Japanese. This individual sentiment does not fit into the frameworks of society."[37]

Individual sentiment was the presumptive basis of morality and the historical development of civilization. The question of romantic love thus became critical to grasping whether Japan was truly or falsely modern. Pursuing love was the way to go to the heart of things, to see the real behind the manners and masks. What would it mean if a civilization with Krupp cannons, French naval officers and silk factories, heavy industry, telegraphs, armies, schools, and railways should be found incapable of love?

As far as French writers were concerned, the weight of this question fell upon knowing about Japanese women. As a *romancier*, Loti was not unique in making a woman, Chrysanthème, a sign for Japan. Bellessort remarked,

"Their land is woman [leur terre est femme] and bewitches us"; an under-standing of women's estate would illuminate "the very essence of their ancient civilization." The line of reasoning directly ranked Japan's modernity according to French ideas of women's station. As Charles Pettit argued it: "We French are accustomed to respecting women by atavism, by tradition, and by education; we've made this the criteria of our civilization and this is why we cannot admit the Japanese claim to be our equal in civilization as long as they have not reformed their customs regarding their women."[38] Had not Juliette Adam herself written, "A people is barbarous to the degree it despises its women and the abasement it imposes on them?"[39]

Primary among French complaints was the Japanese lack of an exalted courtly tradition of romantic love, as the essayist Charles Loonen described it in his studies of Japanese theater and literature: "The characters of their romances battle to keep the mistress which pleases them; they are never heroes that would merit the good graces of their beautiful one by chivalric actions." And real women's lives? Japan was superior only to its own "Ori-ent." Noted Loonen, "One cannot still compare the state of the women in Japan with that of women in Asia; the Japanese woman visits her friends, goes out with her family, participates in public festivities and manages her home . . . if [her situation] is inferior to that of Europeans, she is strongly superior to those of other Asian women." Yet what characterized this supe-riority? According to Charles Pettit, in a phrase strongly echoing Loti, a temperament "sweet, friendly, proper, and fastidious, incredibly devoted to their masters. In brief, the character of a good dog."[40]

For Pettit, the claim against Japan was not that the women were inef-fectual nor decorative. Indeed, he insisted "they are not dolls, these little Japanese women, the force which they possess to dominate their passions, or in any case hide their feelings is the clue to a strong and willing charac-ter." In fact he commented on Japanese women's "ferocious character," their strength in enduring lives filled with "agony, horrible convulsions."[41] The question of Japan's place in modern history was not strictly in the rights and roles of women, but what, through these women, could be understood as acceptable in the emotional civilization of Japan.

Most French writers accepted the thesis articulated by André Belles-sort: "Japanese education proposes less to heal souls of their original mala-dies, than to render them sociable." To be Japanese meant "choking back painful emotions, even the most legitimate."[42] Such apparently antinatural behavior was rooted in the powerful unity of a philosophical fatalism and an aristocratic warrior tradition, a unity and metaphysic distressingly resis-tant to Western notions of love, sentiment, and romantic chivalry. The great distinction with the West lay in the weakness of Christian traditions and the Renaissance Humanist legacy in Japan, which seemed to impress as a faithless land where individuals were not respected, where Buddhism was a consolation of monks and Shinto an ideology of reverence for the long history of emperors.

One French writer recorded a meeting with a man laughing over the death of a friend; "everything created must die," explained the man, leaving the writer to surmise that for the fatalistic Japanese, profound sorrow or emotional loss apparently "excluded sociability, fraternity, and to say all in a word, *charité*"; the summation is telling for the way the Western word for the greatest of possible loves is negated in Japan where "the spirit of Christian charity is foreign."[43] Thus, a land of women who could not cry; a land without charity—that is, without compassionate, brotherly love: Japan was a giant of material progress, but a dwarf in those qualities of sentiment and morality by which the French refined their notion of civilization. In elaborating his disaffection with Meiji Japan, Loti disparaged Chrysanthème for his own inability to experience stirrings of emotion for his colonial position. Although he played the master, her ritualized, formal attentiveness to him, "which I should find amusing in anyone else—anyone I loved—irritates me in her."[44]

~

Loti's mocking account is startlingly distinct from Messager's and Puccini's weeping women in its emotional opaqueness. His vision was not particular; many Western Meiji chroniclers wrote similarly about stereotypically "inscrutable" Japanese. The naval commander Clement de la Roncière le Noury reported, "They excel at discussions lasting for entire days without conclusions and without betraying their innermost thoughts." The American writer Eliza Scidmore also suggested, "They and their outward surroundings are so picturesque, theatrical and artistic that at moments they appear a nation of poseurs—all their world a stage and all their men and women merely players."[45]

Such optics could be reversed as the "players" showed themselves keen exploiters of what they in turn read as Western and French tastes and characteristics. Nakae Chomin had called France a "drama," and the activist and actor Kawakami Otojiro, also a strong partisan of the People's Rights Movement, made his reputation performing satirical and polemical dramas with his troupe throughout western Japan in the 1880s and 1890s. Touring Europe in 1900, he and his celebrated wife Sadayakko adapted their repertoire to strongly dramatize "Japanese" emotions, including wrenching romance leading to despair and gratuitous scenes of ritual suicide. When André Gide enthused, "Sada Yacco gives us the sacred emotion of the great dramas of antiquity, which we seek and no longer find on our own stage," he sought the revitalizing Japan of Regamey and the Japonistes. Yet, he was watching performances that were as much Sadayakko's impressions of France and French passions as they were insights into Japan. As she herself recounted, "Under their grace and beauty all the French people are hungry for blood and tears."[46]

Like Loti after *Madame Chrysanthème*, Sadayakko found journalists pressing her to talk about love in Japan. Her responses about amorous custom and the "very noble, sublime, and sacred" nature of love were couched in a register not—perhaps as hoped for—of romance and passion but of loyalty and propriety. It was a particular historical moment to which the Kawakamis responded, an understanding elaborated by Otojiro to his fellow actors: "The great fame and fortune that our troupe has met with today is by no means due to our own abilities but because, as the Japanese empire won the recent war [the Sino-Japanese war of 1894–1895], many countries have focused their attention on Japan." Parisian rapture over the historical romances of Sadayakko and Otojiro was more than dramatic appreciation: "Our present success is partly due to the fact that foreigners are interested in dramas performed by a victorious nation . . ."[47] Paris audiences may have craved sentimental exoticism yet were increasingly drawn—consciously or not—to stories whose attraction was framed by a rival imperialism.

In this instance, Japanese "love" was made possible by a shifting global order in the Pacific. To ask for love from Sadayakko in 1901 was to seek, as with Gide or Regamey, the deficits in Gallic civilization, and to interrogate the foundations of an exotic stranger's success—both in sentiment and conquest. Sadayakko's artistry, in demonstrating—as one reviewer put it—that "a Japanese woman can love deeply, hate savagely, and then die quietly," provided stereotyped images of "Oriental" female submission for audiences, yet within a dutiful "Japanese ethos" of sacrifice and passion ultimately linked to Otojiro's "victorious nation."[48]

In a notable essay, Charles Pettit summarized his view of Japanese civilization with an image of men departing for military service and the possibility of women's tears. "These poor women contain themselves so as not to weep; it is pitiful to see. But they keep calm and silent as demanded by their proud traditions of the past: women must not cry at the departure of warriors, but must maintain admirable respect."[49] Locating the emotional nexus of Japan at a moment of departing troops and the possibility of female tears was historically astute and unsettling. Along with Sadayakko's dramatic talent and Otojiro's staging of Japanese empire through patriotic, pro-Meiji plays, such crossings would establish Japanese "love" stories as political dramas shifting from colonial submission to imperial sacrifice—and imperial conquest.

Loti himself was forced to modify his 1887 vision of a childish, precious Japan by the turn of the century. Revisiting the islands in 1900 as the Kawakamis toured Paris, he wrote from shipboard, "This bay seems like a pleasant garden, no?" yet in the same letter intoned of the political atmosphere, "It is war first of all between Russia and Japan, war declares itself, soon and inevitable . . . so much it is decided in each yellow brain."[50] The militaristic fervor of 1900 and the frank expression of nationalist passions were no longer commensurable with the Japan of previous decades and the foreign privilege and banalities of the treaty port.

However broadly Loti and others condemned the emotional insincerity of modern Japan, these same commentators still widely agreed that "the most noble sentiment" of love did in fact exist, and quite powerfully, in Japan: it was called *patriotism*. Here was truly the site of Japanese passions, the manifestation of "the sentiments of love and of ardent ambition."[51] Writing in 1895 at the time of the Sino-Japanese War, the political journalist G. Apport, despite his ambivalence about Japanese imperial designs, commented with admiration: "The Japanese love their homeland with a passion that is not always clear, but which necessarily must be respected." In Paris, the Japanese diplomat Baron Suyematsu would concur, "A nation is on the right road when it places its loyalty in the sovereign and love of the country above all other private and petty considerations."[52]

In Japan, what might be love of the emperor and of country was uniquely intertwined with "the private," and French commentators were able to elaborate their arguments about Japanese sentimental life and women's estate through the institutions which intersected all in daily practice: the family and marriage.

Not surprisingly, discussing *amour de la patrie* in Japan was a way of admitting that love could be real while simultaneously, in this case, condemning it. As French political writers intoned that Germany *used to be* a homeland of individual expression, the Japan scribblers also challenged Meiji society as a nightmare of domination and submission. The journalist Félix Martin showed distinctions between East and West by trading on the moral and civil superiority of French domestic life: "Among us the equality of the father and the mother tends more and more to be the constitutive base of the family," whereas the Oriental Confucian system ordained that the woman "must obey her father, her husband, and then her male children."

Unsettled at home by feminist agitation and the emergence of the *nouvelle femme*, writers like Martin held up unequal Japan as an example to demonstrate the *liberté* and *egalité* of women in France. A generation later, in the 1930s, the universitaire Félicien Challaye began to suggest parity, arguing "it is modern feminism which, by raising the moral and social status

of women, permits Japanese men and women to express anew the appreciation of love, the sweetness and sorrow of loving, as did their noble ancestors
in the year one thousand."

As Challaye's temporal reference indicates, even he thought love had
been lost in Japan's modernity—largely to a "Chinese philosophy of feminine inferiority." He extolled the classicism of Sei Shonagan's *Pillow Sketches*
and Murasaki Shikibu's *Genji Monogatari* ("principally an account of amorous adventures") yet concurred that "from the beginning of the seventeenth
century especially, the status of woman begins to drop," and "love plays a less
and less important role . . . the liberty of loving, and of doing as one likes is
allowed to no one but geishas."[53]

Although strong, resourceful, and better off than in the rest of Asia,
Meiji women would become—as far as Europeans were concerned—little
better than servants or slaves. The writer Paul de Lacroix was one of many
who suggested, "The woman must spend her existence obeying; her role
she plays is thus passive. Her duty is to bend her knee and to bow before
her husband." The writer and critic Arthur de Claparède cogently expressed
the similitudes between Meiji politics and the now formalized binding of
patriotism and privacy: "The man is not only the head of the family, he is
the center, or better, the incarnation. Young women are but the servants of
their father, wives the domestic servants of their husbands. Paternal power is
unlimited . . . a small state within a state."[54]

Family replicated nation, in a particular Japanese way—a people under a
divine emperor, linked by a "chain of gods and of spirits." What served the
divine father figure thus served the incarnated lineages of heaven and was
the greatest expression of love; what served only personal matters distracted
from this. As such, romantic love as understood by Europeans would be
dangerous if introduced into Japanese society. Commented André Bellessort, "A family where all of the members are tightly subordinated to each
other considers love as a disorganizing agent and does not base its harmony
on the most unstable of our sentiments, the most diverse, often the most
self-interested." Thus, "It is not by affection . . . that a man should choose his
wife, nor by affection that a wife should obey her husband, because human
inconstancy and other affections could impede duties or lead souls astray."[55]

What Europeans prized as "love" and "affection" were, presumably, alien
to Japan. Suggested Bellessort, "In the eyes of the Japanese a marriage for
love is . . . a sort of forfeiture, at the very least the admission of a con-
temptible weakness." Affection, he argued, "is admitted, but in the manner
of a parasitic plant." When Loti in his novel discovers a possible attraction between "wife" Chrysanthème and his best friend Yves, a moment of
divided love threatens, and he declares, "we might even find here, ready at

hand, the elements of a fratricidal drama." But it is not to be, for "we are in Japan, and under the narrowing and dwarfing influence of the surroundings . . . nothing will come of it all."[56]

For Loti, "narrowing and dwarfing" characterized the oppressive atmosphere of a servile and insincere culture. In Japan, despotic duty and sacrifice were all. In their dutiful role, women obeyed the males of the family, yet this also meant denying comfort to those men except in sacrifice to the principle and the glory of the imperial dynasty. Baron Suyematsu recounted a tale of a dying mother who refuses to see her son—he has abandoned his military regiment to make the journey home. "If you dare approach me, you shall have to break this mosquito netting which is my iron fortress." The mother has no love for a man merely as her son, and he returns to battle without seeing her. Jean Dhasp (pen name of Antony Klobukowski, consul general at Yokohama) recorded a theatrical piece in which a young child upsets an altar while playing and has his throat cut before his mother for his transgression. What impressed and appalled Dhasp was the "mother's" lack of reaction. "The mother, crouching low, has not moved. Remaining alone, she takes a moment and looks out at the audience. Attention! This is the scene of maternal despair!" Perhaps she feels shamed; she certainly does not weep for her unfortunate child.[57]

The apparently fanatical Japanese attachment to duty and sacrifice fascinated French writers. How was it possible? What were its human costs? Diplomatic notes concentrated on distortions of Japanese emotionalism—patriotism become fanaticism. At the outbreak of the Sino-Japanese War in 1894, the French minister at Tokyo wrote Paris, "The Japanese government has been drawn into war almost exclusively for reasons of pure sentiment." Insistent upon the centrality of these misguided passions, such reports focused on the possibilities of Japanese imperial mimicry of Western powers. With grave concern, the report spoke of a Meiji state which "has allowed itself to be carried away by illusions and vanities," while tracing this threat directly to "everything . . . that forms this young Japan of bureaucrats, officers, and scientists artificially subjected to European culture."[58] For the minister, Japanese elites had appropriated all too well the project of shaping a discourse of national love into imperial policy.

Japan's militarism was only one source of interest and disquiet. As ever, young women were a constant focus. Despite—or perhaps because of—the cultural power of Madame Chrysanthème in France, more than a few commentators searched out what the mask of the musumé might be disguising: young women whose energies and bodies shaped Japan's modernity but who were its harsher, uglier side. Japan's startling economic prowess in particular was an opportunity for journalists (and in this case, missionaries) to illuminate the presumed state of civilization in the island nation. The export products with which Japan stunned the world were turned out by cheap labor, "women in the majority," a cruel system of female impoverishment, weeklong workshifts tied to deafening, dangerous, machinery and disease-ridden factories, a system in which "girls compete with women and where the work is twenty four hours a day."[59]

The Catholic journalist L. Joly noted "the development of heavy industry has singularly aggravated the servitude of the woman. She is sought in all the factories because . . . more docile than the man, more able in certain types of work, she is satisfied with a lower salary." For Joly, Japanese women were strong—in ways not enviable: "they carry coal, maneuver cranes to raise heavy pieces of iron from the bottom of boats by the sweat of their brows. They are courageous . . . deformed, bent, ravaged before their time." And as always, marriage, that "solemn act" was for the woman "simply a change of master . . . the consecration of a new servitude."[60]

Thus, another of Japan's illusions; if Madame Chrysanthème were Japan's face to France, the apparent coquettery, the ethereal, playful cheer of her powdered features was once again a mask—this time for the harsh treatment of young women, the sign of an outwardly progressive but inwardly desolate society. Joly sourly noted, "ask a Japanese how many children he has and he will respond, I have three sons and two disappointments."[61] Such disappointments were for sale, to factories, to brothels, to foreigners like Loti whose romantic flourishes did not disguise his own disappointment and disgust with Japan and with himself.

What Loti offered Madame Chrysanthème was a soul and heart—of a modernity he hated, not only in Japan but also in his native France, where home was the retreat of Rochefort, where he created his own Orient. His obtusely bitter vision of Chrysanthème was brutal and also piercingly consistent with versions of France's Japan as a land not truly civilized, a place of tenacious duty and heartless honor, of mothers sending their sons out into Japan's armies and selling off their daughters to brothels, never to know the anguish of loss.

It was here, on the question of the heart—that of Madame Chrysanthème, of Japan, and of France's own "struggle for civilization"—that battle was joined. The artist Félix Régamey, as André Messager and Puccini in their operas, rewrote Loti to accommodate a tragic and romantic rather than ironic and sarcastic history, thus one in which true love was possible. Theater and literary critics took note. Reviewers of the opera for *Piano-Soleil* focused on the ways in which "Madame Chrysanthème, the pretty, insensitive, and unconscious doll of the novel" had become "an intelligent woman, seductive, devoted, and sincerely in love."[62] In the closing act of Messager's opera, Chrysanthème has left Pierre a letter that he reads as his ship sails from Japan:

> I wanted to keep myself a place in your memory
> I don't dare say in your heart
> Alas, I see well that it was never for me
> You said, I was never for you but a doll, a musumé
> But if I was able to see you leave, smile on your lips
> I want you to know that when you are far away
> from me, very far
> That in Japan also there are women who love
> and who cry[63]

Régamey followed this line. He was an enthusiastic traveler in Japan, a serious student of Japanese culture, and a violent critic of Loti. He called Loti, "the ingrate, the deplorable friend of Madame Chrysanthème," and compared Loti's descriptions of "this astonishing land of all sorts of absurdities" with his own celebrations of "superb nature," of bamboo, of the artistry of Buddhist monks. He edited special works on women, art, and Japan in journals such as *La Plume* (October 15, 1893), for which he penned the "Cahier Rose de Madame Chrysanthème," a retelling of Loti's story from Chrysanthème's point of view. Madame's tale, couched in excerpts from her supposed diaries, paints a portrait not of craven mercenary dullness, but of a woman's sufferings, her longings, and her resigned but clearly anguished pain at the insensitivity of the man she knows does not love her.

In his special issue of *La Plume* dedicated to "La Femme au Japon," Régamey collected a deeply sympathetic selection of Japanophile works, translations, art, verse, and essays. None obviously condescended towards its Asian female subject, yet each was steeped in a clear fin-de-siècle historical vision of femininity: woman as bounded by her physical and emotional nature. Régamey follows Messager in pursuing the splendid tautology that closes the latter's opera. As Pierre finishes reading Chrysanthème's letter, his companion Yves comments: "Just as at home, women are always women." What this meant was as clear to Régamey as to Yves and Pierre, and can be transposed to readings of France and Japan in the later nineteenth century.

In *La Plume*, some of that meaning is frivolous. "She is small, petite, obedient," writes one essayist of "the Japanese woman." "I've been much criticized," he notes, for presenting the Japanese woman as "semi-angelic" and a "creature of ivory." Moreover, "she is the woman the most devoted, patient, attentive, the sprightliest, the most attached to her duties in all of the world," a creature of "gentleness in subordination," a "tranquil, satisfied, and delicious person." In tone, the piece recalls the splendidly banal *My Japanese Wife: a Japanese Idyll* by the English writer Clive Holland, who rhapsodised about his paramour, "Japanese women are butterflies with hearts . . . it is very pleasant to have my pretty little musumé flitting about my home and garden."[64]

But much is far from frivolous. At the end of Messager's opera, when the final letter to Pierre declares "in Japan there are also women who love, and who cry," the confession makes apparent that Chrysanthème has been excluded from this possibility, unlike "your European women" who are "willful, capricious . . . more loveable."[65] For Messager, tears will make Chrysanthème a woman. Likewise for Régamey, tears are a means to defend Japan and vilify the poisonous and pointedly modern disillusion—the *ennui*—of Loti's disenchanted vision; ennui, not just boredom, but the spleen, the malaise of nineteenth-century civilization.[66]

In Régamey's version of Loti's invention, Chrysanthème has a history in the best tragic-romantic mode: her father had been a high samurai, crushed by melancholy at the demise of his noble order, ravaged by the spectacle of "foreigners making off with everything in the country." Where Loti saw Japan spoiled by the West, Régamey saw her exploited. The one was disenchanted, the other outraged. Loti's Chrysanthème lacked any touch of aristocratic sensuality; she was a reminder to the Frenchman of a world lost to the decadence of modern Europe. In Régamey's tale, by contrast, it is Japan that preserves true romance, and Westerners who stupidly fail to appreciate the possibilities of renewal in Japanese culture.

Régamey's Chrysanthème stakes out a feminine role as the true Japan—like a true France, unsettled in politics, unconquerable in love: "Women do not count in politics; the heart should be all for them; even geishas at Kyoto, nothing can conquer their love." She dreams of the theater, where hardship leads to resolution in "all of the obstacles that lovers would encounter before finding marriage."[67] Sympathies lie with the one who can love. In her inner monologues, Chrysanthème avows, "Pierre is my master, I have nothing except to please him; I love him . . ." but terror creeps into her diary entries. "I dare not admit it to myself . . . *Il s'ennui*. Everything bores him. What is happening in Pierre's heart?" As Pierre becomes ever more distant, Chrysanthème pictures a wall going up between them. "What will I become if this continues!" She is driven to her wit's end. "He's never asked me if I love him, or only if I could love him one day. One day . . . he'll be far away, I'll never see him again and everything will be finished."

Always, there is the question of tears, the markers of sentiment and civilization. Painfully, feverishly, Chrysanthème marks out the time she and Pierre have left, hoping for a sign of affection from the man who disappears to the port, or who stands watching the sea while she tries not to burst out crying. "Every morning I change the flowers in the house, I put on my most beautiful kimono, and I refuse myself tears so he does not find me ugly when he returns."

Finally, early one morning, comes the moment of desolation: "I see Pierre standing, one hand holding up the mosquito netting, the other holding a small pouch. I stifle a cry." He gives her the pouch and goes: the silver coins to pay off their marriage contract.

For the infamous coin-counting scene, Régamey creates a folkloric alibi; Chrysanthème is singing the sad song of the moneylender, striking the piastres not to test their authenticity, but in anger and despair. "This song, well known in Japan, shows that love of money leads to all crimes and that money is the worst thing in the world." Chrysanthème is devastated that Pierre thinks to have caught her concerned about her payment. "It's the final insult!" she rages.

In the end of Régamey's revision, Chrysanthème is truly a woman, passionate unto self-destruction. Régamey takes her to the edge of the turbulent sea where she throws herself into the deep, attempting to drown with "one hundred pieces of silver tied into a piece of fine silk." The coins are scattered to the sea bottom; found instead are tattered notes, scribblings of Pierre she has saved, half washed away, detailing his profound disillusion with this land "always strange," full of "bizarre smirks," "absurd," cruel details of a land and woman he cannot and does not love.[68]

The dialectic of Chrysanthème's tears is that of Japan written into history through its emotional capacities within a shifting landscape of geopolitical competition on the European continent and in East Asia. Japan could be alternately the Eastern Prussia or the Asian Marianne, the heartless menace or the ravaged, yet dignified victim. For French observers, Japan—the woman—in the nineteenth century embodied a multiplicity of fears and longings: the land of nature and artistic culture, of deception and cruel ambition. Japan was woodblock prints, yet by century's end it was also a preeminent threat to Euro-American global dominance. As Charles Pettit put it for the French: "Japan is the only power that is truly to be feared regarding our empire in Indochina . . . it is to be hoped for the sake of humanity and civilization that the European peoples make all efforts between themselves to allow the white race to maintain its superiority in the Far East."[69]

The possibility of a woman's love played directly into this struggle as the gauge of a shifting civilization, the incarnation of the real and the false, the vehicle for the sacrifice of personal sorrows in the name of uniting loves of family and nation. The Baron Suyematsu quoted Napoleon, "women are the mothers of the nation," and Charles Loonen observed that the search for "the true woman" in Japan was not a matter of chasing eroticism, exoticism, or beauty, but woman as "the mother of the family, the teacher of generations which make the nation." His regret for Japan was that he did not see how Japanese women, crushed by tradition, could exercise a "precious influence, comforting and consoling within the family."[70] They could obey, but never weep; their love was not their own.

"You didn't believe in my love . . ." said Madame Chrysanthème; Frenchmen sought to write the history of an unsettling nineteenth-century Japan by denying or restoring to Madame real tears of loss and separation. Some, like Loti, cynically recorded the base emptiness of modern Japan, seduced, corrupted, and abandoned by the false romance of Western civilization. Others, like Messager and Régamey, reaffirmed a different woman, one crushed but clinging in the end to a world where love was *real*. For critics and journalists in a shaken France, weeping in Japan would be for the sons and husbands marching away in Japan's imperialist wars, for the daughters sold off to treaty ports and industrial modernity, while mothers offered no comfort or consolation, only dutiful sacrifice to the emperor; these are the histories glistening in the tears of Madame Chrysanthème.

AFTERWORD

THE LOST CONTINENT

In his Tahitian tale *The Marriage of Loti*, Pierre Loti's mariner hero takes aside his Polynesian lover and waxes about her historical fate. "I think, O my love, that upon these faraway seas are scattered lost archipelagos, that these archipelagos are inhabited by a mysterious race soon destined to disappear, that you are a child of this primitive race." Despite—or perhaps because of—this grim pronouncement, he appears determined she know "that high upon one of these islands, far from human creatures, in complete solitude, I, child of the Old World, born on the other side of the world, I am here with you, and I love you."[1] As a Diderot, Bougainville, or Dumont d'Urville fashioned a savage and sentimental Oceania of nature and nobility for the Enlightenment, so Loti's words of love resonated through a romance of the Pacific in an age of European empire: historical destiny, Europe and Oceania, passion and possession.

French royal houses and republics projected naval power and maritime strategies upon the Grand Ocean in the nineteenth and early twentieth centuries, and figures such as Loti and Juliette Adam haunted colonial boundary questions, at times inscribing but just as often purposefully erasing the distinctions between love story and imperial ideology. Through them, I have pursued *points de relâche* and *points d'appui*, marking a particular territory of encounters and emotions with locations, not all significant in the same moments, not all captured under one rubric of "colonialism," or even "island," yet all, whether administratively, commercially, militarily, or in ideology and imagination, parts of a drifting current of meanings that at times resonated as an Empire of Love.

Running through the *points de relâche* are the foundations of a European history of the Pacific, tales of grand navigation and adventure, fantasy and exploration fueled by desires for the fabulous East, the uncorrupted isle, and

The end of the world: **Moorea** *(1845), Charles-Claude Antiq.*
Source: National Library of Australia

the search for the *terra australis incognita*, the great Southern Continent of legend. That continent has been something of a figure for what has been presented here, in the way that eighteenth-century European navigators surmised that Oceanic islands and peoples were existing on the peaks of mountains, common formations now submerged beneath fathomless waters, points somehow joined yet isolated.

I have similarly articulated empire: distinct engagements from Rochefort to Noumea to Nagasaki set within overlapping narrations. Some of those narrations, like that of "isolation," drew together assumptions about Oceania and Asia. Not only tropical islands were presumed excluded from global currents of History. In 1889, the future governor of Indochina Jean Louis De Lanessan asserted of Southeast Asia, "The state of communication lines is the same as that of Europe two thousand years ago . . . they are condemned to an impotence as great as their isolation is complete." He even pressed for influence in Meiji-era Japan by vaguely threatening, "If she continues to isolate herself and close her ports, if she shows herself incapable of understanding her destiny, she could very well one day give a stronger and more intelligent government the idea of taking her place."[2]

Despite such presumed similarities, distinctions also asserted themselves within the narratives. Nineteenth-century French accounts of Southeast and East Asia generally detailed great, glacial civilizations in decline, or in Japan, yet unrealized; Melanesia shared images drawn up around a stereotyped Africa, fixed upon adventure and primitivism. Polynesia was also so labeled, yet was especially where Enlightenment ideals were deployed to outshine the conquest and commerce narratives of older Spanish, Portuguese, and Dutch colonies, designating local peoples as generously sensual, strong, indeed enviable. Savagery, innocence, and mystery were unevenly projected onto lands surrounded by a great ocean.

Bounded by such allied, encompassing, yet inconsistent narratives, French empire in the Pacific was never clearly defined or well located. Extended across a huge, fragmented geography, it defied metropole-colony models. From the Panamanian isthmus to the coast of Southeast Asia, from the southern ocean of New Caledonia, Tahiti, and Futuna to the northern archipelago of Japan, the French Pacific was less an enclosed space than a waxing and waning set of locations, some strategic, some symbolic. Distinctive Gallic narrations of sentiment framing a civilizing mission were critical for making colonies and territories commensurable and attractive as objects of rule. Oceanic tales and ministerial policies alike were fashioned to win support for colonial exploits, whether by adventure, interest—or romantic shaping of local histories.

Many of those histories were, and are, disputed. Loti prophesied the day when Oceanic peoples "will have long since disappeared, and will be no more than a distant memory conserved in books of the past."[3] It was for that moment he wrote his fatal imperial romances. He was wrong about the peoples and their increasingly powerful and vital presence across the next century, but he marked well—as one of its creators—the legacy of imperialism as Empire of Love. I have pursued the accommodations and struggles over such contending histories by highlighting cross-talk between Loti's tales of love and voices of plantation workers, contract wives, immigrants, monarchs, settlers, and deportees as they confronted and converged with French fictions of empire.

Some replied and resisted with armed force and left legacies and commemorations of violent anticolonial struggle. Some threatened with their own insistent "modernization" and imperial policies. Others fought yet also embraced an ennobling romance of family, brotherhood, and tutelage, appropriating and adapting religious practices and political ideas, forming alliances, taking partners. Marriage is as much a part of these stories as ministerial decisions, *métis* and *demis* blood signs of both affection and exploitation, sexual relations and military power. Conflicting love stories are historical narratives.

In his *Marriage*, Loti lamented the passing of traditional Polynesian culture as a decadent historical inevitability, one he encapsulated in the tubercular decline of his lover Rarahu. But there were other voices. At his own marriage in 1875, the future King Pomare of Tahiti, then Prince Ariiaue, took as his bride the seventh child of a distinguished couple, Royal Secretary and counselor Alexandre Salmon and his wife Ari'ioehau Ari'ita'ima'i. Family historians described the event as a familiar imperial romance: "Loti, in his *Marriage of Loti*, was able to describe for us one of these receptions and to extol the charm and the brilliant attractions." Yet, they also counterposed the words of the bride, Marau, who would later observe, "And I cannot compare without melancholy the profusions of then with the narrowness of today. The respect with which our traditions were still held, with the oblivion into which they have fallen; the prestige and authority of hereditary chiefs with the erasure of those who have replaced them."

Her voice countered the narrative of the Empire of Love, remembering as part of her own past a culture of excluded traditions and institutions. After the death of her husband, Marau famously championed the vitality of Tahitian culture as the "Last Queen" of her islands. Invoking the ambivalent embrace of France, Marau both recognized and slighted the European agents of empire, "the passing bureaucrats, certainly full of goodwill, but most generally ignorant of our language, of our needs, of our possibilities," and also, as she noted, "of our history."[4]

Marau's historical vision of self-knowledge is one that has marked colonial and postcolonial Pacific questions into the twenty-first century, from Tahiti to New Caledonia, from Aotearoa-New Zealand to Hawai'i. Imperial sites from Oceania to Asia are still contested as points de relâche and points d'appui, and also reclaimed as living, fluid, and historically rich crossings of peoples and cultures in states, nations, and a greater sea of islands.[5] I have tried to look at the tensions in some of those contests within a history of Pacific empire across the nineteenth and early twentieth centuries. The stories have sought to engage Islanders and Asians voyaging the hemisphere, colonial administrators, migrant laborers, defiant chiefs, fervent Catholic priests, wretched prisoners, impoverished Caribbean and American laborers, treaty-port courtesans, and proud Polynesian monarchs.

Together, these are some of the actors who constituted and negotiated an Empire of Love in the Pacific, tenuously bound together by an entangling romance of power and emotion. Their tales are the crossing places of still-resonant waves, spreading outward as small histories borne on brief currents and the deep tides of a deeper ocean.

NOTES

INTRODUCTION

1. Louis Antoine de Bougainville, *Voyage autour du monde*, Paris, 1771; Charlotte Haldane, *Tempest Over Tahiti*, London: Constable, 1963, 2.

2. Archives Territoriales, Tipaerui, Tahiti, 48W/1078, 1–3.

3. Admiral P. Revèillère, in Juliette Adam, ed., *A Vasco de Gama: Hommage de la pensée française, 1498–1898*, Paris/Lisbon: Guillard, Aillaud, 1898, 15; Paul de Deckker and Pierre Yves Toullelan, eds., *La France et la Pacifique*, Paris: Société Française d'histoire d'outre-mer, 1990; Jean Chesneaux and Nic Maclellan, *La France dans le Pacifique: de Bougainville à Moruroa*, Paris: La Découverte, 1993; Stephen Heningham, *France and the South Pacific: A Contemporary History*, Honolulu: University of Hawaii Press, 1992; Deryck Scarr, ed., "France in the Pacific: Past, Present, and Future," special issue of *Journal of Pacific History*, no. 26 (1991).

4. J. Charles Roux, *Colonies et pays de protectorats*, Paris: Exposition universelle de 1900, 1900, 225, 305.

5. Epeli Hau'ofa, "Our Sea of Islands," *Contemporary Pacific* 6, no. 1 (1994), 148–61; for extended commentaries, *A New Oceania: Rediscovering Our Sea of Islands*, ed. Eric Waddell, Vijay Naidu, and Epeli Hau'ofa, Suva: University of the South Pacific, 1994; also Arif Dirlik and Rob Wilson, eds., *Asia-Pacific as Space of Cultural Production*, Durham, N.C.: Duke University Press, 1995; David Woodward and G. Malcolm Lewis, eds., *History of Cartography: Cartography in Traditional African, American, Arctic, Australian, and Pacific Societies*, vol. 2, book 3, Chicago: University of Chicago Press, 1998, esp. Ben Finney, "Nautical Cartography and Traditional Navigation in the Pacific Basin," 419, passim; David Lewis, *We the Navigators: The Ancient Art of Landfaring in the Pacific*, ed. Derek Oulton, Honolulu: University of Hawaii Press, 1994; Otto Winkler, "On Sea Charts Formerly Used in the Marshall Islands with Notices on the Navigation of These Islands

in General," *Annual Report of the Board of Regents of the Smithsonian Institution*, Washington, D.C.: Government Printing Office, 1901, 487–508.

6. See Nicholas Thomas, *Entangled Objects: Exchange, Material Culture, and Colonialism in the Pacific*, Cambridge: Cambridge University Press, 1991. Also, Greg Dening, "History 'in' the Pacific," *Contemporary Pacific* 1, nos. 1 and 2 (1989), 134–9; Dipesh Chakrabarty, *Provincializing Europe: Postcolonial Thought and Historical Difference*, Princeton, N.J.: Princeton University Press, 2000.

7. Bronwen Douglas, "Doing Ethnographic History: Reflections on Practices and Practising," in Brij Lal, ed., *Pacific Islands History: Journeys and Transformations*, Canberra, 1992, 106. In a larger context, see Douglas, *Across the Great Divide: Journeys in History and Anthropology*, Amsterdam: Harwood Academic Publishers, 1998; also Robert Borofsky, ed., *Remembrance of Pacific Pasts: An Invitation to Remake History*, Honolulu: University of Hawaii Press, 2000, 26.

8. Henri Lutteroth, *O-Taiti, histoire et enquête*, Paris: Paulin, 1843, iii; René Pinon, "La France des antipodes," *Revue des deux mondes*, 158 (1900), 784.

9. See Pierre Nora, ed., *Les Lieux de mémoire*, 7 vols., Paris: Gallimard (1984–1992); Jeffrey K. Olick, ed., *States of Memory: Continuities, Conflicts, and Transformations in National Retrospection*, Durham, N.C.: Duke University Press, 2003. For excellent bibliographical notes on the pioneering work and legacies of ethnographic and anthropological "micro-histories" in European studies (works by Emmanuel Le Roy Laduire, Natalie Zemon Davis, Carlo Ginzburg, Robert Darnton, Clifford Geertz, and others), see Edward Berenson, *The Trial of Madame Caillaux*, Berkeley: University of California Press, 1992, 7–8, 251–2. For the Pacific works of Dening and Thomas, see Greg Dening, *Islands and Beaches: Discourse on a Silent Land, Marquesas, 1774–1880*, Honolulu: University of Hawaii Press, 1980; Dening, *History's Anthropology: The Death of William Gooch*, 1988; Dening, *Mr. Bligh's Bad Language: Passion, Power and Theatre on the Bounty*, Cambridge: Cambridge University Press, 1992; Dening, "A Poetics for Histories: Transformations that Present the Past," in Aletta Biersack, ed., *Clio in Oceania: Towards an Historical Anthropology*, Washington, D.C.: Smithsonian Institution Press, 1991, 347–80; Nicholas Thomas, "Partial Texts: Representation, Colonialism and Agency in Pacific History," in his *In Oceania: Visions, Artifacts, Histories*, Durham, N.C.: Duke University Press, 1997, 23–49; Thomas, *Oceanic Art*, London: Thames and Hudson, 1995; Thomas, "The Indigenous Appropriation of European Things," in his *Entangled Objects*, 83–124.

10. Marshall Sahlins, *Islands of History*, Chicago: University of Chicago Press, 1985; on the contested nature of historical narratives, Gananath Obeyesekere, *The Apotheosis of Captain Cook: European Mythmaking in the Pacific*, Princeton, N.J.: Princeton University Press, 1992, and Marshall Sahlins, *How "Natives" Think: About Captain Cook, for Example*, Chicago: University of Chicago Press, 1996. See also Brownen Douglas, "Fracturing Boundaries of Time and Place in Melanesian Anthropology," *Oceania*, 66, no. 3 (1996), 177–84; some scholars have also usefully adapted Richard White, *The Middle Ground: Indians, Empires, and Republics in the Great Lakes Region, 1650–1815*, Cambridge: Cambridge University Press, 1991—see

interview in Borofsky, ed., *Remembrance of Pacific Pasts: An Invitation to Remake History*; also, Bernhard Klein and Gesa Mackentheun, eds., *Sea Changes: Historicizing the Ocean*, New York: Routledge, 2004.

11. Paul de Deckker and Pierre Yves Toullelan, eds., *La France et la Pacifique*, Paris: Société Française d'histoire d'outre-mer, 1990; Jean Chesneaux and Nic Maclellan, *La France dans le Pacifique: De Bougainville à Moruroa*, Paris: La Découverte, 1993; Stephen Heningham, *France and the South Pacific: A Contemporary History*, Honolulu: University of Hawaii Press, 1992; Deryck Scarr, ed., "France in the Pacific: Past, Present, and Future," *Journal of Pacific History*, no. 26 (1991).

12. See Pierre Yves Toullelan, *Tahiti Coloniale, 1860–1914*, Paris: Sorbonne, 1987, 237. Robert Aldrich, *The French Presence in the South Pacific, 1842–1940*, Honolulu: University of Hawaii Press, 1990; Rod Edmond, *Representing the South Pacific*, Cambridge: Cambridge University Press, 1997; Anne Godlewska and Neil Smith, *Geography and Empire*, Oxford: Blackwell, 1994.

13. An excellent overview by John Dunmore, *Visions and Realities: France in the Pacific*, 1695–1995, Waikanae, N.Z.: Heritage Press, 1997.

14. Havelock Ellis, preface to Bronislaw Malinowski, *The Sexual Life of Savages*, New York: Halcyon, 1929, vii. See also the classic by Bernard Smith, *European Vision and the South Pacific: 1768–1850: A Study in the History of Art and Ideas*, Melbourne: Oxford University Press, 1989.

15. Patricia Seed, *Ceremonies of Possession in Europe's Conquest of the New World, 1492–1640*, New York: Cambridge University Press, 1995, 26–9, 70.

16. Stendhal cited by Luisa Passerini, *Europe in Love, Love in Europe*, London: I. B. Tauris, 1999, 206. For comparative work, see Lisa Lowe, *Critical Terrains: French and British Orientalisms*, Ithaca, N.Y.: Cornell University Press, 1991.

17. Dr. Jacobus X (pseud.), *L'Art d'aimer aux colonies*, Paris: Georges Anquetil, 1927, p. 359. Comparatively, especially on Cook, see Kathleen Wilson, *Island Race: Englishness, Empire and Gender in the Eighteenth Century*, New York: Routledge, 2002.

18. "Rapport de Admiral Brossard de Corbigny," C.A.O.M., FM/ SG/ C. 140, doss. A120.

19. See "Interview: In liefde verenigd: het vitale Europa van Luisa Passerini," *Nieuwste Tijd* (March 2002), 6. In detail, Passerini, *Europe in Love, Love in Europe*, esp. introduction, chapters 2, 6, 7. See discussion of Irving Singer and Octavio Paz, who distinguish "between the feeling of love, which belongs to all times and places, and the idea or ideology of love typical of a certain society and epoch," 8–9.

20. Vicente L. Rafael, *White Love and Other Events in Filipino History*, Durham, N.C.: Duke University Press, 2000; John Hirst, *The Sentimental Nation: The Making of the Australian Commonwealth*, Melbourne: Oxford University Press, 2000; Jane Samson, *Imperial Benevolence: Making British Authority in the Pacific Islands*, Honolulu: University of Hawaii Press, 1998

21. Julia Clancy-Smith and Frances Gouda, eds., *Domesticating the Empire: Race, Gender, and Family Life in French and Dutch Colonialism*, Charlottesville: University

Press of Virginia, 1998; Alice Conklin, *A Mission To Civilize: The Republican Idea of Empire in France and West Africa, 1895–1930*, Stanford: Stanford University Press, 1997; Antoinette Burton, *Burdens of History: British Feminists, Indian Women, and Imperial Culture, 1865–1915*, Chapel Hill: University of North Carolina Press, 1994; Ann Laura Stoler, *Carnal Knowledge and Imperial Power: Race and the Intimate in Colonial Rule*, Berkeley: University of California Press, 2002; more generally, William Reddy, *The Navigation of Feeling: A Framework for the History of Emotions*, Cambridge: Cambridge University Press, 2001, an excellent overview and analytic framework. Also, impossible to miss for its breadth and ambition, Peter Gay, *The Bourgeois Experience: Victoria to Freud* (5 vols.), New York: Oxford University Press (1986–1998).

22. *Le Saigonnais*, October 7, 1886, 17. On love as a force, see Vicente Rafael, *White Love;* also, Maurizio Viroli, *For Love of Country: An Essay on Patriotism and Nationalism*, Oxford: Oxford University Press, 1995.

23. Nicholas Thomas, *In Oceania: Visions, Artifacts, Histories*, Duke University Press, 1997, 16–17, 45; Thomas, "The Primitivist and the Postcolonial," in his *Colonialism's Culture: Anthropology, Travel, and Government*, Princeton, N.J.: Princeton University Press, 1994, 170–95; Christophe Charle, *La Crise des sociétés imperiales: Allemagne, France, Grande Bretagne, 1900–1940*, Paris: Seuil, 2001; Robert Young, *White Mythologies: Writing History and the West*, London: Routledge, 1990, esp. chs. 1, 7–8.

24. Pierre Loti, *Impressions*, New York: Brentanos, 1900, introduction by Henry James, 14.

25. Lesley Blanch, *Pierre Loti: Portrait of an Escapist*, London: Collins, 1983; Christian Genet and Daniel Hervé, *Pierre Loti, l'enchanteur*, Gemozac: La Caillerie, 1988; Alain Villiers-Quella et al., ed., *Pierre Loti: Cette eternelle nostalgie, journal intime, 1878–1911*, Paris: La Table Ronde, 1997.

26. *Pierre Loti: The Romance of a Great Writer*, London: Kennikat, 1926, reissued 1970, 41; Paul Bourget, *Physiologie de l'amour moderne*, Paris: Plon, 1889, 22, reissued, 1995; also, Stephen Barney, *Allegories of History, Allegories of Love*, Hamden: Archon, 1979, "allegories of history 'mark time' as they measure the distance from the revealed form of salvation and the not-present fact of salvation. Allegories of love, in analogous fashion, seek out the prelapsarian world for their setting," 177.

27. Saidya V. Hartman, *Scenes of Subjection*, New York: Oxford, 1997, 23–4. See Roland Barthes, *Plaisir du texte*, Paris: Ed. du Seuil, 1973, 9: "ne jamais s'excuser, ne jamais s'expliquer, il ne nie jamais rien, . . . je détournerai mon regard, ce sera désormais ma seule négation." Roland Greene, *Unrequited Conquests: Love and Empire in the Colonial Americas*, Chicago: University of Chicago Press, 1999, 11–14.

28. Homi K. Bhabha, "Of Mimicry and Man: The Ambivalence of Colonial Discourse," *October 28* (1984), 125–33. Edward Said, *Culture and Imperialism*, New York: Vintage, 1993; James Scott, *Domination and the Arts of Resistance: Hidden Transcripts*, New Haven, Conn.: Yale University Press, 1990.

29. Max Radiguet, *Les derniers sauvages: la vie et les moeurs aux Iles Marquises, 1842–59*, Paris: Ed. Duchartre et Van Buggenhoudt, 1929, 234; Ann Laura Stoler,

Race and the Education of Desire: Foucault's History of Sexuality and the Colonial Order of Things, Durham, N.C.: Duke University Press, 1995.

30. Raoul Girardet, *L'Idée coloniale en France*, Paris: La Table Rond, 1972, 271–2.

31. H. Le Chartier and Charles Legrand, *Guide de France en Océanie et Océanie en France*, Paris: Jouvet, 1889, 198

32. Stephen Greenblatt, *Marvelous Possessions* Chicago: University of Chicago Press, 1991; Anthony Pagden, *European Encounters with the New World from Rennaisance to Romanticism*, New Haven, Conn.: Yale University Press, 1993, and Pagden, ed., *Facing Each Other: The World's Perception of Europe and Europe's Perception of the World*, Aldershot/ Hampshire: Ashgate/Variforum, 2000; Stuart B. Schwartz, *Implicit Understandings: Observing, Reporting, and Reflecting in the Encounters Between Europeans and Other Peoples in the Early Modern Era*, Cambridge: Cambridge University Press, 1994; Pierre Loti, *A Pilgrimmage to Angkor*, Bangkok: Ed. M. Smithies, 1996, 90.

33. Stuart Persell, *The French Colonial Lobby, 1889–1938*, Stanford: Hoover, 1983, 3–4; Stephen Roberts, *History of French Colonial Policy, 1870–1925*, London: P.S. King and Son, 1929; Albert Sarrault, *La Mise en valeur des colonies françaises*, Paris: Payot, 1923; Scott Cook, *Colonial Encounters in the Age of High Imperialism*, New York: Harper Collins, 1997.

34. Auguste Pavie, *A la conquête des coeurs*, Paris: Presses Universitaires de France, 1947, 268.

35. Félicien Challayé, *Souvenirs sur la colonisation*, Paris: Picart, 1935, 4 . On the *mission civilisatrice*, see Alice Conklin, *A Mission to Civilize: The Republican Idea of Empire in France and West Africa, 1895–1930*, Stanford: Stanford University Press, 1997.

36. Challayé, *Souvenirs*, 4, 40, 201.

37. *Océanie Française*, no. 123 (January/February 1931); cited and narrated in Robert Aldrich, *The French Presence*, 268. Castex was a major theorist of naval strategy.

ONE: ROCHEFORT

1. Marie-Pascale Bault, ed., *Pierre Loti en Chine et au Japon*, Musée des beaux-arts de Rochefort, see "Les voyages de P. Loti en extreme orient a la fin du XIXe siècle," 4; Suetoshi Funaoka, "Les Itinéraires de Pierre Loti en Extrême-Orient," *Revue Pierre Loti*, no. 18 (April 1984), 31–4. On this chapter title, see Lynn Hunt, *The Family Romance of the French Revolution*, Berkeley: University of California Press, 1992.

2. Emile Bergerat, *L'Amour en République: étude sociologique*, Paris: E. Dentu, 1889, 13.

3. Loti, *Le Roman d'un spahi*, 65; Loti, cited and commented in Alain Quella-Villéger, *Pierre Loti: L'Incompris*, Paris: Presses de la Renaissance, 1986, 239. On French regionalism, see Stéphane Gerson, *The Pride of Place: Local Memories and*

Political Culture in Nineteenth Century France, Ithaca, N.Y.: Cornell University Press, 2003.

4. Pierre Loti, *The Marriage of Loti*; Pierre Loti, André Alexandre, Georges Hartmann, *L'Ile du rêve*, music by Reynaldo Hahn, Paris: Calmann-Lévy, 1898. Opera first presented at the Theatre National de l'Opera Comique, March 23, 1898, directed by Albert Carré. In general, see Tony Chafer and Amada Sackur, eds., *Promoting the Colonial Idea: Propaganda and Visions of Empire in France*, New York: Palgrave, 2002, 1–11.

5. See the analysis of France, Marianne, and Cambodia in Penny Edwards, "Womanizing Indochina: Fiction, Nation, and Cohabitation in Colonial Cambodia, 1890–1930," in Clancy-Smith and Gouda, eds., *Domesticating the Empire*, 108–9, 129–30.

6. Juliette Adam, *La Vie des ames*, Paris: Bernard-Grasset, 1919, 1; Winfred Stephens, *Madame Adam, La Grande française*, London: Chapman and Hall, 1917, 222–3. The Grande Juliette will carry the surname Lambert from birth in 1836, Lamessine from 1853 to 1863, and Adam from 1868 to 1877 and after according to her marriages; her nom de plume will remain an abbreviated Lamber. Also, Christophe Charle, *Les Elites de la République, 1880–1900*, Paris: Fayard, 1987. Other powerful salonnières included the Marquise de Blocqueville for her mondain guest list, and Madame Beulé, who entertained Renan and other writers, artists, and composers.

7. Charles-Victor Crosnier de Varigny, *Fourteen Years in the Sandwich Islands*, 1855–1868, reprinted, Honolulu: University of Hawaii Press, 1981, xxvii.

8. Juliette Adam, *Jean et Pascal*, Paris: A. Lemerre, 1905, 18, 21, 306–7. See also, *La Chanson des nouveaux époux*, Paris: L. Conquet, 1882, 22–3. See also her *Le Mandarin*, Paris: M. Lévy Frères, 1860, or *Païenne: Un Rêve sur le divin*, Paris: A. Lemerre, 1903.

9. Juliette Adam, *Mes souvenirs*, vol. 7, 366, 392; see also accounts in Winfred Stephens, 215, 217, 398.

10. Juliette Adam, in Brigitte Adde, et al., eds., *Et C'est Moi, Juliette: Madame Adam, 1836–1936*, Gif-sur-Yvette: Saga, 1988, 73. On literary varieties of love in this period, see S. Francis Ellen Riordan, *The Concept of Love in the French Catholic Literary Revival*, Washington, D.C.: Catholic University of America, 1952, for readings of Barbey d'Aurevilly (*L'Amour impossible*), Bourget (*Un Crime d'amour, Cruelle enigme d'amour*), and Huysmans (*Les Soeurs Vatard, A Rebours, Là-bas*), 1–11; also Guy Breton, *Histories d'amour de l'historie de France*, vol. 2, Paris: Presses de la Cité (1991).

11. Pierre Loti, "Discours de réception de M. Pierre Loti," Séance de l'Académie française du 1891, Paris: Calmann-Lévy, 1892.

12. See Marius-Ary Leblond (pseud. Aimé Merlo and Georges Athenas), *Après l'exotisme de Loti, le roman colonial*, Paris, 1927; Victor Ségalen, "Essai sur l'exotisme: une esthétique du divers," in Henry Boullier, ed., *Oeuvres complètes*, Paris: Robert Laffont, 1995, 755–9; for an overview, Alain Buisine, Norbert Dodille, Claude Duchet, eds., *L'Exotisme: actes de colloque*, Paris: Didier-Erudition, 1988, featur-

ing thirty-seven essays on "altérités, voyages, colonies, poétiques, ésthetiques," esp. 5–10 and 305–30 on Loti and Ségalen.

13. Bruno Vercier, Alain Quella-Villéger, Guy Dugas, eds., *Cette eternelle nostalgie: journal intime, 1878–1911* (Loti's journal), Paris: La Table Ronde, 1997, 99.

14. British adventure romance has a huge critical literature. See especially, Patrick Bratlinger, *Rule of Darkness: British Literature and Imperialism, 1830–1914*, Ithaca, N.Y.: Cornell University Press, 1988; Robert Dixon, *Writing the Colonial Adventure: Race, Gender, and Nation in Anglo-Australian Popular Fiction, 1875–1914*, Cambridge: Cambridge University Press, 1995.

15. Juliette Lamber (pen name), *Idées Anti-Proudhoniennes sur l'amour, la femme, et le mariage*, Paris: Michel Lévy Frères, 1868, lv–lvi.

16. For a detailed reading of "couples" who invent themselves in love and politics in the nineteenth century, see Marjan Schwegman, "Aardse liefde in een heroisch leven" ("Earthly Love in a Celestial Life: Giuseppe Mazzini and Giuditta Sidoli, 1831–1992"), *Bulletin Geschiedenis Kunst Cultuur* 3, no. 1 (1994), 52–80, esp. discussions of Mazzini's sensitive "female" characteristics and Sidoli's "virile" qualities.

17. Peter Gay, *The Bourgeois Experience, Victoria to Freud*, vol. 2, *The Tender Passion* (New York: Oxford University Press, 1986), 78. On the transformations of French romantic love and sexuality since the Third Republic, a subject far more complex than I can treat here, see Robert A. Nye, "Sexuality, Sex Difference and the Cult of Modern Love in the French Third Republic," *Historical Reflections/ Réflexions Historiques*, 20, no. 1 (1994), 57–76; Guy Breton, *Histoires d'amour de l'historie de France*, vol. 2, Paris: Presses de la Cité (1991), esp. 1052–6 for Gambetta's romance with suspected German agent Léonie Léon and Juliette Adam's political and personal maneuverings to end it.

18. Nguyên Phan-Long, *Le Roman de Mlle Lys*, Hanoi: Imprimerie Tonkinoise, 1921, 103.

19. *Païenne et Un Rêve sur le divin*, Paris: A. Lemérre, 1903, 222, 242–7.

20. *Le Vice-Amiral Bergasse Du Petit-Thouars, 1832–1890, d'après ses notes et sa correspondance*, Paris: Perrin et Cie, 1906, i–iii. Emile Duboc, *35 Mois de campagne en Chine, au Tonkin, 1882–5*, Paris: Charavay, Mantoux, Martin, 1889, 310; this work is a part of "editions for young people."

21. Pierre Loti, *Lettres de Pierre Loti à Madame Juliette Adam*, Paris: Plon-Nourrit, 1924, letter of June 11, 1885; Loti, "La Mort de l'Amiral Courbet," *Revue des deux mondes* (August 15, 1885), republication of *Le Figaro* article; Garnier, in Jules Harmand, *Bulletin de la société de géographie* (March 1875), 290. On the larger erotic context, see multiple works by Robert Aldrich, especially his *Colonialism and Homosexuality*, London: Routledge, 2003.

22. Marlon B. Ross, "Romancing the Nation-State: The Poetics of Romantic Nationalism," in Jonathan Arac and Harriet Ritvo, eds., *Macropolitics of Nineteenth-Century Literature: Nationalism, Exoticism, Imperialism*, Philadelphia: University of Pennsylvania Press, 1991, 56–7; for contexts, Fredrick Cooper and Ann Laura Stoler, eds., *Tensions of Empire: Colonial Cultures in a Bourgeois World*, Berkeley: University of California Press, 1997.

23. Juliette Adam, *La Chanson des nouveaux époux*, Paris: L. Conquet, 1882, 22–3; Adam, *Mes souvenirs*, vol. 7, 366.

24. Pierre Loti, *Les Fleurs d'ennui*, 361–2; *Le Roman d'un Spahi*, 169. Also, Jehan Despert, *Le Douloureux amour de Pierre Loti*, Rochefort: La Malle aux livres, 1995.

25. Loti, in Alain Quella-Villéger, *Pierre Loti: L'Incompris*, Paris: Presses de la Renaissance, 1986, 80.

26. See Stephen Roberts, *History of French Colonial Policy, 1870–1925*, London: P.S. King and Son, 1929, 11–12. For variations, Robert Aldrich and John Connell, *France's Overseas Frontier: Départements and territoires d'outre-mer*, New York: Cambridge University Press, 1992.

27. Pierre Loti, *Madame Chrysanthemum*, 20.

28. Paul Deschanel, *La Politique Francaise en Oceanie*, Paris: Berger-Levault et Cie, 1884, 34; the Maison de Pierre Loti archive keeps a photograph from Deschanel with the inscription, "à Pierre Loti, vive amitié." Also, Marguerite Duras, *Un Barrage contre le Pacifique*, Paris: Gallimard, 1958; Helen Lainé, *Pioneer Days in New Caledonia*, trans. of *Hommage filial, documentaire Calédonien*, Noumea: Imprimeries Réunies, 1942, 62; Albert de Pouvourville, *L'Annamite aujourd'hui*, Paris: Ed. de la Rose, 1932, 113.

29. Loti, *Lettres*, letter (December 9, 1883); pieces for *Le Figaro*, "La Prise de Tonkin," (September 28, 1883); "Prise de Hué" (October 13, 1883); "Au Tonkin," (October 17, 1883)

30. On "exotic war," Pierre Loti, *Cette eternelle nostalgie, journal intime, 1871–1911*, ed. Bruno Verciér, Alain Quella-Villéger, Guy Dugas, Paris: La Table Rond, 1997, 101; on "noble emotion," Emile Duboc, *35 Mois de campagne en Chine, au Tonkin, 1882–5*, Paris: Charavay, Mantoux, Martin, 1889, 310. This work is a part of "editions for young people."

31. Edward Berenson, "Unifying the French Nation: Savorgnan de Brazza and the Third Republic," in Barbara Kelly, ed., *Music, Culture, and National Identity in France, 1870–1939*, Rochester: Rochester University Press, 2005.

32. Juliette Adam, *Le Mandarin*, Paris: Michel Lévy Frères, 1860, 63–5.

33. Krzystof Pomian, *Collectionneurs, amateurs, et curieux*, Paris: Gallimard, 1987, 70.

34. Loti, *A Child's Romance [Le Roman d'un enfant]*, New York: W. S. Gottsberger, 1891, on collecting, possession, and becoming a sailor, 107–9, 261.

35. Loti, *Lettres* (Adam) vi–vii;

36. Loti, *Prime Jeunesse*, 24, 28; see Alain Quella-Villéger, *Pierre Loti: L'Incompris*, 239 on Gustave's memory and "cette sorte de sentiment presque fétichiste." Also, Georges Taboulet and Jean Claude Demariaux, *La Vie dramatique de Gustave Viaud, frère de Pierre Loti*, Paris: Ed. du Scorpion, 1961, for a detailed perspective on Gustave's life, with emphasis on his Indochina mission.

37. Loti, *Journal inédit*, 34; see François Le Targat, *A la recherche de Pierre Loti*, Paris: Seghers, 1974, 35.

38. Loti, *Prime Jeunesse*, 41; *Madame Chrysanthemum*, 14–15.

39. Loti, *A Pilgrimmage to Angkor*, 217.

40. Clotilde Chivas-Baron, *La Femme aux colonies*, Paris: Larose, 1927, 184.

41. Thierry Liot, *La Maison de Pierre Loti à Rochefort*, Chauray: Ed. patrimoines et médias, 1999; Sylviane Jacquemin, "L'Océanie et les musées de la seconde motié du XIXe siècle," in Annick Notter, ed., *Oceanie: Curieux, navigateurs, et savants*, Paris: Somogy Ed. d'Art, 1997.

42. "Promotional Cards for Children," *La France Pittoresque*, Ed. Le Chocolat Suchard (1880–1910), Getty collection, 92.R.55, cards 204, 252, 258, 274, 277–80; also of interest, Le Masson, *Views of Tahiti, 1896–1900*, one album, 46 prints, 93.R.92; Musée des missions évangéliques: *Exposition universelle, Paris, 1867*, one portolio, twenty-six prints, 93.R.102.

43. Pierre Loti, *Pecheur d'Islande [An Iceland Fisherman]*, Paris: Calmann-Lévy, 1886, 317. Loti (translated works) cited here originally published by Calmann-Lévy, *The Marriage of Loti*, 1880 first appeared in Adam's *La Nouvelle Revue*, 1879; *Madame Chrysanthemum*, 1887; *Prime Jeunesse*, 1919.

44. Loti, *Madame Chrysanthemum*, 20.

45. Auction catalogue, *Collection Pierre Loti: Objets d'art et meubles de la Chine provenant du palais impérial, art Océanien, Ile de Paques, Iles Marquises, Nouvelle Calédonie, sculpture Mexicaine*, Paris: Hotel Drouot (January 29, 1929), 18. The boomerang attracted a good deal of attention and a good price (1,120 francs); see press clippings collection Maison Pierre Loti, "Un Flaneur à l'Hotel Drouot," "Un coup d'oeil sur la vente Pierre Loti" (February 7, 1929), "La Curiosité" (January 30, 1929).

46. Loti, *A Child's Romance*, 93; Marcel Sémézies, "Une veillée avec Loti à Rochefort," *Cahiers Pierre Loti*, no. 74 (Dec. 1979), 27.

47. "La Vie qui passe" (January 30, 1929)

48. "On a vendu des souvenirs de Pierre Loti" (January 31, 1929); other press clippings: "Des souvenirs de Pierre Loti aux feux des enchères," "Les Collections de Pierre Loti sont vendues," "La vente Pierre-Loti."

TWO: PANAMA

1. Augustin Garcon, *Histoire du canal de Panama*, Paris: Challamel Ainé (1886), preface by Ferdinand de Lesseps, 3.

2. Willis John Abbot, *The Panama Canal in Picture and Prose*, New York: Syndicate Publishing, 1913, 121.

3. Emile Bergerat, *L'Amour en République: étude sociologique*, Paris, E. Dentu, 1889, 159; Garcon, *Historie*, 80.

4. Winfred Stephens, *Madame Adam, La Grande Française*, London: Chapman and Hall, 1917, 216. On *La Nouvelle Revue*, "Nothing pleased her more than the interest taken in it by M. Ferdinand de Lesseps, a new acquaintance she owed to (Emile) Girardin."

5. Paul Deschanel, *La Politique Française en Océanie*, Paris: Berger-Levrault et Cie, 1884.

6. *La Nouvelle Revue*, 1, no. 1 (Oct–Dec 1879), 9–11.

7. Centre des archives du monde du travail, Roubaix, 7AQ 2–9. *Bulletin du canal interocéanique*, no. 148, October 15, 1885; newspapers collected with the *Bulletin*, no. 29, November 1, 1880.

8. *Bulletin*, no. 30, November 15, 1880, 275. See also, E. W. Dahlgren, *Les Relations commerciales et maritimes entre La France et les côtes de l'océan Pacifique*, Paris: Honoré Champion, 1909.

9. Pierre Loti, *A Child's Romance*, New York: W.S. Gottsberger, 1891, 253–5.

10. Garcon, *Histoire*, 45; *Bulletin*, Archives du monde du travail, no. AJX4 (September 1880); Deschanel, *La Politique Francaise en Océanie*,1; also, Archives de la Marine, BB3814, "mouvements de la flotte," note 27.219 on "the exchange connections between France and the naval division of the Pacific Ocean."

11. Inagaki Manjiro, *Japan and the Pacific*, London: T. Fisher Unwin, 1890, 47, 57; Garcon, 77; Victor Cabrit, *Considerations sur les rivalités internationales dans le Pacifique nord*, Montpellier: Imprimerie cooperative ouvrière, 1910.

12. Félix Belly, *A Travers l'Amérique Centrale: Le Nicaragua et le canal intérocean-ique*, Paris: Suisse Romande, 1867, 37. On "Latin" America, see Paul Edison, *Latinizing America: The French Scientific Study of Mexico, 1820–1920*, Durham: Duke University Press, 2005.

13. Néle de Kantule, "The History of the Cuna Indians from the Great Flood Our Time," in Erland Nordenskiold and Ruben Pérez Kantule, *An Historical and Ethnological Survey of the Cuna Indians*, Goteborgs: Goteborgs Museum, 1925, reprinted New York: AMS, 1979, 193–5.

14. Belly, *A Travers l'Amérique Centrale* , 80, 161; also Cyril Allen, *France in Central America: Félix Belly and the Nicaraguan Canal*, New York: Pageant, 1966.

15. Béatrice Giblin, ed., *Eliseé Réclus, l'homme et la terre*, Paris: F. Maspero, 1982, 22, 132; also Henriette Chardak, *Eliseé Réclus, L'homme qui aimait la terre*, Paris: Stock, 1997.

16. Athanase Airiau, *Canal interocéanique par l'isthme du Darien*, Paris: Chez France, 1860, 38.

17. Athanase Airiau, *L'Achèvement de Canal de Panama: Lettre ouvert addressé á Messieurs les senateurs et deputés*, Paris, 1894; Athanase Airiau, *Canal interocéanique*, Faucher cited 43.

18. Airiau, *L'Achèvement*, 74.

19. Claude Drigon, Marquis de Magny, *Canalisation des isthmes de Suez et Panama*, Paris: Compagnie Maritime de Saint Píe, 1848, 9, 17.

20. Wolf von Schiebrand, *America, Asia, and the Pacific*, New York: Henry Holt, 1904, 144.

21. Juliette Adam, *My Literary Life*, New York: Appleton, 1904, 142.

22. Adam, *My Literary Life*, 138–9.

23. Adam, *My Literary Life*, 146–7; Winfred Stephens, *Madame Adam*, 88; *Oeuvres de Saint Simon et d'Enfantin*, Paris: E. Dentu, 1866, vol. 26, esp. 1–30. See also

Maria Teresa Bulciolu, *L'Ecole Saint-Simonienne et la femme, notes et documents, 1828–33*, Pisa: Goliardica, 1980, 50–5.

24. Saint Simon, lectures, in Jules St. André, *Religion St. Simonienne: enseignement central*, Paris: D'Everat, 1831, 58. *Oeuvres de Saint Simon et d'Enfantin*, Paris: E. Dentu, 1866, vol. 10, 55, vol. 26, 1–30.

25. Prosper Enfantin, *Colonisation de l'Algérie*, Paris: P. Bertram, 1843, 31–2, these and "worthy of nineteenth-century" citations.

26. Maxime du Camp, *Souvenirs littéraires*, Paris: Hachette, 1892, 487; *Oeuvres de Saint Simon et d'Enfantin*, Paris: E. Dentu, 1866, vol. 10, 74–5. also Félix Paponot, *Suez et Panama: une solution*, Paris: Librarie Polytechnique Baudry, 1889; Timothy Mitchell, *Colonizing Egypt*, Berkeley: University of California Press, 1988.

27. *Oeuvres de Saint Simon et d'Enfantin*, letter, 62.

28. National Archives, F72 15978 "Commissariat special-2/10" (1888).

29. Lambert-Bey in Juliette Adam, *Mes Premières armes littéraires et politiques*, Paris: A. Lemérre, 1904, 230–3.

30. *La Phare de la Loire*, July 31, 1879.

31. Eliseé Réclus, "Le Littoral de la France," *Révue des deux mondes* (September 19, 1864), 673–702.

32. *La Nouvelle Revue*, 1, no. 1, 15. See Gerson, *The Pride of Place*, 73–178.

33. See Maron J. Simon, *The Panama Affair*, New York: Charles Scribner's Sons, 1971, 23

34. Renaulat in Jean Bouvier, *Les Deux scandales de Panama*, Paris: Juillard, 1964, 97.

35. Ferdinand de Lesseps, "Discours de réception de M. Ferdinand de Lesseps, Séance de l'Académie française du 23 avril 1885."

36. *Journal Officiel*, Chamber of Deputies (November 21, 1982); see Bouvier, *Les Deux scandales*, 160.

37. Edmond Drumont, *De l'or, de la boue, et du sang*, 1896, 40. See also Drumont, *La France Juive: essai d'histoire contemporaine*, Beiruit: Charlemagne, 1994; Jean-Yves Mollier, *Le Scandale de Panama*, Paris: Fayard, 1991; Bouvier, *Les Deux scandales*, 141–2. For running coverage, see *Le Journal officiel* and *Le Droit: Journal des tribunaux*, issues of 1893, "Affaire du Panama," collected in N.A. C5485. Mention of Freppel, *Le Libre parole* (September 18, 1892).

38. Philippe Bunau-Varilla, *Panama: Le Passé, le présent, l'avenir*, Paris: Gresson, 1892, 6: Bunau-Varilla, *The Great Adventure of Panama*, New York: Doubleday, 1920, 51–61.

39. For American perspectives, Abbot, *The Panama Canal in Picture and Prose*, on wine, women, and the *temps de luxe*, 127; also, Alexander Missal, "In Perfect Operation: Social Vision and the Building of the Panama Canal," in Jaap Verhuel, ed., *Dreams of Paradise, Visions of Apocalypse: Utopia and Dystopia in American Culture*, Amsterdam: VU University Press, 2004, 69–77; James M. Skinner, *France and Panama: The Unknown Years, 1894–1908*, New York: Peter Lang, 1989; Diogenes Arosemena, *Documentary Diplomatic History of the Panama Canal*, Pan-

ama: Republic of Panama, 1961; Lesseps quoted in *La Phare de la Loire* (July 31, 1879).

40. David Sweetman, *Paul Gauguin*, London: Hodder and Stoughton, 148–60; David McCullough, *The Path between the Seas*, New York: Simon and Schuster, 1977, 174.

41. For his own correspondence, see Paul Gauguin, *Noa Noa: The Tahitian Journal*, and *Gauguin's Letters from the South Seas*, New York: Dover (1985, 1992).

42. Archives du monde du travail, 7AQ 3–9, "notes de notre correspondent du *Soir*: voyage de Ferdinand de Lesseps," piece 1464 (April 1886).

43. Abbot, *The Panama Canal in Picture and Prose*, 9.

44. Mary Louise Pratt, *Imperial Eyes: Travel Writing and Transculturation*, London: Routledge, 1992, ch. 2.

45. Adrien Marx, *Le Figaro*, November 26, 1880; Albert Larthe, *Dans l'isthme de Panama: Scenes de la vie indienne, souvenirs et impressions de voyage*, Tours: Alfred Cattier, 1895, 7–9. Lucien Napoléon Bonaparte Wyse, *Le Canal de Panama*, Paris: Hachette, 1886. Also, Charles Autigeon, *De Bordeaux à Panama et de Panama à Cherbourg*, Paris: A. Chio, 1883.

46. Larthe, *Dans l'isthme de Panama*, 20, 122, 146; Autigeon, *De Bordeaux à Panama*, 78–9.

47. Néle de Kantule, "The History of the Cuna Indians from the Great Flood to Our Time," in Erland Nordenskiold and Ruben Pérez Kantule, *An Historical and Ethnological Survey of the Cuna Indians*, Goteborgs: Goteborgs Museum, 1925, reprinted New York: AMS, 1979, 197.

48. Néle de Kantule, "From the Great Flood to Our Time," 199–200.

49. Néle de Kantule, "From the Great Flood to Our Time," 201.

50. Armand Reclus, *Panama et Darien: Voyage d'exploration*, Paris: Hachette, 1881, 405.

51. Wyse, 45; Reclus, 80.

52. Larthe, 17; Autigeon, 49–50, 78; Reclus 66–7.

53. Abbot, *The Panama Canal in Picture and Prose*, 125.

54. Albert Tissander, *Six mois aux Etats-Unis suivi d'un excursion à Panama*, Paris: Grasson, 1886, 255.

55. National Archives, F72 15978 MI 25347, letter of March 28, 1887; on the history of this story, see Robert Tomes, *Panama in 1855*, New York: Harper and Bros. (1855); Luis A. Picard-Ami, Maria Josefa de Melendez, "El Suicido de los Chinos," *Loteria* no. 281 (July 1979), 62–87; Eustorgio Chong Ruiz, *Los Chinos en la Sociedad*, Instituto Nacional de Cultura Panamena, 1992.

56. Walter Leon Pepperman, *Who Built the Panama Canal?* London: J.M. Dent & Sons, 1915, 218; Missal, "In Perfect Operation: Social Vision and the Building of the Panama Canal," passim.

57. Frank Morton Todd, *The Story of the Exposition*, New York: D.P. Putnam and Sons, 1921, 18; Michael Conniff, *Black Labor on a White Canal*, Pittsburgh: University of Pittsburgh Press, 1985; Velma Newton, *The Silver Men: West Indian*

Labor Migration to Panama, 1850–1914, Kingston: Institute of Social and Economic Research, 1984, 123; Henri Cermois, *Deux ans à Panama*, Paris: Flammarion, 1886, 53–8, for description of roulette for Europeans, cards, church, and cricket for West Indians, no theaters, concerts, or cafés, but saloons for everyone.

58. Albert Tissander, *Six mois aux Etats-Unis suivi d'un excursion à Panama*, Paris: Grasson, 1886, 81.

59. Philippe Bunau-Varilla, *Panama: The Creation, the Destruction, the Resurrection*, Paris: Plon, 1913, 724–5.

60. Charles Lemire, *Les Intérêts Français dans le Pacifique*, Paris: Augustin Challamel, 1904, 6–8, 77, 9. Also, *Rapport de la mission chargée d'étudié les consequences de l'ouverture du Canal du Panama en ce qui concerne les colonies françaises*, Paris: *Journaux Officiel*, 1913; Néle de Kantule, "From the Great Flood to Our Time," 195.

THREE: WALLIS AND FUTUNA

1. Claude Rozier, ed., *Ecrits de S. Pierre Chanel*, Rome, 1960, in subsequent notations "EC" where cross-referenced by Rozier; Aléxandre de Poncet, *Historie de l'Ile Wallis: le protectorat français*, Paris: Société des Océanistes, no. 23 (1972); Chanel's personal journal at the Archives des Pères Maristes, Padri Maristi, Rome, doc. no. 112.1 (1838), entry of Friday, December 14, concerning his work and reputation with the *maison des malades* and sick children.

2. Thanks to Hugh Laracy; see especially his "Saint-Making: The Case of Pierre Chanel of Futuna," *New Zealand Journal of History*, 34, no. 1 (2000), 145–61. For a comprehensive overview, Frédéric Angleviel, *Les Missions à Wallis et Futuna au XIXe siècle*, Bordeaux-Talence: Centre de Recherche des Espaces Tropicaux, 1994; also, Robert Aldrich and Isabelle Merle (eds.), *France Abroad: Indochina, New Caledonia, Wallis and Futuna*, Sydney: University of Sydney Press, 1997.

3. L. C. Servant, *Ecrits de Louis Catherin Servant*, Paris: Pierre Tequi (reprint, 1996), 143; René Pinon, "La France des antipodes," *Revue des deux mondes*, 158 (1900), 807.

4. Petelo Leleivai, "Le berceau polynésien," in Elise Huffer and Petelo Leleivai, eds., *Futuna: Mo Ona Puleaga Sau (Aux deux royaumes)*, Suva and Sigave: Institute of Pacific Studies, University of the South Pacific, and Service des Affaires Culturelles de Futuna, 2001, 12.

5. Servant, *Ecrits*, 102–7. For images of the martyrdom (some extremely rare) and commentary, Archives des Pères Maristes, Padri Maristi, Rome, files nos. 511.1, 512.1, 512.1, "prima effigies," 520/521, "Eius Orta et Martyrium," 514.1, "Tableau official."

6. Roman Catholic Church, *Tonga Station Correspondence 1844–70*, Pacific Manuscript Bureau, Australia National University , Canberra (PMB), 192.

7. Loti, *Le Roman d'un enfant (A Child's Romance)*, 116–7, 130–2.

8. *Annales de la congrégation des sacres coeurs de Jesus et de Marie*, vol. 5, Paris: Rue de Picpus, 1879, 45; Servant, *Ecrits*, 96 (1840); also J. Coste, *Lectures on Society of Mary History (Marist Fathers)*, Rome: Society of Mary, 1965; for chronicles and histories: *Annales de la propogation de la foi* (receuil périodique des lettres des éveques et des missionaires), vol. 51, Lyon: Pélagaud, 1879; J. B. Biolet, ed., *Les Missions Catholiques Françaises au XIXe siècle*, 5 vols., Paris: Armand Colin, 1902.

9. Methodist Missionary of Australia, Fiji District, MMSA/M-20, *Papers Re: Friction between the Catholic and Wesleyan Missions*, National Archives of Fiji.

10. See Hugh Laracy, *Marists and Melanesians*, Honolulu: University of Hawaii Press, 1976, 17; also on islander views, Raymond Mayer, *200 Legendes de Wallis et Futuna: éléments de la tradition orale*, ms, University of Hawaii, UH PACC GR 395 W3M4; Ruth Finnegan and Margaret Orbell, *South Pacific Oral Traditions*, Bloomington: Indiana University Press, 1995.

11. Rev. Samuel Worcester, in Char Miller, ed., *Missions and Missionaries in the Pacific*, Lewistown: Edwin Mellen, 1985, 68–73; Maggie Whitecross Paton, *Letters and Sketches from the New Hebrides*, New York: A. C. Armstrong, 1895, 31; Vicente Diaz, *White Love and Other Events in Filipino History*, Durham, N.C.: Duke University Press, 2000; Margaret Rodman, *Houses Far From Home: British Colonial Space in the New Hebrides*, Honolulu: University of Hawaii Press, 2001.

12. Teio Faateni, on his great-grandfather Tefaatau Faatemi, "Le Bible/ Histoire 38," Musée de Tahit et des îles, Punaauia, Tahiti.

13. Henri Rivière, *Souvenirs de la Nouvelle Calédonie*, Paris: Calmann-Lévy, 1880, 63; Victor Ségalen, "Journal des iles," in Henry Bouillier, ed., *Oeuvres complètes*, Paris: Robert Laffont, 1995, 421–2; Frédéric Angleviel, *Les Missions à Wallis et Futuna au XIXe siècle*, Bordeaux-Talence: Centre de Recherche des Espaces Tropicaux, 1994, passim; Claire Laux, *Les Théocraties Missionaires en Polynésie aux XIXe siècle*, Paris: L'Harmattan, 2000.

14. Archives des Pères Maristes, Padri Maristi, Rome, files nos. 113.3–4, "Sermon sur la Passion (EC 22, 1835), "Sermon sur le désir du Ciel (EC 21, 1828).

15. Servant, *Ecrits*, 143; René Pinon, "La France des antipodes," *Revue des deux mondes*, 158 (1900), 807.

16. Laracy, *Marists and Melanesians*, 279, 15; Gabriel Michel, *Frère François et la reconnaissance legale des frères Maristes 1840–1851*, Paris: G. Michel, 1991; Gerald Arbuckle, "The Impact of Vatican II on the Marists in Oceania," James A. Boutilier et al., eds., *Mission Church and Sect in Oceania*, Ann Arbor: University of Michigan, 1978.

17. Kenneth Woodward, *Making Saints*, New York: Simon and Schuster, 1990; Vicente M. Diaz, *Repositioning the Missionary: The Beatification of Blessed Diego Luis de Sanvitorres and Chamorro Cultural History*, Santa Cruz, 1992 (UM Microfilm, 1993).

18. Letter from Mission St Jean d'Ombrym (May 17, 1895), University of Hawaii microfilm; Servant, *Ecrits*, 102–7.

19. Servant, *Ecrits*, 102–3.

20. Le Reverend Père J. A. Bourdin, *Vie du venerable Pierre Marie Louis Chanel, prêtre de la Société de Marie*, Paris: Jacques LeCoffre, 1867, 564

21. Servant, *Ecrits*, 105

22. Servant, *Ecrits*, 106–7

23. Chanel's Personal Journal, Archives des Pères Maristes, Padri Maristi, Rome, entry of Sunday, 21 July, "These poor natives . . . ten pigs for a gun; the purchase of four guns transports them with joy." Also, Chanel, in Servant, *Ecrits*, 45, 84–5.

24. D. Frimigacci, M. Keletaona et al., *Ko Le Fonu Tu'a A Limulimua/ La Tortue au dos mossu: textes de tradition orale de Futuna*, Louvais: Peeters, 1995, 487–8. See Johannes Fabian, *Power and Performance: Ethnographic Explorations though Proverbial Wisdom and Theater in Shaba, Zaire*, Madison: University of Wisconsin Press, 1992.

25. Servant, *Ecrits*, 103; Archives des Pères Maristes, Padri Maristi, Rome, files nos. III.11 and III.12 (EC 40–1), Chanel's letters on Niuliki: "the king gave me the best possible welcome"; Dorothy Shineberg, *They Came for Sandalwood: A Study of the Sandalwood Trade in the South-West Pacific 1830–1865*, London: Melbourne University Press, 1967, and Shineberg, *The People Trade: Pacific Island Laborers and New Caledonia, 1865–1930*, Honolulu: University of Hawaii Press, 1999. Also, Peter Corris, ed., William T. Wawn, *The South Seas Islands and the Queensland Labor Trade*, Honolulu: University of Hawaii Press, 1973; Edward W. Docker, *The Blackbirders*, London: Angus & Robertson, 1970.

26. *Sydney Morning Herald*, May 22, 1869; see Captain George Palmer, *Kidnapping in the South Seas*, London: Dawsons (original 1871; reprint 1971), 168.

27. Maggie Paton, 310–11; also Albert Hastings Markham, *The Cruise of the Rosario*, London: Dawsons (original 1873; reprint 1970), 74.

28. Benjamin Goubin, *Lifou, Pacifique-Sud*, Annonay: Jean-Luc Chavlet, 1985, letter of 1877, 26. For Moncelon, see Shineberg, *The People Trade*, 113.

29. Chevron, in Servant, *Ecrits*, 45, 99; William Tagupa, *Father Chanel and Futuna Island: A Study in Missionary Martyrdom and Change in a Traditional Polynesian Society*, ms. (1972) University of Hawaii: BX 4700 C55T3.

30. Meitala's letter, reprinted in Bourdin, *Vie du venerable Pierre Marie Louis Chanel*, 594.

31. M. Morel, *Dernière Journée et Martyre du Bienheureux Pierre Louis Marie Chanel, drame en vers*, Lyon: E. Vitte, 1889, 11.

32. Roman Catholic Church, *Tonga Station Correspondence 1844–70*, Pacific Manuscript Bureau, Australia National University, microfilm reels PMB 192, BMICR MF 2330, reel two.

33. D. Frimigacci, M. Keletaona, et al., *Ko Le Fonu Tu'a A Limulimua/ La Tortue au dos mossu: textes de tradition orale de Futuna*, Peeters: Louvais/Paris, 1995, 481–3.

34. Servant, *Ecrits*, 176. Odom Abba, "Faut-il réhabiliter Musumusu?" *Les Cahiers de Wallis et Futuna*, no. 1, March 2001, Ono: Les Amis de Wallis et Futuna, 2001.

35. Servant, *Ecrits*, 197. See Odom Abba, 33.

36. Paul Barré, *Revue française de l'etranger et des colonies*, 24 (1889), 459; Alphonse Bertillon, *Ethnographie moderne: les races sauvages*, Paris, 1883, 236.

37. D. Frimigacci, M. Keletaona et al., *Ko Le Fonu Tu'a A Limulimua/ La Tortue au does mossu: textes de traditions orale de Futuna*, Louvais: Peeters, 1995, 39, 66.

38. Chevron, in Servant, *Ecrits*, 91.

39. *Triduum solennel et inauguration du pèlerinage en l'honneur du Bienheureux Pierre-Louis Marie Chanel*, Bourg, 1890 BNF: Ln27.39398, 9–10. For details, Jean-Claude Marquis, *St. Pierre Chanel: De L'Ain au Pacifique*, Bourg-en-Bresse: La Taillanderie, 1991.

40. *Annales de la congrégation des sacres coeurs de Jesus et de Marie*, 45.

41. Victor Poupinel, in Bourdin, *Vie du venerable Pierre Marie Louis Chanel*, 603.

42. Adrien Dansette, *The Religious History of Modern France, Vol II: Under the Third Republic*, New York: Herder and Herder, 1961, 432; Bernard Plongeron, ed., *Catholiques entre monarchie et république: actes du colloque nationale de l'université catholique de l'ouest*, Angers, 1992, 117, 138; James Tudesco, *Missionaries and French Imperialism: The Role of Catholic Missionaries in French Colonial Expansion, 1880–1905* (UM Microfilm, 1983); F. Soulier-Falbert, *L'Expansion française dans le Pacifique-Sud*, Paris, 1911.

43. Jacques Bozon, ed., *Faut-il un nouveau concordat?* Paris: Ed. Presse-Française, 1913, 8–10, 99–100.

44. Goubin, *Lifou*, 157; Bouzige cited in Angleviel (A.P.M. OW 208), 188; on "points de relache," René Pinon, "La France des antipodes," *Revue des deux mondes*, 158 (1900), 784. For comparative work, see Peter Hempenstall, *Pacific Islanders under German Rule: A Study in the Meaning of Colonial Resistance*, Canberra: Australia National University Press, 1978; Russell Berman, *Enlightenment or Empire: Colonial Discourse in German Culture*, Lincoln: University of Nebraska Press, 1998; Samson, *Imperial Benevolence*.

45. Lamaze at Poi, in Poncet, *Histoire de l'Ile Wallis*, 25.

46. John Williams, *Christianity and Civilization in the South Pacific*, London: W. Allen Young, 1922, 20.

47. Avner Ben-Amos, *Funerals, Politics, and Memory in Modern France, 1789–1996*, Oxford: Oxford University Press, 2000, esp. 226–30 on Bishop Freppel and the funeral rites for Admiral Courbet.

48. *Triduum solennel*, 7, 9, 33; objets de piété, 44–5.

49. *Quelques guerisons et graces signalées obtenus par l'intercession du Bienhereux Pierre Louis Marie Chanel*, Lyon: Librarie générale Catholique et classique, 1891, testimonies of Félix T., M. L'Abbé F., Soeur M. Saint-Brune, 9, 37, 44–5.

50. *Triduum solennel*, 38.

51. Archives des Pères Maristes, Padri Maristi, Rome, file no. 111.42, August 29, 1839 (EC48), "Lettres à divers, 1837–1840."

52. Flag noted in Poncet, *Historie de l'Ile Wallis*, 208; Morel, *Dernières jours*, 11, 16, 60.

53. Letter, signed "Parizat," September 29, 1881, C.A.O.M. FM/ SG/ c. 140, doss. A120.

54. Documents with original signatures, C.A.O.M. FM/ SG/ NCL/ c. 176, doss. 1.

55. C.A.O.M. FM/SG/NCL/c. 176, doss. 1.

56. "Incident Piho," Pacific Manuscripts Bureau/ Oceania Marist Province Archives 313, Catholic Archdiocese of Noumea, AAN 112.3–112.9.57.

PMB/OMPA 313: Catholic Archdiocese of Noumea, AAN 112.3, 112.9.

58. René de la Bruyère, *Contes et legendes de l'océan Pacifique*, Paris: Pierre Roger, 1931, 12–14.

59. *Enosi*, part of program *Sermons et explications touchant la vie du Bienheureux Chanel et celle de Mgr. Bataillon*, in Poncet, *Historie de l'Ile Wallis*, 133.

FOUR: SOCIETY ISLANDS

1. Guy de Maupassant, "L'Amour dans les livres et dan la vie," *Gil Blas* (July 6, 1886). Every Pacific collection has copies of Bengt Danielsson's *Love in the South Seas*, London: George Allen & Unwin, 1956. The author notes, "the most famous south seas novel, *Le Mariage de Loti* . . . does not end in a wedding in the Western sense, but starts instead with a Polynesian wedding," 11. Also, Robert Langdon, *Tahiti: Island of Love*, Sydney: Pacific, 1954; Daniel Maurer, *Aimer Tahiti*, Paris: Nouvelles Editions Latines, 1972; France Guillain, *Maïma: Des Iles de l'amour à l'amour de la vie*, Paris: Plon, 1987; Charles Teriiteanuanua Manutahi, *Le Don d'aimer*, Pirae: Polytram, 1983.

2. Pierre Loti, André Alexandre, Georges Hartmann, *L'Ile du rêve*, music by Reynaldo Hahn, Paris: Calmann-Lévy, 1898, 25.

3. Jules Garnier, "Excursion autour de l'île de Tahiti," *Bulletin de la Société de Géographie*, (November-December 1869), 3; Margaret Jolly, "From Point Venus to Bali Ha'i: Eroticism and Exoticism in Representations of the Pacific," in L. Manderson and Jolly, eds., *Sites of Desire, Economies of Pleasure: Sexualities in Asia and the Pacific*, 1997, 99–122.

4. *Le Vice-Amiral Bergasse Du Petit-Thouars, 1832–1890, d'après ses notes et sa correspondance*, Paris: Perrin et Cie, 1906, letter of March 23, 1854.

5. Paul Deschanel, *La Politique Française en Océanie*, Paris: Berger-Levault et Cie, 1884, 34.

6. C.A.O.M. FM/SG/c. 140, doss. A120, "confidential letter" Dec. 14, 1883. On this metaphor applied to general history, Pierre Yves Toullelan and Bernard Gille, *Le Mariage Franco-Tahitien*, Tahiti: Polymages-Scoop, 1992.

7. Colin Newbury, "Resistance and Collaboration in French Polynesia: The Tahitian War: 1844–7," *Journal of the Polynesian Society*, no. 82 (1973), 5–27; Newbury, *Tahiti Nui: Change and Survival in French Polynesia, 1767–1945*, Honolulu: University of Hawaii Press, 1980; also Miriam Kahn, "Tahiti Interwined: Ancestral Land, Tourist Postcard, and Nuclear Test Site," *American Anthropologist* 102, no. 1 (2000), 7–26.

8. For a postwar look at a key moment in Tahitian "nationalism," see Jean-Marc Regnault, *Te Metua: L'Echec d'un nationalisme Tahitien*, Papeete: Polymages, 1996.

9. Ministère des Finances, no. 8012 (December 26, 1881), C.A.O.M. "authorizes the monthly payment of pensions registered with the public treasury of France by

the law of December 30, 1880 in the name of King Pomare V and the members of his family . . ."

10. C.A.O.M. FM/ SG/ c.29/ doss. A10–15 "correspondance génerale Océanie, 1842," on Dupetit-Thouars's missions to the Marquesas.

11. Martin, Edward Dodd, *The Rape of Tahiti*, New York: Dodd, Mead, 1983, 122–5; also Charlotte Haldane, *Tempest Over Tahiti*, London: Constable, 1963, ch. 9 "Royal Correspondence."

12. Pomare Letter (January 23, 1843), in Paul DeDeckker, ed., George Pritchard, *The Aggressions of the French at Tahiti and Other Islands in the Pacific*, Auckland: Auckland University Press, 1983; 133–4, MS pages of Pritchard 98–9, copies in Foreign Office documents, FO 58/23 and FO 27/664. Also, 122–3, MS pages 84–5 for Pomare's declaration, "I did not sign of my own free will." On narratives and counternarratives, Kareva Mateata-Allain, "Ma'ohi Women Writers of Colonial French Polynesia: Passive Resistance Towards a Post-Colonial Literature," *Jouvert: Journal of Postcolonial Studies*, 7, no. 2 (2003).

13. *Appeal of the Natives of Tahiti to the Governments of Great Britain and America* (January 1846), Admiralty Papers I/5561, Hammond to Seymour (February 11, 1846), see Colin Newbury, "Aspects of French Policy in the Pacific 1853–1906," *Pacific Historical Review*, 27, no. 1 (1958); also Newbury, "Resistance and Collaboration in French Polynesia: The Tahitian War: 1844–7," appendix 1, 21–5.

14. Archives Musée de Tahiti et des îles, 77.5.22.2.C, *Procés-verbal de la réunion qui s'est tenue à bord du naivre de guerre anglais Talbot dans la rade de Papeete à Tahiti*, 3, 5.

15. Archives Musée de Tahiti et des îles, 77.5.22.C, *Procés verbal*, 5–6.

16. DeDeckker, ed., Pritchard, *The Aggressions of the French at Tahiti and Other Islands in the Pacific*; see DeDeckker's introduction.

17. Jean-Marc Regnault, Jean-Marie Dubois, director and coordinator, *Histoire au cycle 3*, Polynésie Française: CTDRP-ETAG, 1998, 123. See "Le 29 Juin, symbole d'amitié et de solidarité," *Te Fenua: Journal d'information du gouvernement de Polynésie Française*, no. 2 (June 22, 2001), 7.

18. Bruat, in "Rapports sur les combats qui ont eu lieu à Tahiti de 1844 à 1846," in *Bulletin de la Société des Etudes Océaniennes*, no. 57 (1936), 606, 622; T. Deman, *La Révolte aux Iles sous le Vent (Tahiti)*, Douai: Union Géographique, 1897, 41–2; Caroline Ralston and Nicholas Thomas, eds., *Sanctity and Power: Gender in Polynesian History*, special issue of *Journal of Pacific History*, 22 (1987).

19. Captain Martin in Dodd, *Rape of Tahiti*, 122–5.

20. E. Watbled, "La France en Océanie," *Nouvelle Revue*, 3 (April 1898), 466.

21. Archives Musée de Tahiti et des îles, 77.5.22.C, *Procés verbal*, 7.

22. Giraud has been recently revisited; see the catalogue *Tahiti 1842–1848: Oeuvres de Charles Giraud*, Musée de Tahiti et des îles/Te Fare Iamanaha (November 15, 2001–January 27, 2002). General scholarly works have appeared especially since the 1980s. See, for example, Pierre Yves-Toullelan, ed., *La France en Polynésie, 1842–1960*, part of *L'Encyclopédie de la Polynésie*, Gleizal: Multipress, 1986.

23. Charles Crosnier de Varigny, *L'Océan Pacifique*, Paris: Hachette, 1888, 67–8; F. V. Picquenot, *Géographie physique et politique des Etablissements Français de l'Océanie*, Paris: A. Challamel, 1900; French occupation is explained this way: "By request of Queen Pomare and the great chiefs, Admiral Du Petit-Thouars established the French protectorate over Tahiti and its dependencies."

24. Pomare Vedel, "Tahiti," Etablissements Français du Pacifique Austral, *Exposition Coloniale Internationale de Paris*, Paris: Société d'Editions Géographiques, Maritimes, et Coloniales, 1931, 16–17

25. Vedel, "Tahiti," 17; Wragge, *Romance*, 165.

26. Dr. L. Sasportas, "Tahiti," *Exposition*, 31.

27. "Les Colonies Françaises," *L'Illustration* (June 4, 1864), 122.

28. Bishop Museum Archives, MS 5-S9, Apo of Atimaha, *Encouagement aux indigènes Huahine qui vont aux combats*, trans. by Reverend Orsmond (September 20, 1849) ms.

29. See Michael Panoff, *Tahiti Métisse*, Paris: Denoël, 1989, 103.

30. See the reports in "Correspondance générale: fin de la révolte de Raïatea," C.A.O.M. FM/SG/Océanie/ c. 92/ doss. A149; Haldane, *Tempest*, 231

31. Apo of Atimaha, *Encouagement*, 20, 14, 22, 8.

32. Capitain Michel Jouslard, "Papiers Hautefeuille," Archives de la Marine, 147 GG2, 1–4, 36–7.

33. Jean-Jo Scemla, *Le Voyage en Polynésie*, Paris: Robert Laffont, 1994, from Jacques Arago, "Deux Océans," 606; see also Commandant le Hussard, Rapport, "Tahiti" (September 24, 1881), C.A.O.M., 140 A120, on continuing relations between monarchs and chiefs; Jocelyn Linnekin, *Sacred Queens and Women of Consequence: Rank, Gender, and Colonialism in the Hawaiian Islands*, Ann Arbor: University of Michigan Press, 1990.

34. Service des Archives Territoriales, Tipareui, Tahiti, 48W/1132, "Etat nominative des fonctionnaires;" 48W/ 581 no. 1.1, no. 29 (March 3–June 28, 1893).

35. Jouslard, "Papiers Hautefeuille," 34, 47–8. See the report of Chief Inspector of Services Nesty complaining of "personnel recruited by chance . . . composed of those who come from who knows where and leave at their whim. . . . " Letter, C.A.O.M., FM/SG/ c. 140, doss. A 120.

36. "Délégation de pouvoirs adressée à M. Chesse," Papeete (November 11, 1881, and March 14, 1882), C.A.O.M. Géo-Océanie, 140/ A-120.

37. Archives de la Musée de Tahiti et des îles, 77.5.101P, *Assemblée Législative de Tahiti* (June 24, 1881).

38. E. Watbled, "La France en Océanie," *Nouvelle Revue*, 3 (April 1898), 474–5.

39. Letter, "Gov. Tahiti á Ministère de la Marine et Colonies, Paris" C.A.O.M. FM/ SG/ c. 140, doss. A120, January 12, 1883.

40. Letters, "Mouvements de la flotte," Archives de La Marine, BB 3–814; reports from BB4 366–1, 7–8.

41. Service des Archives Territoriales, Tiapaerui, Tahiti, 48W/ 1078/ no. 3 (February 7).

42. BB4 366–1, 7–8; Pierre Yves Toulellan, "La longue durée Tahitienne," 222.

43. Pierre Benoit, *Les Grands Escales*, Paris: Alpina, 1933, 73; Robert Nicole, *The Word, the Pen, and the Pistol: Literature and Power in Tahiti*, Albany: SUNY Press, 2000, 99–129 on Loti, Gauguin, Ségalen. For a commanding overview, Daneil Margueron, *Tahiti dans toute sa littérature: Essai sur Tahiti et ses îles dans la littérature française de la decouverte à nos jours*, Paris: Editions l'Harmattan, 1989.

44. Edward D'Auvergne, *Pierre Loti: The Romance of a Great Writer*, New York: Fredrick Stokes, 1926; see Lesley Blanch, *Pierre Loti: Portrait of an Escapist*, London: Collins, 1983, 37, 41; Pritchard, *The Aggressions of the French at Tahiti*, "Joint Declaration of Tati and Utami," ms. piece 50, 92.

45. René La Bruyère, in Haldane, *Tempest*, 230. Naval infantry batallion officer Brea, Report printed in *Bulletin de la Société des Etudes Océaniennes*, no. 57 (1936), 612.

46. Service des Archives Territoriales, Tipaerui, Tahiti, 77.5.26.2P, *Journal du gouverneur*, Papeete (May 31, 1896), 3; Edouard Thomas Deman, *La Révolte aux îles sous le vent (Tahiti)*, Douai: Union Géographique, 1897, 41–2.

47. C.A.O.M. FM/ SG/ c. 140, doss. A125.

48. *L'Illustration* (June 4, 1864), 122

49. M. Cartailhac, E. Hamy, and P. Topinard, eds., *L'Anthropologie*, vol. 1, Paris: Masson, 1890, 532–6.

50. François Guillot, *Souvenirs d'un colonial en Océanie, 1888–1911*, Annecy: Dépollion, 1935, 9; Jules Garnier, *Voyage autour du monde: Océanie*, Paris: Plon, 1871, 35, 348–9; Deschanel, *La Politique Française en Océanie*, 145–6.

51. Jean-Marc Regnault, *Te Metua: L'Echec d'un nationalisme Tahitien*, Papeete: Polymages, 1996; Robert Aldrich, *France and the South Pacific Since 1940*, Honolulu: University of Hawaii Press, 1993; Stephen Henningham, *France and the South Pacific: A Contemporary History*, Sydney: Allen and Unwin, 1992; Nic McLennan and Jean Chesneaux, *After Moruroa: France in the South Pacific*, Melbourne: Ocean Press, 1998; more generally, Jocelyn Linnekin, "The Politics of Culture in the Pacific," in Linnekin and Lin Poyer, eds., *Cultural Identity and Ethnicity in the Pacific*, Honolulu: University of Hawaii Press, 1990, 149–174; Margaret Jolly, "Specters of Inauthenticity," *The Contemporary Pacific: A Journal of Pacific Affairs*, 4, no. 1 (1992), 49–72.

52. Henri Lutteroth, *O-Taiti, histoire et enquête*, Paris: Paulin, 1843, 294.

53. Archives Musée de Tahiti et des îles, 77.5.22.2.C, *Procés verbal de la réunion des chefs presidée par la Reine Pomare* (February 9, 1843).

FIVE: NEW CALEDONIA

1. Clement L. Wragge, *The Romance of the South Seas*, London: Chatto and Windus, 1906, 25–6.

2. Juliette Adam, *Nos amitiés politiques avant l'abandon de la revanche*, Paris: A. Lemerre, 1908, 21–2; also, Henri de Rochefort, *Retour de la Nouvelle Calédonie: de Nouméa à Europe*, Paris: F. Jeanmare, 1877.

3. Louis Proal, "Les Crimes d'amour," *Nouvelle Revue*, no. 116 (Jan.–Feb. 1899).

4. Victor de Malherbe, Rapport, 1859, microfilm C.A.O.M., Aix-en-Provence, 26MI OM23; see the commentary by Joel Dauphiné, *Les Dèbuts d'une colonisation laborieuse, Le Sud Calédonien, 1853–1860*, Paris: L'Harmattan, 1995, 122; for a grand and detailed overview, Isabelle Merle, *Expériences coloniales: La Nouvelle Calédonie, 1853–1920*, Paris: Ed. Belin, 1995; also Barbara Creed and Jeanette Hoorn, eds., *Body Trade: Captivity, Cannibalism, and Colonialism in Australia and the Pacific*, Dunnendin: University of Otago Press, 2001.

5. Alice Bullard, *Exile to Paradise: Savagery and Civilization in Paris and the South Pacific, 1790–1900*, Stanford: Stanford University Press, 2000, chs. 1–2.

6. Charles Victor Crosnier de Varigny, *L'Océan Pacifique*, Paris: Hachette, 1888, 55.

7. Juliette Adam, *Nos amitiés politiques*, 95.

8. René Pinon, "La France des antipodes," *Revue des deux mondes*, 158 (1900), 784–5.

9. République Française, *Notices Coloniales*, 167.

10. Alain Saussol, "Une Experience Fouriériste en Nouvelle Calédonie: Le phalanstère de Yaté," *Société d'Etudes Historiques sur la Nouvelle Calédonie*, no. 38 (1978), 29. Also "Guillain, Premier Gouverneur de la Nouvelle Calédonie, 1862–70," in Bernard Brou, *Memento d'historie à la Nouvelle Calédonie: les temps modernes, 1774–1925*, Noumea: Ed. de Santal, 1993, 129–42.

11. Michel Reuillard, *Les Saint-Simoniens et la tentation coloniale: les explorations Africaines et le gouvernement Néo-Calédonien de Charles Guillain, 1808–1875*, Paris: L'Harmattan, 1995, 462–516; C.A.O.M. Fonds Nouvelle Calédonie, carton 26, letter 218 (April 30, 1863).

12. On the financial difficulties of the "model farm" and the "shops, construction sites, and workshops," see the "Boutan report," C.A.O.M. FM/ SG/ 56/ doss. 6. Also, Saussol, "Une Experience Fouriériste," 31–3; also Jean Guillou, "L'Infernal utopie de La Nouvelle France en Nouvelle Guinée, 1879–1881," *Société d'Etudes Historiques sur la Nouvelle Calédonie*, no. 42 (1980), 17–49, on the ill-fated settlement projects of the Marquis de Rays.

13. "Bagnes," Ministère de l'Intérieur, C.A.O.M. H 1834, no. 3065 (October 30, 1872); Report, "Nécessité d'introduire dans la colonie des femmes," C.A.O.M. H 1834 (September 14, 1881), 11.

14. "Femme Barat," Ministère de la Marine et des Colonies, C.A.O.M. H 32, no. 1806 (October 1, 1867).

15. "Famille Fournier,"Ministère de la Marine et des Colonies, C.A.O.M. H 32, no. 2023 (November 8, 1867); "Ordre de service général," C.A.O.M., H 1834 no. 10 (July 6, 1869); M. le Vice-Amiral Krantz, *Notice sur la transportation à la Guyane Française et La Nouvelle Calédonie: Rapport pour l'année 1885*, Paris: Ministère de la Marine et des Colonies, 1889, telegrams, "reclamation de la femme," "envoi de familles," (March 5 and October 24, 1885), 445, 515, 550.

16. Correspondence, C.A.O.M., H 1834, no. 502 (July 11, 1873); Adam, *Nos amitiés politiques*, 21.

17. Henri Rochefort, *De Noumea en Europe*, Paris: Jules Rouff, 1881, 3, 41–2, 113.

18. "Interrogation de M. Higginson," C.A.O.M. FM/ SG/ NCL/ c. 56, doss. 7, vi. Escaping along with Rochefort were other ex-leaders of the Commune: Paschal Grousset, Minster of Foreign Affairs; Francis Jourde, Minister of Finance; Olivier Pain, Secretary for Foreign Affairs; Achille Ballière, Aide to the General Staff; Bastien Grandthille, Commander of the National Guard.

19. Bellmare, 1854 and Longomazino, 1851, C.A.O.M. FM/ H8, doss. 26.

20. Notes C.A.O.M. H56-H32 (February 1875); Admiral Ribourt, C.A.O.M. FM/ SG/ NCL/c. 56, doss. 6 (1874); Théodore Ozeré, *Carnets et lettres d'un déporté de la Commune à l'Ile des Pins, 1871–9*, Noumea: Pub. de la Société d'Etudes Historiques de Nouvelle Calédonie, no. 50 (1993), see letters of 1873 with sentiments to Ozeré's family, "you will write me so that each mail delivery will bring me a letter."

21. Correspondence, C.A.O.M., H 1834, no. 947 (October 4, 1873), no. 532 (November 19, 1872).

22. Johannes Caton, *Journal d'un deporté de la Commune à l'Ile du Pins, 1871–1879*, Paris: Ed. France-Empire, 1986, letter of October 23, 1873, 224.

23. Augustin Bernard, *L'Archipel de la Nouvelle Calédonie*, Paris: Hachette, 1895, 303.

24. "Femmes Canaques," Gouverneur de la Nouvelle Calédonie, C.A.O.M. H 1834 (August 4, 1862).

25. M. le Vice-Amiral Krantz, *Notice sur la transportation*, telegram, "request for approval of marriage" (January 13, 1881), 218.

26. "L'Introduction dans les colonies des femmes," Ministère de la Marine et des Colonies, C.A.O.M. H 1834 (September 1878).

27. Report, "Nécessité d'introduire dans la colonie des femmes," C.A.O.M. H 1834 (September 14, 1881), 1–5.

28. République Française, *Notices Coloniales de l'exposition universelle d'Anvers*, tome 1, Paris, 1885, 168. Dorothy Shineberg, *The People Trade: Pacific Island Laborers and New Caledonia, 1865–1930*, Honolulu: University of Hawaii Press, 1999. Also, Peter Corris, ed., William T. Wawn, *The South Seas Islands and the Queensland Labor Trade*, Honolulu: University of Hawaii Press, 1973.

29. Report, "Nécessité," 3; Isabelle Merle, *Expériences coloniales: La Nouvelle Calédonie, 1853–1920*, Paris: Ed. Belin, 1995, 54; James-Nathan, *Essais sur la réforme penitentiaire*, Paris: Société générale des prisons, 1886, 40.

30. Helen Lainé, *Pioneer Days in New Caledonia*, trans. of *Hommage filial, documentaire Calédonien*, Noumea: Imprimeries Réunies, 1942, 19.

31. Avner Ben-Amos, *Funerals, Politics, and Memory in Modern France*, Oxford: Oxford University Press, 2000, 228.

32. Lainé, *Pioneer Days*, 53.

33. Lainé, *Pioneer Days*, 60-1.

34. Lainé, *Pioneer Days*, 63-4.

35. Marc Le Goupils, *Comment on cesse d'être colon*, Paris: Grasset, 1910, 150.

36. Ribourt, C.A.O.M. FM/ SG/ NCL/c. 56, doss. 6 (1874); *La Calédonie* (July 1, 1897); discussion of Feillet in Isabelle Merle, *Expériences coloniales: La Nouvelle Calédonie, 1853–1920*, Paris: Ed. Belin, 1995, 280–1.

37. Augustin Bernard, *L'Archipel de la Nouvelle Calédonie*, Paris: Hachette, 1895, 288; Margaret Jolly, "Colonizing Women: the Maternal Body and Empire," In Sneja Gunew and Anna Yeatman, eds., *Feminism and the Politics of Difference*, Sydney: Allen and Unwin, 1993, 103–27.

38. Bernard, *L'Archipel de la Nouvelle Calédonie*, 288, 298.

39. Merle, *Expériences coloniales*, 54–5.

40. Edouard Payen, "La Colonisation libre en Nouvelle Calédonie," *Annales des sciences politiques*, tome XIV (January 1899), 198, 214.

41. *Etude sur la Nouvelle Calédonie* (February 1860), C.A.O.M. 42; see commentary by Daphiné, *Les Dèbuts d'une colonisation laborieuse*.

42. Jules Durand, "Chez les Ouébias en Nouvelle Calédonie," *Le Tour du monde*, 6, Hachette, 1900, 503. For a sophisticated overview of historical representations and meanings, see Bronwen Douglas, *Across the Great Divide: Journeys in History and Anthropology*, Amsterdam: Harwood Academic Publishers, 1998.

43. Durand, "Chez les Ouébias," 512.

44. Durand, "Chez les Ouébias," 495–7.

45. C. de Varigny, *L'Océan Pacifique*, C. Durand, "Chez les Ouébias," 513.

46. Isabelle Merle, *Expériences coloniales*, 152.

47. Arthur de Trentinian, "Rapport sur les causes de l'insurrection canaque en 1878," C.A.O.M. FM/ SG/ NCL/ c. 43, doss. 8, with signatures. Also, Dossier Trentinian, Archives de Vincennes (February 4, 1879), first published by Roselène Dousset-Leenhardt, *Colonialisme et contradictions*, Paris: La Haye, Mouton, 1970, annex, 127–59.

48. Reports, "Capitaine du Frégate Matheiu," and "Le Gouverneur," C.A.O.M. FM/SG/NCL/c. 43, doss. A7 and "Rapport no. 79," January 16, 1879.

49. For contemporary records, see C.A.O.M. FM/SG/NCL/c. 43, doss. 8, report no. 160, "The massacre by the canaques of the brigade of the gendarmerie of La Foa (July 6, 1878)"; for Mauger, "Extrait du 'Journal de M.J. Mauger' Fonctionnaire de la Direction de L'Intérieur à Noumea, Aout 1877–aout 1878," in Roselène Dousset-Leenhardt, *Terre natale, terre d'exil*, Paris: G.P. Maisonneuve and Larose, 1976, 231; from the journal MS "Nouvelle-Calédonie, insurrection canaque de 1878."

50. Trentinian, C.A.O.M. "Rapport sur les causes de l'insurrection canaque en 1878," 68.

51. Widely cited; see Nouet, "La Colonisation et les Canaques," *La Grande Revue*, no. 1 (January 1, 1903), 185; citation in Dousset-Leenhardt, *Terre natale, terre d'exil*, 93.

52. Apollonaire Anova Ataba, *D'Ataï à l'independence*, Noumea: Edipop, 1984, 52–3. Reading for broad implications, see Dousset-Leenhardt; new works continue on this subject. See Claude Cornet, *La Grande Révolte, 1878*, Noumea: Editions La Boudeuse, 2000; F. Bogliolo, J. Labarbe, L. Letierie, eds., *Jours de colère,*

jours d'Ataï, Noumea: Ile de Lumière, 2000; on historical transmission, Geoffrey White, *Identity Through History: Living Stories in a Solomons Islands Society*, Cambridge: Cambridge University Press, 1991.

53. Apollonaire Anova Ataba in Marc Coulon, *L'Irruption Kanak: De Calédonie à Kanaky*, Paris: Messidor, 1985, 42–3; works by Anova Ataba, *D'Ataï à l'independence*, Noumea: Edipop Press, 1984 and "The New Caledonian Revolt of 1878 and its Consequences Today," *Pacific Perspectives*, 1973, I: 20–7. Anova Ataba greatly influenced Kanak leader Jean-Marie Tjibaou. See Alain Rollat, *Tjibaou le Kanak*, Lyon: La Manufacture, 1989, and Tjibaou's own, *La Présence Kanak*, Ed. établie et présentée par Alban Bensa et Eric Wittersheim, Paris: Odile Jacob, 1996; also Tjibaou's "Recherche d'identité melanesienne et société traditionelle," *Journal de Société des Océanistes*, 32 (1976), 281–92, and "The Renaissance of Melanesian Culture in New Caledonia," *Ethnies*, 4 8–9-10 (1989), 74–78; also Jean Guiart: "Forerunners of Melanesian Nationalism," *Oceania*, 22–2 (1951), 81- 90, and "Progress and Regress in New Caledonia," *Journal of Pacific History*, 27–1 (1992), 3–28.

54. "Lettre de R.P. Hillerau au R.P. Fraysse-Provicaire, 5 Dec. 1878," in *Jours de colère, jours d'Ataï*, 196; Anova Ataba: *D'Ataï à l'independence*, 51.

55. Archives Territoriales de la Nouvelle Calédonie, 23 WA6 1879 (July 21).

56. Archives Territoriales de la Nouvelle Calédonie, 23 WA6 1879 (December 27).

57. In Lainé, *Pioneer Days*, 43. For context, see "family stories" features ("every day brings us new information . . . ") in papers like *La Nouvelle-Calédonie*, e.g. no. 12, July 31, 1878. Good collection in C.A.O.M. FM/ SG/ NCL/ c. 43, doss. 10. Also, *La France Coloniale*, doss. 12.

58. Because of its peculiar history, New Caledonian love stories often lead to death. See Sonia Faessel, "Eros aux colonies: fantasmes et pulsions de mort," Sonia Faessel and Michel Pérez, eds., *Eros et Thanatos dans le Pacifique Sud*, Noumea: C.O.R.A.I.L. (2001), 157–71.

59. Telegram from the Governor, "Chef Ataï et son fils Baptiste tués," C.A.O.M. FM/ SG/ NCL/ c. 43, doss. 4, September 12, 1878; Bronwen Douglas: "Conflict & Alliance in a Colonial Context: Case Studies in New Caledonia," *Journal of Pacific History*, 15–1 (1980), 21–51.

60. Marc Le Goupils, *Dans la brousse Calédonienne: souvenirs d'un ancien planteur*, Perrin, 1928, 207.

61. *La Nouvelle Calédonie* (October 1879); see John Connell, *New Caledonia or Kanaky? The Political History of a French Colony*, Canberra: Australia National University Press, 1987, 68; Connell also surveys multiple interpretations of the violence from "national emancipation" and "local struggle," to "clash of cultures," and "revolutionary war."

62. Bernard, *L'Archipel*, 297.

63. Henri Rivière, *Souvenirs de la Nouvelle Calédonie: L'insurrection canaque*, Paris: Calmann-Lévy, 1881, 281–2; Anon. (1878), in Alain Saussol, *L'Héritage: essai sur le problème foncier mélanésien en Nouvelle Calédonie*, Paris: Musée de l'homme, 1979, 189, note 216.

64. Rivière, *Souvenirs*, 139–42, 159.

SIX: INDOCHINA

1. Pierre Loti, *Un Pèlerin d'Angkor*, Paris: Calmann-Lévy, 1912, trans. *A Pilgrimmage to Angkor*, 49, 56; also Albert Flament, "Pierre Loti et les ruines d'Angkor," *Paris Excelsior* (March 9, 1912); Eugène Pujaniscle, "Comment on fait de la littérature coloniale: Pierre Loti, pèlerin d'Angkor," *La Grande Revue*, 1927.

2. Bui-Thanh-Vân, *Les Temples d'Angkor*, Huê: Dac-LaPress, 1923, 16–18.

3. Loti, *Un Pèlerin* d'Angkor, 1; Loti, *Propos d'Exil*, Paris, Calmann-Lévy, 1887, 53, 70. See also Panivong Norindr, *Phantasmatic Indochina: French Colonial Ideology in Architecture, Film, and Literature*, Durham: Duke University Press, 1996, 1–51, and Louis Malleret, *L'Exotisme Indochinois dans la littérature française depuis 1860*, Paris: Larose, 1934, 39.

4. Pierre Loti, *Les Fleurs d'ennui*, 361–2; *Le Roman d'un Spahi*, 169. Also, Jehan Despert, *Le Douloureux amour de Pierre Loti*, Rochefort: La Malle aux livres, 1995.

5. Maurice Rondet-Saint, *Dans notre empire jaune*, Paris: Plon, 1917, 82; Pierre Loti, *A Pilgrimmage to Angkor*, 1.

6. Bui-Thanh-Vân, *Les Temples d'Angkor*, Huê: Dac-Lap, 1923, 20–2.

7. Loti, reports from Tonkin for *Le Figaro*, "La Prise de Tonkin," (September 28, 1883); Loti: *Lettres de Pierre Loti à Madame Juliette Adam*, letter, 1884, 40.

8. Bui-Thanh-Vân, *La France: Relations de voyage*, Huê: Dac-Lap, 1923, 37–41.

9. Nguyên An Ninh, *La France en Indochine* (pamphlet, 1925), 1–5, 10–12.

10. M. Pierre Nicolas, *Notices sur l'Indochine: Exposition universelle*, 1900, 27; for context, Pierre Brocheux and Daniel Hémery, *Indochine: La Colonisation ambiguë, 1858–1954*, Paris: La Découverte, 2001; for broader comparisons, Robert Aldrich and Isabelle Merle (eds.), *France Abroad: Indochina, New Caledonia, Wallis and Futuna*, Sydney: University of Sydney Press, 1997; Eric T. Jennings, *Vichy in the Tropics: Pétain's National Revolution in Madagascar, Guadeloupe, and Indochina, 1940–1944*, Stanford: Stanford University Press, 2001.

11. M. Declassé, "Delimitation entre les possessions Chinoises et Indo-Chinoises," Ministère des Affaires Etrangères, no. 1698 (October 1894), C.A.O.M., INDO-NF, 60–692. On Tonkinese and Annamite laborers sent to Oceanic colonies, C.A.O.M. FM/ SG Nouvelles Hebr. 34, doss. E9–10, "hundreds of indentured Annamite coolies," and "the poor treatment of Tonkinois coolies." Also, Christopher Goscha, *Vietnam or Indochina? Contesting Concepts of Space in Vietnamese Nationalism, 1887–1954*, NIAS, 1995.

12. Clotilde Chivas-Baron, "Thi-Vinh," *Trois femmes annamites*, Paris: Eugène Fasquelle, 1922, 73, 38–9.

13. Archives de la Marine, 77 GG/ c. 1, Blancsubé, article in *Le Mé-Kong: Organe des intérêts français en Extrême Orient*, November 24, 1882; Letter to Jules Ferry, m.s. December 16, 1883.

14. Jean Léra, *Tonkinoiseries: Souvenirs d'un officier*, Paris: H. Simonis Empis, 1896; on shifting imaginaries, Nicola Cooper, *France in Indochina: Colonial Encounters*, New York: Berg, 2001.

15. M. Brennier, "L'Indochine Economique," *Bulletin: Société de Géographie de Toulouse*, no. 369 (April 15, 1907), 3.

16. Commandant Berthe de Villers, in Dick de Lonay, *Au Tonkin, 1883–5*, Paris: Garnier-Frères, 1886, 16; Paul Antonini, *Au Pays d'Annam*, Paris: Bloud et Barral, 1889, 225.

17. Maxime Petit, *La France au Tonkin et en Chine*, Paris: Librarie Illustrée, 1885, 99 on Garnier; Jean Baptiste Eliacin Luro, in Georges Taboulet, ed., *La Geste Française in Indochine: histoire par les textes de la France en Indochine des origines à 1914*, vol. 2, Paris: Adrien-Maisonneuve, 1956, 599; Emile Duboc, *35 Mois de campagne en Chine, au Tonkin, 1882–5*, Paris: Charavay, Mantoux, Martin, 1889, 223. This work part of "editions for young people."

18. Duc de Montpensier, *En Indochine: mes chasses, mes voyages*, Paris: Pierre Lafitte, 1912.

19. Léopold Pallu de la Barrière, *Historie de l'éxpedition de Cochinchine in 1861*, Paris, 1888, 179; Dick de Lonay, *Au Tonkin, 1883–1885*, Paris: Garnier Frères, 1886, 24–5; A. Bouinais and A. Paulus, *La France en Indochine*, Paris: Challamel Ainé (1886), 130; De Lanessan, *L'Indochine Française*, 756.

20. Archives de la Marine, 77 GG/ c.1. ms. "réglementation des pouvoirs du Gouverneur," 2.

21. *Débats Parlementaires*, May 26, 1883 (Cuneo d'Ornano), December 9–11, 1883 (Leon Renault and Georges Clemenceau), August 16, 1884 (Eugène Farcy); Blancsubé stories in *Le Parlement illustré*, August 1883; *Le Saigonnais*, October 7, 1886.

22. *Le Mé-Kong, organe des intérêts français en Extrême-Orient*, November 24, 1882.

23. Nicolas, *Notices sur l'Indochine*, 269. For the multi-volume works and reports, see Auguste Pavie, *Exposé des travaux de la mission par Auguste Pavie*, Paris: E. Léroux (1901–6). These quotes from André Masson, introduction to Auguste Pavie, *A la Conquête des coeurs*, Paris: PUF, 1921, revised edition 1947.

24. Pavie letters, C.A.O.M. INDO/ GI/ 26.664.

25. Papiers Pavie, C.A.O.M. 46/ APC/ 1/ doss. 1 piece 2, notebooks, 51.

26. Auguste Pavie, *A la Conquête des coeurs*, Paris: PUF, 1921, revised edition 1947, xxxi-xxxii. On Pavie as minister, C.A.O.M. 46 APC/ c. 1, doss. 4: press clippings "M. Pavie est rentrée."

27. Pavie, *A la Conquête des cœurs*, 214–215, 268, 370, xxxii.

28. Deo Van Tri, letter to Pavie, C.A.O.M. 46 APC/ c. 1, doss. 4.

29. Blancsubé letter, Archives de la Marine, 77GG/ c.1, PT 28.

30. M. Pierre Nicolas, *Notices sur l'Indochine: Exposition universelle*, 1900, 4; also J. Charles Roux, "Notice sur les etablissements français de l'Océanie," *Exposition universelle de 1900: Colonies et pays de protectorats*, Paris, 1900.

31. Nicolas, *Notices sur l'Indochine*, sections "Le Palais des arts," and "grotto dioramas," 313.

32. Nicolas/Pavie, 307

33. Albert Savine, "Le Roi de Cambodge," *La Nouvelle Revue*, no. 161 (June 15, 1906), 566.

34. *La Geste Française in Indochine: histoire par les textes de la France en Indochine des origines à 1914*, tome II, Paris: Adrien-Maisonneuve, 1956, notes, 914. Also, Bui-Thanh-Vân, *Les Temples d'Angkor*, 33.

35. Nicolas/Pavie, 306–7. For more detail, see Auguste Pavie, *Contes populaires du Cambodge, du Laos, et du Siam*, Paris: E. Léroux, 1903.

36. Bui-Thanh-Vân, *Les Temples d'Angkor*, 20, 33.

37. Bui-Thanh-Vân, in *Les Temples d'Angkor*, 25; and *La France: Relations de voyage*, 42.

38. Nguyên Phan-Long, *Le Roman de Mlle Lys: Essay sur l'évolution des mœurs Annamites contemporains*, Hanoi: Impr. Tonkinoise, 1921, i, 85.

39. Augustin Bernard, *L'Archipel de la Nouvelle Calédonie*, Paris: Hachette, 1895, 297.

40. Blancsubé, "Notes sur le Tong-kin," Archives de la Marine, 77GG1, doss. PT 12; Auguste Pavie, *A la conquête des cœurs*, 1921, first appearances in the *Revue de Paris* (May, 1898); A. Bouinais and A. Paulus, *La France en Indochine*, Paris: Challamel Aîné (1886), xiii.

41. J. L. Dureuil de Rhins, *Le Royaume d'Annam et les Annamites*, Paris: Plon, 1879, 87.

42. Clotilde Chivas-Baron, "Madame Hoa's Husbands," *Trois femmes annamites*, Paris: Eugène Fasquelle, 1922, 188, 202; similar views in Dr. Morice, *The French in Indochina* (trans.), Paris: F. Garnier, 1891, 74, "(their) character is that of a people whom slavery, ignorance, and sloth have rendered poor, timid, and apathetic," "shrill monotonous music . . . terrible to a cultured ear . . . of sculpture they know only the rudiments; their poetry is indifferent, they cannot dance . . ."

43. Chivas-Baron, "Madame Hoa's Husbands," 188, 193–4, 202–3.

44. C.A.O.M. INDO/ GI/ 1625, "M. Jolly/ Hoan-Thi-Kiêt," 1677, "M. Riberio/ Nguyên-Thi-Lily," note from resident superior of Tonkin to the governor general, March 13, 1912.

45. C.A.O.M. INDO/ GI/ 26.648, "Au sujet du marriage."

46. C.A.O.M. INDO/ GI/ 1673.

47. Bui-Thanh-Vân, *La France: Relations de voyage*, 110–11.

48. Clotilde Chivas-Baron, *La Femme aux colonies*, Paris: Larose, 1927, 186–7. On the "Empire of the Home," see Anne McClintock, *Imperial Leather: Race, Gender, and Sexuality in the Colonial Contest*, New York: Routledge, 1995.

49. Albert de Pouvourville, *L'Annamite aujourd'hui*, Paris: Ed. de la Rose, 1932, 113–17; Clotilde Chivas-Baron, *Confidences de métisse*, Paris: Charpantier and Fasquelle, 1927, 211. See also, Julia Clancy-Smith and Frances Gouda, eds., *Domesticating the Empire: Race, Gender, and Family Life in French and Dutch Colonialism*, Charlottesville: University Press Virginia, 1998. Note the important similitudes in Alice Conklin's "Redefining Frenchness: France and West Africa," and Penny Edwards's "Womanizing Indochina: Colonial Cambodia," for insights that only a white wife could "satisfy the end for love in the superior and ideal sense," and that "the congaï [was] a purely physical object incapable of the tender emotions and maternal instincts of la Française (the French woman)," 79, 117.

50. Chivas-Baron, "Madame Hoa's Husbands," 196.

51. Phan Bôi Châu, "The New Vietnam," in Lam Truong Buu, *Colonialism Experienced: Vietnamese Writings on Colonialism, 1900–1931*, Ann Arbor: University of Michigan Press, 2000, 107–9, 119. Pro-French Vietnamese also used the same language, lamenting " the stay-at-home mind of the Annamites, their patriotism that stops at the front door." See Trân-Tan-Binh, C.A.O.M. 9 PA/c.5/doss. 8 "temoignages Annamites."

52. Chivas-Baron, "Madame Hoa's Husbands," 198; Ann Laura Stoler, "Tense and Tender Ties: The Politics of Comparison in North american History and (Post) Colonial Studies," *Journal of American History* 88, no. 3 (2001): 829–873.

53. Chivas-Baron, *Confidences de métisse*, Paris: E. Fasquelle, 1927, 7, 211, 217, 223. Also, Robert J. C. Young, *Colonial Desire: Hybridity in Theory, Culture, and Race*, London: Routledge, 1995, 90–118.

54. "Situation légale des métis non reconnus par leurs pére et mère," C.A.O.M. INDO/ GI/ 1669, no. 3836X18.

55. Poirot/ Hai-Lôc, C.A.O.M. INDO/ GI/ 1662, no. 1372. See also the intriguing case of Louis Hâu of an "Annamite mother and unknown father," which attempts to distinguish between Annamite, French, and European qualities through Hâu's registration (or not) with an état-civil. C.A.O.M. INDO/GI/1669.

56. Maurice Rondet-Saint, *Dans notre empire jaune*, 15. For comparisons, see Owen White, *Children of the French Empire: Misceginatin and Colonial Society in French West Africa, 1895–1960*, New York: Oxford University Press, 1999.

57. De Lanessan, *L'Indochine Frânàise*, 56, 756.

58. C.A.O.M. 9 PA 5, Papiers Sarrault, doss. 8, letter signed by Lê-Van-Trung and five others, October 8, 1913; *Midi Coloniale* and La *Cochinchine Libérale*, press clippings and newspapers.

59. C.A.O.M. 9 PA 5, Papiers Sarrault, doss. 8, Letter on duty, and conference by Trân-Tan-Binh, "temoignages annamites, 1907–1916." Also Nguyên Phan Long, *Le Roman de Mlle Lys*, 377.

60. Trân Van Tung, *Rêves d'un campagnard annamite*, Paris: Mercure de France, 1940, esp. i–iii, 190, 193–7.

61. Nguyên An Ninh, *La France en Indochine* (pamphlet, 1925), 10–12.

62. Challayé, *Souvenirs sur la colonisation*, 24, also, 40, 201; on maintaining European status, M. Jules Besançon, "Rapport sur l'enseignement en Indochine," (1889), National Archives, F17 2939, dossier "Besançon." The director of the Collège Mytho warns that the French bureaucrat will "no longer be master of his own domain if ever, thanks to the French language, communcations could be made directly between the villages and Saigon," 4.

63. Chau Kim Dang, *Leçons d'historie d'Annam á l'usage des écoles normales et primaries supérieurs franco-annamites*, Saigon: Duc-Luu-Phuong, 1930, i, 5, 142.

64. *La Dépêche coloniale*, August 7, 1913; C.A.O.M. PA 93, Papiers Sarrault, "Affaires Indigènes." Report by Nguyên Van Ngô, 6–7.

65. Lemire in Pierre Singaravélon, *L'Ecole française d'extrême orient, ou l'institution de marges, 1898–1956*, Paris: L'Harmattan, 1999, 62.

66. Charles Meyniard, *Le Second empire en Indochine*, Paris: Societe d'Editions Scientifiques, 1891, xii; Duc de Montpensier, 175.

67. J. L. Dureuil de Rhins, *Le Royaume d'Annam et les Annamites*, 3.

68. Clotilde Chivas-Baron, "Thi-Vinh," *Trois femmes annamites*, Paris: Eugène Fasquelle, 1922, 36. See Henri Copin, *L'Indochine dans la littérature française des annés vingt à 1954*, Paris: L'Harmattan, 1996, 162–75, on Chivas-Baron, exotisme, alterité; Copin, *L'Indochine des romans*, Paris: Kailash, 2000.

69. Loti, reports from Tonkin for *Le Figaro*, "La Prise de Tonkin," (September 28, 1883); also Loti, *Impressions*, New York: Brentanos, 1900, 161. Huu Ngoc and François Corrèze, *Anthologie de la literature populaire de Viêt-Nam*, Paris: L'Harmattan, 1982, 223.

SEVEN: JAPAN

1. André Messager, *Madame Chrysanthème* Paris, 1893, lyrics, G. Hartmann and A. Alexandre, collection of Bibliothèque de l'Opéra, Paris, no. 2199, 263–4.

2. For the overlapping histories of John Luther Long, David Belasco and Puccini's *Butterfly* with Loti's and Messager's *Chrysanthème*, see Jacques Legrand, "Madame Chrysanthème au théâtre," *in Le Japon de Pierre Loti*, Rochefort: *Revue Pierre Loti*, 1988 and Sophie Daniel, "De Chrysanthème à Butterfly: Chronique d'un malentendu" (ms., collection Maison Pierre Loti). For insights into Loti's Japanese/French writings, see Suetoshi Funaoka, *Pierre Loti et l'extrême-orient*, Tokyo: France Tosho, 1988; Pierre E. Briquet, *Pierre Loti et l'Orient* (Neuchatel: Ed. de la Baconnière, n.d.), and the collective work in *Colloque de Paimpol: Loti et son temps* Rennes: Presses Universitaires de Rennes, 1994, esp. Damien Zanone, "Bretagne et Japon aux antipodes: les deux moments d'un même roman d'amour pour Yves: lecture de *Mon frère Yves* et *Madame Chysanthème*," 97–109, and Irma d'Auria, "Les Contradictions du Japon dans l'expérience de Loti," 111–21. Also, the essays collected in Alain Quella-Villéger, *Le Japon de Pierre Loti*, Rochefort: Revue Pierre Loti, 1988; Marie-Pascale Bault, *Pierre Loti en Chine et au Japon* Rochefort: Musée Municipal des Beaux Arts, 1985. The last two are limited collections courtesy of the Maison de Pierre Loti, Rochefort.

3. Pierre Loti, *Madame Chrysanthème*, original edition Calmann-Lévy, 1887/1888, reprinted Paris: Flammarion, 1990, 225–6. Julien Viaud's (Loti) other writings on Japan include *Japoneries d'autonme* Paris: Calmann-Lévy, 1923.

4. Patrick Beillevaire, "L'autre de l'autre: contribution à l'histoire des représentations de la femme japonaise," *Mots: Parler du Japon*, no. 41 (Dec 1994), 56–98. For specific analyses of Japan/Woman as colonial and romantic object, see Irene L. Szykiowicz, *Pierre Loti and the Oriental Woman* New York: St. Martin's Press, 1988.

5. A. S. Doncourt, *Les Français dans l'extrême orient: Chine, Japon, Indochine, Annam, etc.*, Lille and Paris, 1884, 115.

6. E. Lamairesse, *Le Japon*, Paris: Augustin Challamel, 1892, 1; M. Courant, *Bulletin Périodique de la Presse Japonaise*, no. 30, Ministères de la Guerre et des Affaires Etrangères (July 1917), 3.

7. Félix Martin, *Le Japon Vrai*, Paris: Bibliothèque Charpantiér, 1898, 1–2; I. Hitomi, *Le Japon: Essais sur les moeurs et les institutions*, Paris: Librarie de la société du recueil general des lois et arrets, 1900, 259; Paul Monconduit, "Rapport de mission d'études au Japon," Archives de la Marine, SSE a(1) 152 (1911), 58; Lt. Col. Péroz, *France et Japon en Indochine*, Paris: R. Chapelot, 1907, 77; William L. Schwartz, *The Imaginative Interpretation of the Far East in Modern French Literature*, Edinburgh: Librarie Ancienne, 1926, 131.

8. I. Hitomi, *Le Japon: Essais sur les moeurs et les institutions*, Paris: Librarie de la société du recueil general des lois et arrets, 1900, 259. Baron Suyematsu, *Un Songe d'été à Paris: le Japon hier et aujourd'hui*, Paris: Félix Juven, 1906, 49.

9. Loti, *Madame Chrysanthème*, 182. See also Gèrard Siary, "The Image of Japan in European Travelogues from 1853 to 1905," *Transactions of the Asiatic Society of Japan*, 4th series, 2 (1987).

10. Félix Régamey, *Le Japon Pratique*, Paris: Bibliothèque des professions (1888?), 19–20.

11. Loti, *Madame Chrysanthème*, 63.

12. See Gérard Siary, "La représentation littéraire du Japon dans *Madame Chrysanthème*," in *Le Japon de Pierre Loti*, 15–30. Note that in John Luther Long's *Madame Butterfly*, the narrator comments "there are no terms of enderament in the Japanese language." *Madame Butterfly*, New York: Century (1897), 11.

13. Emmanuel Benezeit, *Dictionnaire critique et documentaire des peintres, sculpteurs, dessinateurs et graveurs*, vol. 8 Paris: Librarie Grund, 1976, 650.

14. Edmond and Jules de Goncourt, *Journal II 1866–1886*, Robert Ricatte, ed., Paris: Robert Laffont, 1956, letter of December 3, 1870, 476.

15. Félix Régamey, *Le Japon Pratique*, 2. For context, see Debora L. Silverman, *Art Nouveau in Fin-de-Siècle France: Politics, Psychology, and Style*, Berkeley: University of California Press, 1989, 129–33.

16. Adolphe Buisson (review of Loti) *Les Annales politiques et littéraires* (1 December 1887), 1. Marie-Pascale Bault, "La pagode japonaise de la maison de Pierre Loti à Rochefort," in *Le Japon de Pierre Loti*, 37–45.

17. Nakae Chomin, *A Discourse by Three Drunkards on Government*, New York: Weatherhill, 1992, 76–7.

18. Teruko Craig, ed., *The Autobiography of Shibusawa Eiichi*, Tokyo: University of Tokyo Press, 1994, 162–3; Richard Sims, *French Policy Towards the Bakufu and Meiji Japan*, 1854–1895, London: Japan Library Survey, 1998, 274–5.

19. Messager, *Madame Chrysanthème*, 23–4.

20. Félix Martin, *Le Japon Vrai*, Paris: Bibliothèque Charpantiér, 1898, 1–5.

21. Loti, *Madame Chrysanthème*, 215.

22. Charles Pettit, *Pays de Mousumés, Pays de Guerre,* Paris: Félix Juven, 1905, 9–10.

23. Reginald J. Farrar, *The Garden of Asia,* London: Methuen, 1904, 186.

24. Loti, *Madame Chrysanthème,* 42.

25. Edmond Cotteau, *Un Touriste dans l'extrême orient,* Paris: Hachette, 1885, 17.

26. Paul d'Estournelles de Constant, "Le Péril Prochain," *Revue de deux mondes* (April 1, 1896) 670; Pettit, 6. For similar views, Henri Stamm, "Concurrence et chômage," *Revue de deux mondes* (July 15, 1897).

27. G. Apport, "Deux Révolutions au Japon," *Revue de deux mondes* (March, 1895) 639; *Le Vice-Amiral Bergasse Du Petit-Thouars, 1832–1890, d'après ses notes et sa correspondance,* Paris: Perrin et Cie. (1906), letter of September 2, 1868, 222; Loti, *Madame Chrysanthème,* 228; mimicry and subversion in Homi K. Bhabha, "Signs Taken for Wonders: Questions of Ambivalence and Authority under a Tree Outside Delhi, May 1817," *Critical Inquiry 12:1* (1985).

28. Petit, 5. Loti, *La Troisième Jeunesse de Madame Prune,* letter of October 5, 1900, reprinted, Paris: Editions Proverbe, 1994, 135.

29. Ourel Reshef, *Guerre, mythes, et caricature: au berceau d'un mentalité française,* Paris: Presses de la fondation des sciences politiques, 1984, 67, and Digeon, 64.

30. The key here is "large-scale" conflict. French and Japaneses forces had been in direct military conflict in the infamous 1867 "Incident at Sakai" most notably recorded by Mori Ogai, in which sixteen French sailors were killed, and twenty Japanese condemned to seppuku. Nine of the latter carried out their own executions before the ceremonies were suspended by the abrupt departure of Léon Roche and the French diplomatic party.

31. Petit, 34. Loti, *Madame Chrysanthème,* 229; Clement de la Roncière le Noury, "Note sur la puissance militaire du Japon," Archives de la Marine (April, 1864), GG2 408 17GG2–8; also Monconduit, "Rapport de mission d'études au Japon," SSE a(1) 152 (1911), 57, "son adaptation à la civilisation occidentale est très superficielle . . ."

32. Victor Bérard, *La Révolte de l'Asie* Paris: Armand Colin, 1904, 101–2; Loti, *Madame Chrysanthème,* 182.

33. Bérard, 60–1; Loti, *Madame Chrysanthème,* 225.

34. M. L. Gagneur, *Chair à canon* Paris, 1873, 225

35. Loti, *Madame Chrysanthème,* 97; "Un Bal à Yeddo," in *La Nouvelle Revue* 45 (January 1, 1888).

36. Edmond and Jules de Goncourt, *Journal II,* letter of December 5, 1870, 352.

37. Ludovic Naudeau, *Le Japon moderne: Son évolution,* Paris: Flammarion, 1909; 345–7. André Bellesort, *La Société Japonaise,* Paris: Perrin & Cie. (1904), 302, 315; on theater, Shionoyo Kei, *Cyrano et les samurai,* Paris: Société Franco-Japonais, 1986.

38. Bellesort, 292; Petit, 34. This was not a strictly "Western" construction. Meiji thinkers readily debated the status of Japanese women and Japanese civilization as part of a continuing dialogue with Europe and the United States. To read some of the original documentation in English translation, see William Reynolds Braisted,

trans., *Meiroku Zasshi: Journal of the Japanese Enlightenment,* Tokyo: University of Tokyo Press, 1976, see particularly Mori Arinori's multipart "On Wives and Concubines"; Eiichi Kiyoka, *Fukuzawa Yukichi and Japanese Women,* Tokyo: University of Tokyo Press, 1988, chs. 1–3.

39. Juliette Adam, *La Vie des ames,* Paris: Bernard-Grasset, 1919, 24.

40. Charles Loonen, *Le Japon Modern,* Paris: Librarie Plon, 1894, 120; Petit, 12.

41. Pettit, 15.

42. Bellesort, 310; Pettit, 14.

43. Loti, *Madame Chrysanthème,* 182; Jacques Flach, "L'Ame Japonaise d'après un Japonais" *Annales des sciences politiques* 4 (July 15, 1904), 447–8.

44. *Madame Chrysanthème,* 180.

45. *Madame Chrysanthème,* 187; Clement de la Roncière le Noury, "Note sur la puissance militaire du Japon," Archives de la Marine (April 1864), GG2 408 17GG2–8; Eliza Scidmore, from *Jinriksha Days in Japan,* in K. Kiyoshi Kawakami, ed., *Japan and the Japanese as Seen by Foreigners Prior to the Beginnings of the Russo-Japanese War,* Tokyo: Keiseisha, 1904, 10–11.

46. Citations collected and narrated in Lesley Downer, *Madame Sadayakko: The Geisha Who Bewitched the West,* New York: Gotham, 2003, 166–9; on Gide, André Gide, *Lettres à Angèle,* in *Pretextes,* Paris: Ed. de Mercure de France, 1903, 134; on the French, Yone Noguchi, "Sada Yacco," *New York Dramatic Mirror,* Feburary 17, 1908. Extensive analyses and documentation in Ayako Kano, *Acting Like a Woman in Modern Japan: Theater, Gender, and Nationalism,* New York: Palgrave, 2001; also Shelley Berg, "Sada Yacco in London and Paris: 1900: Le rêve realisé," *Dance Chronicle,* 18, no. 3 (1995), 343–404. For an overview of the Paris exploits, see Matsunaga Goichi, *Kawakami Otojiro: Kindaigeki, hatenko na yoake,* Tokyo: Asahi Shinbunsha, 1988, 173–81.

47. Sadayakko on love in Louis Fournier, *Kawakami and Sada Yacco,* Paris: Brentano's, 1900, 19–20; Kawakami Otojiro cited by Downer, 175; see Shirakawa Nobuo, ed. *Kawakami Otojiro, Sadayakko: shimbun ni miru jinbutsu zo,* Tokyo: Yushodo, 1985, for newspaper articles and essays related to the couple.

48. Downer, 142; Kano, esp. chapter 5, "Reproducing the Empire."

49. Bellesort, 310; Pettit, 14.

50. Pierre Loti, *La Troisième jeunesse de Madame Prune,* Paris: Proverbe, 1994, 30–1.

51. Charles Loonen, 120.

52. G. Apport, "Deux Révolutions au Japon," 661; Suyematsu, 139.

53. Martin, 38; Félicien Challayé, *The Soul of Japan,* London: Routledge, 1933, 65–66.

54. Paul de Lacroix, *Le Japon* (n.d., Musée Guimet, no. 52184-E10 (4)); Claparède, 101. See also Louis Frédéric, *La Vie quotidienne au Japon au debut de l'ere moderne (1868–1912),* Paris: Hachette, 1984, ch. 3, "La Maison et la famille," 4, "l'individu japonais."

55. Bellesort, 315–6.

56. Madame Chrysanthème, 165.

57. Bellesort, 316; Suyematsu, 32;

58. M. Harmand to M. Hanotaux, August 10, 1894, Ministère des Affaires Etrangères, *Documents diplomatiques français* 15 (January 2–November 14, 1894).

59. The classic scholarship is E. Patricia Tsurumi, *Factory Girls: Women in the Thread Mills of Meiji Japan,* Princeton, N.J.: Princeton University Press, 1990. See also Janet Hunter, "Textile Factories, Tuberculosis, and the Quality of Life in Industrializing Japan," in Janet Hunter, ed., *Japanese Women Working,* New York: Routledge, 1993, 69–97.

60. L. Joly, "La Femme Japonaise," *La Science catholique* (April 1906), 18–22.

61. Joly, 14.

62. *Piano-Soleil* (26 February 1893), 1.

63. Messager, *Madame Chrysanthème,* 263–4.

64. Félix Régamey, ed., "L'Art et la femme au Japon: litteraire, artistique, sociale," *La Plume,* no. 108 (October 15, 1893), 439; Clive Holland, *My Japanese Wife: A Japanese Idyll,* London: R. A. Everett Co. (1903), 43–4.

65. Messager, *Madame Chrysanthéme,* 263.

66. For insights into what I consider Loti's "Baudelarian" tendencies, see especially his epistolary novel, *Fleurs d'ennui,* Paris: Calmann-Lévy, 1925, and his "longue saison d'ennui" in Paris as a youth, 18–19. Régamey declared his "unbreakable faith in the future of Japan," even in 1905 with an editorial piece, "Le Péril jaune: les responsables," *Mercure de France* (November 15, 1905).

67. Régamey, "Le Cahier rose de Madame Chrysanthème" in *La Plume,* 445.

68. Régamey, "Le Cahier rose de Madame Chrysanthème," 446–8.

69. Petit, "Tableau," 102; "Indochina," 236; also "Negotations commerciales Franco-Japonsaises," Ministère des Affaires Etrangères (June 1895), C.A.O.M., INDO/NF/107/1019, 14–15.

70. Suyematsu, 32; Loonen, 127.

AFTERWORD

1. Pierre Loti, *Mariage de Loti* (*The Marriage of Loti*); also Pierre Loti, *Pages choisies des auteurs contemporains,* Paris: Calmann-Lévy, 1910, 415.

2. Jean Louis De Lanessan, *L'Indochine Française,* Paris: Alcan, 1889, p. 3; Ministère des Affaires Etrangères, INDO/NF 834 B3, "Délimitation de la frontière," INDO/NF 837 COO, 1894 "Mission d'éxploration Haut-Mekong"; also, République Française, *Notices Coloniales de l'exposition universelle d'Anvers,* vol. 1, Paris, 1885, p. 33; connections imagined through Robert Aldrich and Isabelle Merle, eds., *France Abroad: Indochina, New Caledonia, Wallis and Futuna,* Sydney: University of Sydney Press, 1997.

3. Loti, *Mariage de Loti*; also Loti, *Pages choisies,* 416.

4. *Alexandre Salmon et sa femme Ariitaimai: deux figures de Tahiti a l'epoque du protectorat,* Papeete: Société des Etudes Océaniennes, 1982, Loti, 162–3; melancholy, 166. Marau's (1860–1934) full title with family name, Queen Joanna Marauta'aroa Tepa'o Salmon. See Nicholas Thomas, "Partial Texts: Representation, Colonialism

and Agency in Pacific History," in *Oceania: Visions, Artifacts, Histories*. Durham, N.C.: Duke University Press, 1997 23–49; Vilsoni Hereniko: "Representations of Cultural Identities," in K. Howe, R. Kiste and B. Lal, eds., *Tides of History: The Pacific Islands in the Twentieth Century*, Honolulu: University of Hawaii Press, 1994, ch. 17; Judith Binney, "Maori Oral Narratives, Pakeha Written Texts: Two Forms of Telling History," *New Zealand Journal of History* (April 1987), 16–28. R. Finnegan and M. Orbell, eds., *South Pacific Oral Traditions*, Bloomington: Indiana University Press, 1995; David Hanlon, "Beyond "the English Method of Tattooing": Decentering the Practice of History in Oceania," *Contemporary Pacific* 15, no. 1 (2003).

5. Epeli Hau'ofa, "Our Sea of Islands," *Contemporary Pacific* 6, no.1 (1994), 148–61; for extended commentaries, *A New Oceania: Rediscovering Our Sea of Islands*, ed. Eric Waddell, Vijay Naidu, and Epeli Hau'ofa, Suva: University of the South Pacific, 1994, especially Tarcisius Kabutaulaka, "The Bigness of our Smallness," 91–93. See also David W. Gegeo, "Cultural Rupture and Indigineity: the Challenge of (Re) Visioning 'Place' in the Pacific," *Contemporary Pacific* 13, no. 2 (2002); on migration, travel, and diaspora questions, David Chappell, *Double Ghosts: Oceanian Voyagers on European Ships*, New York: M.E. Sharpe, 1997; P. Spickard, J. Rondilla, and D. Hippolite Wright, eds., *Pacific Diaspora: Island Peoples in the United States and Across the Pacific*, Honolulu, Hawaii: University of Hawaii Press, 2002; Paul de Deckker and Pierre Yves Toullelan, eds., *La France et la Pacifique*, Paris: Société Française d'histoire d'outre-mer, 1990.

INDEX

CPSIA information can be obtained
at www.ICGtesting.com
Printed in the USA
FSOW04n1735041115
12967FS